03 JUN. 1999 184

SALIDA

ARTMENT OF IMMIGRATION
PERMITTED TO ENTER
AUSTRALIA.

24 APR 1986

on

For stay of *12 Month*

SYDNEY AIRPORT 54

IMMIGRATION & ETHNIC AFFAIRS

·········Person

30 OCT 1989
DEPARTED
AUSTRALIA

SYDNEY 32

A
72
DEPARTED
ENTRY
- 9 FEB 1987
SIGNED

IMMIGRATION DIVISION BANGKOK THAILAND

T R A V E L E R ' S
PERU
C O M P A N I O N

中华人民共和国

广东省公安厅

上陸許可
ADMITTED
15. FEB. 1986
4
Status: 4-1-
Duration: 90 days
NARITA(N)
Immigration Inspector
日本国

ADMITTED
20 OCT. 1988
Status: 4-1-16
Duration 180 days
Port: HANEDA
Signature

№ 011278

THE UNITED STATES
OF AMERICA
NONIMMIGRANT VISA
ISSUED AT

U.S. IMMIGRATION
170 HHW 1710

JUL 20 1983

USED Air Port

HONG KONG
(1038)
- 7 JUN 1987
IMMIGRATION
OFFICER

The 1999–2000 Traveler's Companions

ARGENTINA • AUSTRALIA • BALI • CALIFORNIA • CANADA • CHILI • CHINA • COSTA RICA • CUBA • EASTERN CANADA • ECUADOR • FLORIDA • HAWAII • HONG KONG • INDIA • INDONESIA • JAPAN • KENYA • MALAYSIA & SINGAPORE • MEDITERRANEAN FRANCE • MEXICO • NEPAL • NEW ENGLAND • NEW ZEALAND • PERU • PHILIPPINES • PORTUGAL • RUSSIA • SOUTH AFRICA • SOUTHERN ENGLAND • SPAIN • THAILAND • TURKEY • VENEZUELA • VIETNAM, LAOS AND CAMBODIA • WESTERN CANADA

Traveler's PERU Companion

First Published 1999 in the United Kingdom by
Kümmerly+Frey AG,
Alpenstrasse 58, CH 3052 Zollikofen, Switzerland
in association with
World Leisure Marketing Ltd
Unit 11, Newmarket Court, Newmarket Drive, Derby, DE24 8NW, England

Website: http://www.map-world.co.uk

ISBN: 1-84006-067-0

© 1999 Kümmerly+Frey AG, Switzerland

Created, edited and produced by
Allan Amsel Publishing, 53, rue Beaudouin
27700 Les Andelys, France.
E-mail: Allan.Amsel@wanadoo.fr
Editor in Chief: Allan Amsel
Editor: Anne Trager
Original design concept: Hon Bing-wah
Picture editor and designer: David Henry

Printed by Samhwa Printing Co. Ltd., Seoul, South Korea

TRAVELER'S
PERU
COMPANION

by Joe Yogerst and Maribeth Mellin

photographs by Mireille Vautier

Kümmerly+Frey

Contents

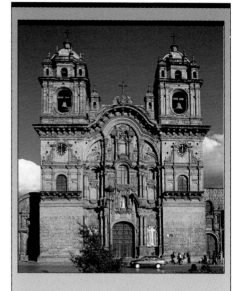

TRAVELER'S
PERU
COMPANION

Machala
Tumbes Huaqu
T U M B E S
Máncora Punta Sal
Atascadero
Talara
Sullana
Colán **Puira**
Paita Vic
Catàcaos P I U
Sechura Li
Bayovar
Reventazón
L A M B A Y E
Lambayeque Sip
Chiclayo
Pa
Pacas
Puerto C

UNITED STATES OF AMERICA

MEXICO

CUBA

JAMAICA

HONDURAS

GUATEMALA NICARAGUA

COSTA RICA VENEZUELA

PANAMA

COLOMBIA

GALAPAGOS
ISLANDS ECUADOR
(Ecuador)

BRAZIL

PERU

BOLIVIA

CHILE

ARGENTINA

LEGEND

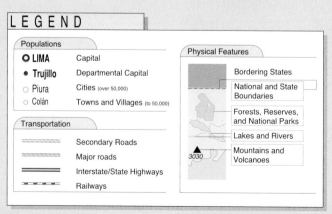

Populations

⊙ **LIMA**	Capital
● **Trujillo**	Departmental Capital
○ Piura	Cities (over 50,000)
○ Colán	Towns and Villages (to 50,000)

Transportation

Secondary Roads
Major roads
Interstate/State Highways
Railways

Physical Features

Bordering States
National and State Boundaries
Forests, Reserves, and National Parks
Lakes and Rivers
3030 Mountains and Volcanoes

TOP SPOTS

Mingle with the Spirits of Machu Picchu

DAWN SEEPS THROUGH THE CHILLED MOIST AIR IN THE PERUVIAN ANDES, SLOWLY ILLUMINATING TERRACES ETCHED IN GRANITE 500 YEARS PAST. A sunbeam slithers toward Intihuatana (the Inca Hitching Post to the Sun). A trio of drowsy-eyed alpaca ruffle their matted fur and pose insouciantly beside an ancient gateway high above the temples and dwellings of Machu Picchu.

My first visit to South America's most famous ruined city occurred on a dry September morning at 7 AM. Looking about for the highest spot above structures and lawns etched beneath the twin peaks of Machu and Huayna Picchu, I headed up a trail.

Below me lay a city that once housed hundreds of residents and pilgrims, all bustling about cooking, cleaning, farming, praying, and burying their dead. John Hemming, the Canadian explorer who spent six years writing *The Conquest of the Incas*, describes the city as "a place of magical beauty."

"…the house groups are set amid banks of tidy agricultural terraces, and Machu Picchu is bound together by a web of paths and hundreds of stairways. Its location is fantastic, with the city clinging to the upper slope and crest of a narrow ridge. The sheer sugarloaf of Huayna Picchu rises like a rhinoceros horn at the end of the spur, and the Urubamba roars in a tight hairpin bend around the site, trapped in a green canyon hundreds of feet below. Steep forested hills rise all around Machu Picchu, and its mystery is heightened by ghostly wisps of low cloud that cling to these humid mountains."

Spiritual seekers are drawn to Machu Picchu as they are to Stonehenge, considering the ruins to be one of the most sacred spots in the world; more than a few believers are convinced Machu Picchu was constructed by extraterrestrial beings. The precision of Incan masonry certainly evokes thoughts of an otherworld artistry — human elements seem almost invisible. None of the creativity of the Maya or other fifteenth-century Latin American cultures is evident here, no elaborate carvings of jaguars, snakes, and human skulls.

OPPOSITE: Terraced gardens and roofless huts lead to the ruins of Machu Picchu. ABOVE: Huayna Picchu peaks above the landscape of ruins of Machu Picchu.

Instead, the structures echo the natural landscape, built of angular piles of granite held together by gravity. The subtleties of man's influence on the terrain appear gradually as you witness the sun cast shadows beneath a long *mesa de piedra* (table of rock) or against the *piedra sagrada* (sacred stone).

Though anthropologists still argue over the city's purpose, there can be little question that Machu Picchu was used by priests, astronomers, emperors, and warriors for ceremonies, strategy sessions, and intellectual pursuits. But the city was home to the common man as well. Gardeners tended corn, potato, and *quinua* (grain) plots strictly divided by a series of agricultural terraces. They developed a tool called the *cahqui taclla*, a foot plow helpful in cultivating their steep gardens. Caretakers oversaw clay-mortared, thatch-roofed granaries stocked with the harvest. Female virgins lived amid overseers in the Palace of the Sun Virgins: according to Pedro Sueldo Nava, author of *A Walking Tour of Machupicchu*, 75% of the human remains found at the ruins are female. A thought worth pondering over from above the scene.

As I wandered the ruins that first sunny morning, I watched other travelers discover their favorite perspectives, their ways of approaching this overwhelming site. A group of French pilgrims in white clustered around a shaman by the Sacred Stone; backpackers picnicked and slept in the Upper Cemetery; hikers headed for the Temple of the Moon and the path up Huayna Picchu, the "Young Peak" dwarfed by its higher companion. There was little idle chatter; wanderers passed each other at several junctures with a nod of recognition, occasionally stopping to exchange cliches.

I thought about spirits, energy centers, and all the facts and rumors I had heard and read about the powers of this mystical place, how just being here is supposed to lift your spirits, clear your mind, and focus your thinking, allowing the human spirit to soar to new levels of perception or go inward toward introspection. I wondered what it would be like to feel this place at night, to sense the darkness and wonder at unseen mysteries. Later, I found the answer in *There's More to Life than Surface*, by Australian journalist Kate Turkington.

"The air is pure, the silence profound. Our little group…is totally alone in Machu Picchu — one of the great holy places of the world, one of its most sacred sites. We each find a solitary place under the stars. I feel divorced from here and now, my mind floating somewhere above the dimly seen but intensely felt mountains. There is much spiritual energy here, and great peace."

Blood Cults and Golden Treasure

THE INCA ARE THE BEST KNOWN OF PERU'S ANCIENT PEOPLE, BUT THEY ARE FAR FROM BEING THE MOST ARTISTIC OR RUTHLESS. Both of those mantles could fall on the Mochica, a culture that thrived along the north coast between AD 200 and 1100. Little was known about the Moche people until fairly recently because their empire had passed away long before the arrival of the Spanish conquistadors, but recent archaeological finds reveal they reached a higher plateau of civilization than any other ancient people in the western hemisphere save the Maya of Central America.

As Peru's first true urban culture, they built great cities like Sipán and Túcume, garnished with fabulous palaces, awesome temples and huge mudbrick pyramids called *huacas*. Their artisans produced a wealth of intricate gold and silver pieces as well as an abundance of pottery that depicted everyday life among the Moche. But there was also a brutal side to their realm. There is new evidence that Moche rulers and high priests engaged in bloody sacrificial rites that included the execution of war prisoners. But the Moche didn't stop there: they actually drank the blood of their victims from golden chalices. In fact, researchers now surmise that their culture declined because the hierarchy became too obsessed with these gruesome religious rites and ignored the advance of militant tribes who would soon surpass them.

Today the glory of the Mochica or Moche culture can be seen at half a dozen major sites around Peru.

OPPOSITE: The sun casts a golden glow on the precise architecture of Incan terraces. ABOVE: Mochica funeral mask at the Brüning Museum.

The most renowned of these is Sipán, 30 km (20 miles) east of Chiclayo, where the first of a dozen royal tombs was uncovered in 1987. The first corpse — dubbed the Lord of Sipán by the archaeologists who excavated the site — was clad head to toe in golden ornaments the likes of which had never been seen in South America. The treasure was so rich that people immediately compared it to another great twentieth-century wonder: King Tutankhamen's tomb in Egypt. Since that first discovery, the tombs of generals, shamans, and other aristocrats have been unearthed on the same necropolis.

Much of the Sipán gold treasure and a profusion of Moche pottery are currently on display at the Brüning Museum in Lambayeque. Other good examples can be seen at the Museo de la Nación (Museum of the Nation) and the Museo de Oro (Gold Museum) in Lima. The private Cassinelli Museum in Trujillo also boasts a very good collection of Moche ceramics. Other Moche sites open to visitors include the ruined city of Túcume with its 26 pyramids and the giant Huaca del Sol (Pyramid of the Sun) south of Trujillo.

Search for the Perfect Mountain

THERE ARE A LOT OF ANDES TO CHOOSE FROM, LITERALLY THOUSANDS OF PEAKS SPREAD BETWEEN COLOMBIA'S NORTHERN EXTREMES AND THE SOUTHERN TIP OF CHILE. But nearly anyone who knows this range would be hard-pressed to find a more impeccable mountain than Alpamayo. Why is it so perfect? Foremost is the shape: an almost ideal triangle that rises to a staggering height of 5,947 m (19,506 ft) in the Cordillera Blanca north of Lima. Covered in perpetual snow and ice, Alpamayo stands like a pyramid against the deep-blue highland sky. It offers a daunting challenge to even the most serious climbers, but for photographers the mountain is an absolute dream. Is it possible to snap a bad picture of this peak? I don't think so.

Perfection also comes in the nature that thrives around the mountain's feet. Alpamayo is the northern linchpin of Huascarán National Park, one of Peru's most important nature reserves. The park scenery is incredible, a mosaic of alpine lakes, meadows, glaciers, and deep-green

forest where a diversity of native plants and animals thrive. One of the more remarkable inhabitants is the *Puya raimondi*, a high-altitude desert plant that grows to 12 m (36 ft). Among other denizens are deer, fox, and viscacha (rabbit-like rodents), and numerous bird species including the great Andean condor.

The area is also an adventure-sports paradise. There are several hundred kilometers of trails, including many ancient Indian routes, ideal for hiking, horseback riding, and mountain biking. The cordillera's vertical rock walls and other snowcapped peaks are an open invitation to climbers, while the Río Santa down in the Callejón de Huaylas valley works up enough speed to produce a great whitewater rafting run. You can sleep beneath the stars at some primitive campsite or in a cozy room at some mountain lodge in Huaraz. You can explore the area for just one day or ramble through the park for several days or weeks without ever having to retrace your steps along the same trail. In so many respects, the Cordillera Blanca offer the Andes of our dreams: crisp mountain air, extraordinary vistas, daring adventures… in the shadow of that perfect pyramid mountain.

OPPOSITE: Mochica corn goddess rendered in ceramic LEFT. Isolated Indian homestead RIGHT. ABOVE: Shepherds move their herd across the *altiplano* near Cusco.

Step Back into the Middle Ages

FROM GREAT CATHEDRALS AND ORNATE PALACES TO SPRAWLING PLAZAS AND HACIENDAS, PERU HAS MANY SPANISH COLONIAL TREASURES. But my favorite, the place that really summons up a feeling of the past, is Santa Catalina Monastery in Arequipa. Unveiled in 1580 as a retreat for nuns from wealthy colonial families, the monastery was completely shut off from the world until 1970 when the municipal government decreed that the good sisters must comply with local building and sanitation codes just like everyone else in Arequipa. In order to pay for modernization of electricity and plumbing, the nuns opted for tourism on a limited scale.

Stepping beyond the front doors of Santa Catalina is like unlocking a treasure chest that hasn't been opened in four hundred years, a rare peek into a way of life that has largely vanished with the onslaught of modern times. Alexandra Revilla, my English-speaking guide, was a cache of information on both the building's history and the lifestyle of the people who lived within. Our first destination was the Court of Silence, where novice nuns spent their first year. "For a young woman to get into here, her family had to pay a thousand silver coins and provide a dowry of 25 things that she could use during her life," Alexandra explained. Displayed in the "cells" around the courtyard were various dowry items including furniture, kitchenware, and religious artwork.

Our next stop was the Cloister of the Oranges, the point of no return for novices who had decided to commit their entire life to Santa Catalina. Very few nuns ever saw the outside world again. "To leave was a great shame for the family," Alexandra continued. "It was better to say that you didn't have a daughter than to admit that she had left the convent."

The rest of Santa Catalina gradually unfolded before us, pastel buildings arranged along six streets named after Spanish cities because of their resemblance to Iberian architecture. For all intents and purposes it was a small city; with its own hospital, cemetery, plaza, and public baths. In one large room I carefully studied the portraits of 13 mothers superior, the paintings were rendered after their death with the artist staring at the corpse.

"The size of a nun's cell depended on how much money the family had," Alexandra continued. Some were quite opulent, with splendid furnishings and artwork. Servant's quarters are attached to many of the cells, for in bygone days few of the nuns did their own cooking and cleaning. When I remarked on how spacious and comfortable the cells must have been, Alexandra smiled. "Yes," she said, "but you must remember she had to stay here all her life. The only people that you ever see or talk to are your servants or other nuns." That sobering thought stayed with me until I had made my exit back into the world outside. A couple of hours in the Middle Ages was enough for me.

ABOVE: Arequipa's Santa Catalina Monastery flaunts its Iberian heritage. RIGHT: Jesuits built Arequipa's seventeenth-century La Compañía.

Ponder the Mysteries of Nazca

"ARE YOU READY FOR ADVENTURE?" ASKS PEPE AS HE PULLS OUR SINGLE-ENGINE PLANE ONTO THE SMALL RUNWAY AT NAZCA. Clad in a black leather jacket and aviator sunglasses, he is the very picture of a dashing young pilot. Moments later we are airborne, slowly climbing over the verdant fields of the Nazca Valley and then out into the vast desert that surrounds this oasis city in southern Peru. It's early morning and the wind is still, the sun just peeking over the Andes as we level off at 300 m (900 ft) above the plain. Our destination is the famous Nazca Lines, strange geometric shapes and zoomorphic forms created by some ancient people on the Pampas de San José more than a thousand years ago.

The Nazca Lines are one of Peru's enduring mysteries, accidentally discovered in 1929 by Paul Kosok during his aerial investigation of the Inca irrigation network, and studied by eccentric German Maria Reiche for nearly 50 years. Many theories have been put forth as to their origin. Some researchers feel they have religious significance while others claim they are some sort of ancient astronomical observatory with the various trapezoids and figures related to overhead constellations. Others maintain the lines were created by visiting extraterrestrial beings — a carefully demarcated landing zone. Most likely they were rendered by master artists of the Nazca culture that flourished in this region from 300 BC to AD 700. But the riddle of their origin only adds to the magical allure of the place.

Ten minutes after takeoff, Pepe banks the plane sharply. The G-force nearly pushes my stomach up into my throat, but the view out the port-side window overwhelms any physical discomfort: a perfectly rendered figure of a whale sketched on the desert floor. Over the next 40 minutes we buzz over least a dozen other images including a giant spider, a condor, a hummingbird, a dog, llamas, a lizard, and the bizarre humanoid form dubbed "the astronaut" because of its likeness to an alien being. Each time we approach a new figure, we circle slowly until everyone has snapped the perfect picture and we've all had our bird's-eye view. Pepe levels off again and we slowly sink over Nazca city before a perfect landing at the airstrip.

Flights over the Nazca Lines average US$45 to US$60 dollars per person. My journey was on **AeroCondor** ((34) 522402, the first airline to offer scenic aviation in this area. You can book through your hotel front desk or the AeroCondor office at Nazca Airport.

Drop by for Breakfast with the Macaws

A CANOE DRIFTS ALONG A LOW RIVER AND STOPS AT A MUDDY SANDBAR FACING A CRUMBLING CLIFF. Passengers bundled in windbreakers, pockets stuffed with cellophane-wrapped crackers, settle their campstools on dry ground. Chirping sounds fill the sky as small bodies flutter toward treetops in the faint glimmer of the sun. Binoculars rise. A faint buzz of muttering precedes a formation of parrots; cawing signals the descent of scarlet macaws. Within fifteen minutes the rust-colored cliff serves as a backdrop for flapping green wings, bobbing yellow heads, and mottled beaks in constant motion. Patches of iridescent emerald feathers cover the hillside, but all human eyes are focused on the golden chests of brilliant blue macaws gliding overhead. Parrots and swifts shift position, making way for the royal visitors to this clay café.

Peru's Amazon Basin is dotted with *collpas*, hillsides rich in a salty clay that nourishes animals and birds. The most famous are located in the Manú National Park, a remote, highly regulated reserve that sprawls through high cloud-forest on the

LEFT: This ancient Nazca farmer decorates a wooden vase. OPPOSITE: Nazca sculpture TOP at Lima's Amano Museum. ABOVE: Gold and blue macaws swoop to clay hillsides and hang around remote camps in the Amazon basin.

eastern banks of the Andes to the jungles of the Amazon basin. Birdwatchers come to experience Blanquillo, Peru's most famous clay lick in the southern end of the park, revered by naturalists from all over the world much as spiritualists praise Machu Picchu. To visit the country without coming here is viewed by some as akin to sin.

But Blanquillo is inaccessible if you're on a tight schedule, while the clay licks in the southern part of the country at Tambopata can realistically be visited in a day or two. The Tambopata Research Center, six hours by boat from Puerto Maldonado, was my base for experiencing a *collpa*. I returned every morning for three days, ending my visits at a blind that had been built above the cliff for photographers. I sat in absolute rigidity for over an hour, taping bird sounds and wishing for a giant telephoto lens. The noise above my head in the rainforest canopy was nearly deafening; when hundreds of birds took flight in fear of some invisible prey, I envisioned Alfred Hitchcock lurking in the trees.

Most of the time I focused my binoculars on a single tree midway down the clay lick, where blue and yellow macaws took refuge between courses at the natural mineral bar. Macaws mate for life, and in this pocket of wilderness they seem to survive despite cruel hunting and poaching.

But my first visit to the lick was the most dramatic, due to the company of *los chicos* (the kids), a group of free-flying, semi-tame scarlet macaws who are the raison d'être for the research center. As our guide explained the scientific reasons for the clay lick's popularity, our study was rudely interrupted by *los chicos*, who have grown quite accustomed to humans; hence to crackers in cellophane. Merely rustle the paper and you've got five and a half kilos (12 lb) of bird on your shoulders, neck, and arms.

I now find it impossible to visit Peru without spending time with macaws. Fortunately, they're not hard to find, if you have a bit of time, and there are *collpas* to be explored throughout southeastern Peru. The more remote ones are favored by tapirs and jaguars.

Witness a Regeneration

FRIENDS AT HOME AND IN PERU AT FIRST EXPRESSED CONCERN WHEN THEY HEARD I WAS DETERMINED TO VISIT AYACUCHO AND OTHER ANDEAN CITIES. But I found this region to be among the most moving and rewarding destinations in Peru. I felt as though I had stumbled upon ghost towns coming back to life. I reveled in my presence as a welcome and valued tourist. Children stopped me in the street to ask the time of day, a universal conversation starter. Artists welcomed me into their homes and studios to show me weavings, sculptures, and paintings based on ancient techniques and designs. Poets took note of my pens and papers and offered their works for my perusal. Cab drivers refused to stop until I'd seen their favorite parts of their cities.

Peru was riddled with bombs, bullets, and insensible brutality less than a decade past. Like many countries throughout the world, it now sits on the cusp of peace.

Nowhere is this more evident than in Ayacucho, center of the *Sendero Luminoso* (Shining Path) movement of the 1970s

and 1980s. Travelers still wisely shun smaller Andean cities where kidnappings, robberies, and murders were the norm far too recently. But the fighting has ended in Ayacucho and similar cities including Huancayo and even Cusco (the largest tourist trap in Peru). These regions, once populated by army troops and armed revolutionaries, are among the best places to explore the soul of Peru.

Ayacuchanos probably suffered more than any other populace during the Sendero Luminoso years. Many ended up in *cuidades jovenes* (young cities constructed without infrastructure or creature comforts) outside Lima when they fled their homes during the worst battles between rebels and the military. Young people, many of them students at one of the country's most prestigious universities, were targeted as rebels, spies, and secret police agents. Artists, writers, and intellectuals who had been nourished by the region's cultural climes were suspect as well. To see them surviving and thriving today nurtures the traveler's soul.

Quechua artisans in the Andes now have money to purchase supplies to create elaborate tapestries. Some of the country's finest universities are back up to speed, graduating well-educated business and agricultural managers, journalists and writers, artists and historians. Mingle with students outside schools in Ayacucho and Cusco and you're bound to be drawn into discussions about computers, the Internet, and the global economy. One precaution — steer away from political or Marxist talk. Intellectual freedom is still a fragile human right. But you can talk with adults who feel they have been reborn and know much about hope.

Carlos Manco, a microbiology student turned hotelier, was my guide to the emotional undercurrents in Ayacucho. "We are a sentimental people," he told me as we dined on pizza at a trendy café near the plaza one night. He proceeded to tell the story of the night in 1984 when he studied for a university biology exam as bombs exploded in the streets. "We all have sad stories," Carlos said before launching into a lecture replete with drawings on the reconstruction of his city.

OPPOSITE: Ayacucho's Plaza de Armas, once the scene of violent demonstrations, is now a peaceful gathering spot. ABOVE: Artist Palomino creates fanciful *retablos* depicting village revelry.

Similar sentiments echo throughout the Andes. "Forget Machu Picchu," adventure guide Lucho Hurtado told me as we sat in a disco in Huancayo. "We are living history right here."

Make it to Market Day

THE BUS FROM YUCAY TO PISAC IN THE SACRED VALLEY IS PACKED TO AND ABOVE THE ROOF ON THURSDAYS, market day for vendors and shoppers from small mountain towns. Grain sacks stuffed with tiny potatoes are jammed against rugs and clay pots bundled in plastic tarps. A sign by the bus driver's seat bears a picture of a roadrunner and the saying "Mas vale perder un minuto que la vida en un minuto" (It is better to lose a minute than life in a minute). No one seems in a particular hurry.

Pisac's market is one of the most famous in the valley; hence the bumper-to-bumper tour buses from Lima clogging the town's tiny streets on market day. Stalls sprawl along the tiny plaza and up hilly streets beside the stern granite church backed by mountains and Inca ruins. Locals doing their weekly shopping congregate in one area, sniffing garlic and onions, eyeing bundles of herbs. Those with disposable cash wander the maze of stalls, looking over woolen weavings in Inca designs, alpaca sweaters and hats, and one-of-a-kind pottery.

I did nearly all my Peru shopping in Pisac one Thursday morning after having compared similar items from Cusco to Lima. I ended up with two stylish sweaters in soft mauves and blues (usually they're all bright or brown); three mysterious water jugs that you fill from the bottom and set upright without the water flowing back out; a gallery-quality, hand-painted pottery plate and bowl with winged-warrior designs; and a pink and purple *manta*, the shoulder wrap Andean women use to carry their babies and purchases. None of the items resembled anything I had seen elsewhere. This is the beauty of Peruvian markets.

The best occur in small towns and cities where centuries-old traditions still hold sway. Huancayo's Sunday market is like an open-air, folk-art museum where artisans sign their wares with pride. Gourd carvers from Cochas Chico and Cochas Grande display dried golden gourds covered with incredibly intricate miniature scenes; weavers spin alpaca yarn beneath the finest blankets to be found in Peru. Belts, or *chumpas*, made on backstrap looms depict the region's famous train; the finest have the weaver's name and date in the scenes.

Juliaca's Sunday and Monday markets are the best place to purchase knitted stuffed animals called *animalitos* and reproductions of Lake Titicaca's famed reed *totora* boats. If you're really lucky, you may find amusingly grotesque *diablada* masks, worn by dance groups in the lake region of Peru and Bolivia. The painted plaster masks are enormous, replete with dragon-fire plumes, bug eyes, horns, and tusks, and are actually far prettier than they sound.

Market days are less common in the Amazon basin; traders here usually travel from village to village along the rivers, making sales along the way. From the looks of the luggage on planes from Puerto Maldonado to Lima, blowguns are big sellers. I preferred the tribal weavings and simple balsa-wood carvings in the daily market at Belén outside Iquitos.

Market days are held in every region of the country; serious collectors plan their itineraries accordingly. See SHOP TILL YOU DROP, page 45 in YOUR CHOICE, for a list of important market days.

Market displays present an intriguing array of regional produce.

YOUR CHOICE

The Great Outdoors

From the snowcapped peaks of the Andes to the sun-baked plains of the Nazca desert to the verdant amazon rainforest, Peru is endowed with some of South America's most spectacular scenery. The country presents ideal terrain for long-distance backpackers, hardcore climbers and would-be jungle explorers, a wealth of routes that can take anywhere from a day to a couple of months to negotiate.

In most areas, including national parks and nature reserves, facilities are primitive at best. Unless you sign on with an adventure-travel outfit you will have to provide everything yourself — food, water, tent, medical supplies, etc. And don't expect a helicopter to pluck you off a mountain top or out of the jungle if you get into trouble. This is wilderness in the true sense of the term.

Peru's most renowned walk — and also its most crowded — is the famed **Inca Trail** between Cusco and the Inca ruins at Machu Picchu. Most people take the train up to a station called Km 88 and start from there. The trek takes anywhere from three to six days depending on your physical fitness level, ability to acclimatize to the altitude, and inclination to linger along the trail. The "high season" is June to September when thousands of Europeans and North Americans take to the Inca Trail. October to May is much less crowded, but seasonal rains can turn the trail into a muddy quagmire and the mountains are often shrouded in clouds.

Northwest of Cusco, a much more rugged journey is the three-day **Espíritu Pampa Trail** from the Vilcabamba river valley to the lost city of Espíritu Pampa (Sacred Plain) in the Andes. It's best accomplished with a local guide or through a Cusco-based adventure-travel company.

For a completely different type of wilderness adventure try the **Callejón de Huaylas** region north of Lima. This beautiful Andean valley is flanked by towering mountain ranges: the Cordillera Negra in the west and the Cordillera Blanca in the east. Most of the latter is

OPPOSITE: Lake Titicaca brings a touch of blue and green to the otherwise stark *altiplano*. ABOVE: Lichen thrives at an altitude of 5,000 m (over 16,000 ft) between Arequipa and Ayacucho.

protected within the confines of Huascarán National Park which contains some of the country's highest and most spectacular peaks. The terrain is ideal for hiking, climbing and mountain biking, especially from April through November when there is minimal rainfall. Much of the park hangs above 4,000 m (13,100 ft) and several places there are vertical drops of 1,000 m (3,200 ft), the sort of rock faces that challenges even the most experienced climbers.

The best places to explore Peru's desert terrain is the vast arid expanse between Lima and Arequipa. **Colca Canyon** is one of the world's deepest gorges, a vertical drop of one kilometer (half a mile) from rim to river. Thee several ways to explore the canyon include whitewater rafting and hiking. Many of the paths are poorly marked, so hikers should only venture into this vast, arid wilderness with an experienced local guide. The best places to locate a guide are in Arequipa and Chivay village on the canyon's south rim.

Another desert wonderland is the **Valley of the Volcanoes** which boasts 80 extinct cinder cones and craters. Overlooking the valley is still active Coropuna Volcano, highest in Peru and tenth-tallest in the Andes.

Paracas National Reserve near Pisco is Peru's premier coastal park with over 280,000 hectares (700,000 acres) of shoreline, mountains, and desert. This is realm of myriad sea creatures including dolphins, whales, sea lions and penguins. Unpaved roads and tracks lead to isolated beaches, lagoons and animal breeding sites. This is ideal terrain for anyone who wants to backpack and camp through a pristine coastal wilderness.

The famed **South American Explorer's Club (SAEC)** (/FAX (1) 4250142 E-MAIL montague@amauta.rcp.net WEB SITE www.samexplo.org, Avenida Portugal 146 (near Alfonso Ugarte) in the Breña district in Lima, is your best source of information on hiking trails, mountain climbing, current weather conditions and other

Snowcapped peaks surround Cusco like a defensive cordon.

outdoor matters in Peru. SAEC members pen regular "trip reports" on major destinations and the club also sells guide books and maps. Another map source is the **Instituto Geografico Nacional** ((1) 4759960 or (1) 4743030, Avenida Aramburu 1198, Surquillo district in Lima, which produces topographic maps of major trekking areas.

As an alternative to outfitting one of your own trips you might consider signing on with an adventure travel company. Lima-based **Explorandes** ((1) 4450532 FAX (1) 4454686, San Fernando 320, Miraflores, offers several interesting options including eight days of trekking in the Cordillera Blanca and a seven-day walk through Colca Canyon.

Sporting Spree

Other than soccer — which is played with fervor in every town and village — Peru didn't offer much in the way or organized or adventure sports until fairly recently. But the advent of a stronger middle class following the end of the Terror Years and a profusion of foreign tourists with a penchant for adventure is spurring an outdoor revolution.

One of the more popular organized sports is **tennis**. The country's first tennis club (Las Terrazas) was founded shortly after World War I and the sport continues to prosper. Las Terrazas in Lima's Miraflores district remains the most

stages horse races four times each week throughout the year while the nearby Lima Polo Club offers its own sort of pony action nearly every weekend.

Despite its lengthy coast, it's actually difficult to charter **boats** along the Peruvian shore. Lima flaunts two yacht clubs — in Barranco and Callao — but you really must have your own craft to take advantage of their hospitality. One outfit that bucks this trend is Expediciones Viento Sur ((1) 9617994 or (1) 9614867, in Callao which offers guided tours to offshore islands and weekly/monthly sailboat charters. **Deep-sea fishing** trips can be arranged at several places, including Paracas in the south, and Tortugas Bay (near Casma) and Punta Sal (near Tumbes) in the north. Another possibility is **trout fishing** on Lake Titicaca, organized through outfitters in Puno.

River running is a different matter. **Whitewater rafting** is possible on at least half a dozen Peruvian rivers including the Río Santa through the Callejón de Huaylas, the Río Colca and Río Majes near Arequipa, the Río Tambopata in the southern Amazon, and the Río Cañete in the Lunahuaná region of the Andes foothills south of Lima. Rapids can range up to Class V and the scenery along these routes is nothing short of spectacular.

With its almost endless summer and perpetual waves, Peru has become a major destination on the world **surfing** circuit. On any given day, at almost any given daylight hour, you can see surfers bobbing up and down in the swell on Lima's Waikiki Beach. Some of the more renowned surf spots include Cabo Blanco and Puerto Chicama along the north coast; Punta Hermosa, Pico Alto and Punta Rocas along the south coast. Chicama is supposed to have the world's longest left break, a long, smooth ride into the beach. Pico Alto, on the other hand, boasts powerful, pounding surf that can reach seven meters (20 ft) on a regular basis.

prestigious tennis facility, but you can also find action at the capital's Lawn Tennis Club and at an expatriate haven called the Lima Cricket & Football Club. Resort hotels in the provinces are also starting to offer tennis courts, including the Hotel Paracas near Pisco and the Gran Hotel Tacna in the far south.

Golf is slowly gaining momentum but is still mainly played in the national capital and its environs. The top spots to tee off are the plush Lima Golf Club in San Isidro and Los Incas Golf Club in Monterrico district. One of the few provincial hotels with its own course is Las Dunas Resort near Ica. **Equestrian sports** are also popular in the national capital. The Hipódromo de Monterrico

The mighty Urubamba River presents a challenge to even the most experienced rafters.

Punta Rocas' claim to fame is that it hosted the World Championships in 1964.

The professional **soccer** season runs March to November with matches at all of the big municipal stadiums around Peru. It's especially entertaining to watch coastal teams struggle with the altitude at away games in Puno, Juliaca, and Cusco. Peru's paramount **bullfighting** arena is Plaza de Acho in Lima, but on Saturday and Sunday afternoons in October and November you can find matadors strutting their stuff in just about any local *plaza de toros*. **Cockfighting** in all its bloody glory is best seen at the Coliseo de Gallos in Lima's Barranco district.

The Open Road

Peru's urban roads are veritable "parking lots" of bumper-to-bumper traffic. But don't get discouraged. With thousands of kilometers of rural routes and highways, the country offers plenty of open roads. In fact, the automobile is an ideal way to explore Peru's hinterlands — assuming that you are familiar with third-world driving conditions.

Many of the roads are in poor condition, riddled with potholes and plagued by rockslides and shifting sand. No matter how fast Peruvians drive, slower speeds are advised for anyone not used to these conditions. Four-wheel drive is highly recommended if you're venturing off major highways. As a general rule, the farther you get from major urban areas and tourist attractions, the more primitive the driving will be.

Never pass unless it's absolutely safe, and be on the lookout for drivers coming in the opposite direction who are passing on a blind curve or other dangerous situation. If the vehicle in front of you flashes its left turn signal or indicator, that doesn't necessarily mean the driver is going to turn left — more likely it's a friendly signal that it's okay to pass, that the road ahead is clear. Avoid driving at night when it's difficult to see on dark country roads and when bandits are more likely to be active outside urban areas. And watch out for speed traps: Peruvian highway patrols on enormous Harley Davidson motorcycles are always on the lookout for speeders.

That said, there is also a positive side to motoring around Peru. Service stations are plentiful along the major routes, many of them brand new with cafés or snack counters, small convenience stores, and clean restrooms. They're almost always full service, which means someone to pump the gas, check the oil, and clean your windshield at no extra cost.

Peru's best route is the Pan-American Highway, which stretches from the Ecuadorian frontier in the north to the Chilean border in the south, nearly 3,000 km (2,000 miles) in total. And the best part of the Pan-American are the spans north and south of Lima, where four-lane divided highway stretches for more than a 100 km (62 miles).

Heading north from Lima you can construct an open-road itinerary that includes a number of interesting cities and top sights including Trujillo and the ancient city of Chan Chan, Chiclayo and its many archaeological sites, and the fabulous beaches north of Piura. It's easy to extend your northern motoring adventure to the Callejón de Huaylas and the Cordillera Blanca from some spectacular mountain scenery.

More adventures await along the Pan-American Highway south of Lima including the Paracas Reserve with its abundance of coastal wildlife, the wine country and stunning sand dunes around Ica, the Nazca Lines (the Pan-American actually cuts one of the images in half), the wonderfully rugged desert coast between Chala and Camaná, and then into Arequipa, the "white city" of the south. Once again, extensions off the main highway are a distinct possibility if you have a few extra days to kill.

OPPOSITE: Urcos nestles in the upper Urubamba Valley TOP. Inca stonework at Sacsayhuamán BOTTOM.

One of the most popular is the five-hour drive from Arequipa to the southern rim of Colca Canyon.

The highway linking Cusco and Puno is another prospect. Much of this route was repaved in 1998 and in excellent repair, affording spectacular vistas of the southern Andes, the desolate *altiplano* and the northwest shore of Lake Titicaca.

Backpacking

In many respects Peru is a backpacker's paradise: a deluge of cheap hotels and restaurants, plentiful bus and train connections, inexpensive clothing and souvenirs, and plenty of places where you can just get lost — "drop out" for a week, a month, or a year. There's also a mystical, magical ambience that embraces ancient cultures and celestial power nodes. So it's not hard to fathom why so many young Europeans and North Americans flock here.

Every major tourist destination is well endowed with inexpensive lodging, usually clustered around the train station, bus terminal or Plaza de Armas (central square). These hostels and small hotels are usually nothing to write home about: dank rooms, cold water, and a toilet down the hall are the norm. But many of them are situated in lovely old colonial buildings with bygone ambience. And the price is hard to beat, usually US$5 to US$10 dollars per night. Lima tends to be more expensive, but even there you can usually find a bed in that price range if you know where to look. Don't be afraid to dicker: you can usually get at least a dollar knocked off the price of any room. Peru also has more than two dozen youth hostels including outlets in Lima and Cusco. A list of youth hostels can be obtained at the **Asociación Peruana de Albergues Juveniles** ((1) 4465488 FAX (1) 4448187 in Lima's Miraflores district.

Likewise, the major destinations also boast a wealth of cheap food, cafés, and snack bars that cater especially to young foreigners; with menus that might include burgers and sandwiches, fruit juices and yogurt, omelets and french fries. Peruvians like to eat out, so there's also no shortage of modest cafés that offer simple and economical priced "Creole" dishes like *ceviche* (marinated seafood), deep-fried *corvina* (sea bass), *pollo asado* (fried chicken), and *lechón* (roast pork).

Camping is another cost-conscious alternative. Unlike Europe and North America there are few organized campgrounds, so camping is really only viable in remote places where no one cares if you pitch a tent and cook your meal over an open fire. The Inca Trail and other trekking routes around Cusco offer prime opportunities for camping, as do protected areas like Paracas National Reserve on the south coast, Huascarán National Park in the Cordillera Blanca, and Manú National Park in the Amazon. But even in these places you won't find organized campsites. Camping equipment is difficult to purchase in Peru, so you should bring everything you anticipate needing including backpack, tent, sleeping bag or hammock, mosquito net, butane stove and gas canisters, some sort of mess kit and water container, and water-purification tablets or device. Beware of inclement weather, especially in the high mountains, the jungle, and along dry riverbeds in desert areas. And please remember to pack out your trash: there are no rangers to clean up after you've moved on to the next campsite.

For cost-conscious travelers, the biggest challenges to traveling around Peru are time and space — that fact that so many of the country's travel highlights are scattered so far apart with vast distances to cover in between. Machu Picchu in the Andes and Manú National Park in the Amazon may look close together on a map, but the reality is that it takes a good four days to travel between them if you're doing things on the cheap (bus, truck, and boat rather than small plane).

Minibuses transport tourists to the Inca Trail.

Luckily the local public transportation is usually efficient and cheap, especially the long-distance buses and shared taxis that ply between the major cities. Luxury high-speed bus lines like the Cruz del Sur (Southern Cross) offer comfortable reclining seats, meal and drink service, restrooms, videos, and even lotto tickets. Shared taxis are called *colectivos*. They are usually station wagons or vans that speed between towns, picking up and letting off passengers at just about any place along the road. They cost more than buses but are usually the best way to reach isolated ruins, beaches, or nature areas if you don't have your own vehicle.

Peru also offers inexpensive rail travel, although the local trains can be as agonizing as they are romantic. The train from Lima into the Central Andes was suspended in 1991, but there is still service between Arequipa, Puno, and Cusco. The journeys between these cities average 10 to 12 hours and cost in the region of US$15 to US$30 one way, depending on the class. I strongly recommend "Pullman" or "Inka" class, which offer reclining seats, secure compartments, and cleaner toilets.

Other than the popular and high-priced Lima–Cusco route, domestic air travel is generally quite reasonable. For instance, a one-way ticket from Juliaca (Puno) to Lima runs around US$70. That's about twice as much as a luxury long-distance bus but the journey will take you two hours rather than two days. You can calculate the savings in hotel and meal costs.

Hitchhiking isn't a viable alternative unless you are prepared to wait hours for a free ride. Most local motorists are not familiar with the concept and will not pick up strangers. Truck drivers are more amenable but they usually expect some sort of token payment that should be worked out beforehand. There is also the issue of personal safety: the type of motorists who are likely to pick you up are also the most likely to rob you.

Living it Up

The high life isn't readily evident in Peru. In many places, consistent hot water, soundproofed walls, and electricity are welcome luxuries. Even Lima's high life is somewhat hidden — you must hit the suburbs to check it out. The fanciest hotels and restaurants in the country are located in Lima's prosperous neighborhoods including Miraflores and San Isidro. Cusco and Arequipa are less trendy than the capital city, but do have some fine upscale establishments and a smattering of international flavor. Once you hit the Amazon Basin the basics become precious commodities, though ultra-deluxe adventure cruises provide an alternative to roughing it (see TAKING A TOUR, page 56). In the countryside, luxury translates into a few tasteful lodges and inns tucked amid gardens and farms, the kind of places you wish you could inhabit for weeks. Advance reservations are strongly advised for the places mentioned below, as luxury is still an anachronism in the Andes, Amazon, and coast. Entrepreneurs are investing in small inns throughout the country, however, and the quality of tourism services is increasing constantly. We stumbled upon pockets of quality in the unlikeliest places. So will you.

EXCEPTIONAL HOTELS

Our choice for utmost luxury and efficiency in Lima is the **Hotel el Olivar** in San Isidro. Facing one of Lima's most serene parks, the hotel is a study in the preferences of upscale Peruvians and international travelers. The rooms contain all the amenities needed for conducting business or relaxing in style, all provided amid a tasteful wood-and-mirror decor. Check out the shops and the bar. For the sense of home-away-from-home, our vote goes to the **Hotel Antigua Miraflores**, just a few blocks from the waterfront. Owner David Wroughton, a Peruvian who was in the hotel business in Costa Rica a few years back, has turned a 1918 mansion into a comfortable haven. Each room has

a different view or amenity (microwave, whirlpool tub) that makes it special, and the staff do their utmost to make you comfortable.

A building boom is on in this area. The Spanish Meliá chain is building an enormous compound on the waterfront near Parque del Amor (Lover's Park), and Mexico's Quinta Real group is opening a hacienda-style elegant hotel near San Isidro's country club. Closer to the historic center of Lima, the most intriguing hotel is the **Gran Hotel Bolívar**, which was being used as a stage set for a turn-of-the-century film when we visited. It's the kind of place so filled with crystal, carved beams, and art that you wish someone would invest in making it live up to its buried charm. The guest rooms and staff are less accommodating than one might wish, however. Still, it's a great place for a meal or drink.

Cusco has a few exceptional hostelries, most operated by small Peruvian hotel-chain companies. **Posada del Inca**, which has hotels in Lima and the Sacred Valley, manages to provide serenity and civility just a block from Cusco's noisy main plaza. It's a convenient, comfortable, well-managed

base where porters and receptionists remember your name. Another chain property, the **Hotel Libertador** is one of the company's best efforts. The accommodations, pool, and restaurant win rave reviews, and the building has all the right colonial touches to give a sense of character. History seeps through the walls of the **Hotel Monasterio de Cusco**, a seventeenth-century monastery worth touring. The chapel, gardens, and lobby are worth checking out; ask to see a few rooms before accepting what you're given.

The pickings are very slim at Machu Picchu, though the area has one of the loveliest hotels in the country. The **Machu Picchu Pueblo Hotel** with its hillside orchid gardens, hummingbirds, views of the Andes, and superb restaurant and cozy rooms is outstanding. The very expensive **Hotel Machu Picchu Ruinas** at the entrance to the archeological site is best avoided unless you're determined to be close to the ruins at night. The Sacred Valley is a good option for those who want Andean immersion and access to

Simple lodges provide surprising comforts in the midst of the jungle.

other Incan sites. The **Posada del Inca Yucay**, located in a small village near all the valley's attractions, is lovingly set against a mountain backdrop: golden, tiled buildings glow in the changing sun. The rooms, many with balconies and peaceful views, are designed with culture and comfort in mind. The **Hotel Valle Sagrado de los Inkas** is the best choice if you want a swimming pool, tennis courts, and a resort-like ambience. Spiritualists, gardeners, and folklorists favor the serene **Willka-T'ika Garden Guest Lodge**, which only accepts small groups of like-minded guests.

Arequipa, which many call Peru's most beautiful city, has an exceptional **Hotel Libertador**, a picture of colonial-era lifestyle and architecture opposite Selva Alegra park. The food is excellent and the service impeccable and kind. The city's finest historic inn is **La Hosteria**, a colonial mansion upgraded for comfort.

The smaller Andean cities have less to offer when it comes to luxury, though there are some fine moderately priced inns. Puno and the Lake Titicaca region are sadly underserved; even the chain hotels are hampered by lack of maintenance and management. In Trujillo, the **Libertador** redeems itself with a Plaza de Armas Spanish-style building, a fine restaurant, a pleasant pool, and amiable personnel. Near the Colca Canyon, a late-1990s lodge called **Fundo Puye** in Llanque overlooks spectacular vistas of silvery rivers against stone. Rivers and jungle terrain hamper the offerings at Amazon Basin inns. In the north, **Exploranda** provides the most amenities at its lodges; the company is even thinking of building an air-conditioned, full-scale hotel with relatively easy wildlife access.

EXCEPTIONAL RESTAURANTS

Seafood reigns in Lima, where the most lavish restaurants are huge establishments on the coast. The **Costa Verde** is dazzling in size; its buffet of nearly 500 exquisite dishes is worth the staggering price tag. Many of the clients are obviously using business accounts.

Much farther down the pay scale is **Don Beta Cebichería** in Miraflores, a trendy yet unassuming café specializing in squid, octopus, shrimp and other delights in several different *cebiches* and *ceviches* (see GALLOPING GOURMETS, page 50, for the fine distinctions between the two). Cooked fish dishes, tempura, and sushi are also tempting. Spread your visits out rather than trying to taste everything at once. Lima's best French restaurant is **Le Bistrot de Mes Fils**, where pasta, seafood, and snails all get a distinctive touch amid a sleek black-and-white decor.

Cusco is a good place to sample Andean cuisine in buildings constructed by the Inca, though such restaurants are typically so geared to tourists that they can be disappointing. Those that have folkloric shows (traditions sadly lacking in the city's streets and plazas) usually charge a cover fee if you just want to take in the music and dancing. Actually, the best restaurant in an Incan building is **Café Roma**, which specializes in excellent, filling pasta dishes at reasonable prices. Outside Lima, Cusco has the best internationally influenced dining scene, and new restaurants come and go like the notes from a flute. **Señoritas**, with a few seats overlooking the plaza, is a newcomer with promise. Everything is so fresh and carefully prepared that you end up wanting to sample more. The long-lasting **Pucara** is one of the best places in the country for salads, soups, and standard Peruvian dishes served to local families and visitors amid a background of soft Andean music. The best restaurant in the Cusco region is in the small town of Aguas Calientes by Machu Picchu. **El Indio Feliz** makes you want to stay longer in the area. The fresh mountain trout *ceviche* is amazing, as is the ginger chicken. And the owners and clientele are fascinating.

Arequipa's residents demand a certain sophistication in their dining experiences, as evinced by **Le Bistrot**, which specializes in delicate, delightful crêpes (called *panqueques* in Peru).

Family Fun

Like most developing countries, Peru is not an easy place to travel with young children, especially those who don't adapt well to exotic foods, primitive toilets, and long walks. However, that doesn't mean it's an impossible dream. The trick is tailoring your itinerary to include destinations and attractions that make at least a token attempt to cater to children. As a general rule, the more visual and/or active the experience, the more they will get from it.

Depending on their ages and interests, ruins may not be ideal for your children. Younger ones are more likely to be interested in the grazing llamas than the majestic stones of Machu Picchu. But that doesn't mean you shouldn't expose them to archaeological sights. I find that most kids take gruesome interest in anything that involves skeletons, which means that the ancient cemetery of Chauchilla (outside Nazca) and the Tombs of Sipán (outside Chiclayo) should be at the top of your list. Most kids will also delight in a chance to fly over the Nazca Lines —

many of the images resemble something that a child might draw, and of course any kid can relate to pictures of monkeys, lizards, and birds.

Speaking of animals, anything that involves wildlife is also a big winner. The boat trips from Paracas to the Islas Ballestas are ideal for children, giving them a close-up look at sea lions, sea birds, and maybe even whales or dolphins. Another boat trip they will probably enjoy is a cruise among the Floating Islands of Lake Titicaca where they can mingle with genuine Indians, shop for small trinkets, and learn about another culture.

Peru's beaches are more problematic: many are cursed with rip tides and perilous waves, and most are not staffed by lifeguards except during the Peruvian summer holidays in December and January. Beaches closer to urban areas tend to be fouled by litter and pollution. The best beaches for kids are in the far north, at Punta Sal and Máncora, where the water is much warmer and the surf less treacherous.

A Yagua Indian boy paddles his dugout into Iquitos.

Museums are another good bet, although once again you should tailor your choice of collections to your child's tastes (fine art usually goes unappreciated). The Museo de Oro (Gold Museum) in Lima is a case in point. Girls are often enchanted by the gold collection, a glimmering showcase of ancient necklaces, earrings, and other jewelry. Boys, on the other hand, tend to flock to the military collection on the upper floor with its swords and rifles, armor suits, and uniforms. The Museo de la Inquisición (Museum of the Inquisition) in downtown Lima offers an underground torture chamber with spooky wax figures, sort of a South American version of the London Dungeon. And there's always the

catacombs beneath San Francisco Convent if you want to continue the creepy theme. Another collection that's perfect for kids is the Brüning Museum in Lambayeque with its many scale models of ancient life.

Children always like music and dance, too. Try to take them to at least one *peña* to hear some traditional Andean or Creole music. There are several dozen in Cusco to choose from, but you can also find them in Lima, Arequipa, Puno and smaller towns. And don't forget the parade and flag-raising ceremonies that take place in many town squares on Sunday mornings. Among the best I've seen are at the Plaza de Armas in Arequipa and Trujillo, with marching bands, military salutes, beauty queens, and local children's groups.

Cultural Kicks

When it comes to ancient culture, Peru offers a greater wealth of opportunity than just about any nation on the face of this planet. In fact, it would be difficult to find a country that boasts the remnants of so many distinct civilizations over such a long period of time. The country is littered with pyramids, tombs, palaces, citadels, and other archaeological sites created from adobe and stone over the last 4,000 years.

The most obvious is the Inca culture as personified by Machu Picchu, the lost city of the Andes and Peru's most celebrated cultural icon. Inca stonework, accomplished without machines or modern measuring techniques, is still a miracle of engineering. But the Incas are just the tip of the iceberg when it comes to Peru's cultural heritage. Chan Chan on the outskirts of Trujillo represents the crowning achievement of the Chimú culture that flourished along the north coast for several hundred years before

LEFT: Ancient faces from the National Museum of Anthropology and Archeology in Lima. RIGHT: The seaside ruins of Chan Chan near Trujillo ABOVE. The annual Fiesta de la Virgen de Carmen in Paucartambo BELOW.

the Inca ascendancy. The Nazca Lines in the southern desert may have been rendered by alien visitors from other planets to mark landing sites for their space craft. More likely they are the paramount statement of a mysterious Nazca culture that flourished between AD 600 and 700. Ancient artistic expression and royal flamboyance reached its height with the Mochica, or Moche, people who dominated the north coast for nearly a thousand years after the birth of Christ. The fabulous tombs at Sipán with all of their gold ornaments have exposed just a fraction of their aesthetic wonders. Older still are the ghoulish granite friezes at Sechín that probably show the torture and mutilation of ancient prisoners of war.

As the first place on the South American continent to be settled by the Spanish, and the seat of a viceroyalty that extended from northern Chile to the Caribbean, Peru is also rich in Spanish colonial relics. The most obvious manifestations of the colonial are the churches, monasteries and convents that crown nearly every city and town in Peru. Some of them impress by sheer size, like the massive Lima Cathedral where conquistador Francisco Pizarro is buried and the sprawling Santa Catalina Monastery in Arequipa where nuns are still shuttered away from the modern world. Other holy places impress in a much more sublime manner, especially

Lima's lovely Santo Domingo Convent with its quiet chapels and elegant cloisters.

Peru's rich colonial heritage also comes across in secular structures. Lima's claim to fame is the ornate wooden balcony, literally hundreds of them in the neighborhoods around the Plaza de Armas gracing the façades of lovely colonial buildings like the Torre Tagle Palace and the Casa de Osambela. Having suddenly rediscovered its past, Lima's municipal government has launched a fund-raising drive to restore many of these fragile architectural treasures. Many of the most striking colonial mansions survive in the provinces. Trujillo sports several of the best examples; charming old houses like Casa Orbegoso and Casa Urquiaga that have been lovingly restored and are now open to the public.

Many of the treasures of the various pre-Columbian civilizations and the Spanish colonial realm are showcased at Peru's museums, which are among the

finest of their kind in Latin America. Best place to start is the Museo de la Nación (Museum of the Nation) in Lima, an exhaustive collection where you can scrutinize 2,000 years of the nation's archeological and cultural heritage. Among its treasures are Chavín stone carvings, Nazca pottery, Paracas weavings, Inca stonework, and gold artifacts from Sipán. History comes to life through the use of scale models, life-size replicas, and diagrams. Perhaps even more impressive is the nearby Museo de Oro (Gold Museum) with more than 40,000 pieces of ancient treasure. Everywhere you look there's shimmering gold: ceremonial daggers and funeral masks, huge nose plugs and earrings, jaguar and puma effigies, even wallpaper and chain-mail uniforms forged from solid gold.

All around Peru you will discover small museums that showcase artifacts of ancient cultures that thrived in those particular regions. Most famous is the Brüning Museum in Lambayeque, where many of the priceless artifacts excavated from the tombs at Sipán are now on display. The Tello Museum near Paracas offers a small but fascinating insight into the life and times of the culture that flowered along the south coast more than a thousand years ago.

Peru's premier art collection is the Museo de Arte (National Museum of Art) in central Lima, which flaunts four centuries of colonial accomplishment — from baroque religious paintings to Spanish colonial furniture. Another showcase of the colonial period is the Pedro de Osma Colonial Art Museum in Barranco with its fine collection of Spanish colonial painting, sculpture, furniture, and silver. Santa Catalina Museum in Cusco is also rich in colonial art and artifacts — perhaps the country's top showcase for paintings of the Cusqueña School.

LEFT: Shaman dolls in a Chinchero market. ABOVE: Llamas in the Colca Valley don their "Sunday best" for a rainmaking ceremony.

Shop till You Drop

Be sure to leave space in your luggage when traveling to Peru. You're bound to come home with a bundle of precious purchases. Fortunately, every souvenir shop and market displays cleverly designed backpacks and duffel bags stitched from brightly colored cloth — I managed to stuff a bag with bags.

Alpaca sweaters are probably the leading souvenir from Peru; few travelers seem to leave without at least one soft, warm wrap. Cusco is the headquarters for alpaca shoppers, though there are excellent designer-quality boutiques in the Miraflores area of Lima as well. Baby alpaca, nearly as soft as cashmere with a furry nap, is used in the best clothing, from floor-length capes to sweaters, scarves, and gloves. Cusco's streets are filled with boutiques selling only the best; a simple cardigan can run well over US$100 and last a lifetime. Even the airport has a branch of Alpaca III, the finest shop in the area (with branches in Lima). It's often packed with last-minute shoppers picking up scarves for gifts. Outside Cusco, the best places to shop for alpaca are in the department (state) of Huancavelica (check the market and shops in Huancayo) and the Puno and Juliaca areas.

The uninitiated have trouble discerning the difference between alpaca, llama, and sheep's wool, and all three are often combined with acrylic. Sheep's wool and llama are usually more coarse than alpaca: talk with shopkeepers for a quick lesson before buying from the ladies who set up instant markets in the street. Alpaca is often used in its natural colors of brown, beige, white, and black, and woven in simple designs depicting llamas and Incan scenes. It is possible to dye the fiber, however, and I have found gorgeous purple, green, and blue sweaters in shops and markets. Cheap garments are bound to disappoint the shopper in the long run — they disintegrate with alarming speed. Check the fabric closely for a tight weave; try it on to make sure it's not too scratchy. And never dry clean an alpaca garment. The process eliminates the fiber's oil content. Just wash and dry flat and your sweater or cape will last for years.

Woolen knitted hats called *chullos* are favored by Andean men and children; their ear flaps and ties are practical necessities in the cold winds. *Chullo* designs vary with the region in which they are produced; true aficionados can identify a man's village by the hat he wears. The caps sold in shops and markets throughout the Cusco region are big sellers; keep in mind, however, that they may look a bit strange on the ski slopes of the United States or Europe. Peruvian wool gloves, on the other hand, are fashionable anywhere, and come in a wide range of colors and designs. Again, be sure to try them on; some are unbearably rough. Ponchos are a practical purchase, especially if you're traveling by bus or train through the highlands. If you start out in a warm climate and are traveling to higher elevations never pack your poncho away with your luggage. It will come in handy as the temperature drops. You can also use them as blankets in chilly rock-walled hotel rooms. One with a particularly fine design makes a nice wall hanging once you're home. Knitted and woven woolen goods are readily available in the Cusco, Huancavelica, Puno, and other highland areas.

Tapestry weavings used as rugs, blankets, and wall hangings are irresistible. Ayacucho's weavers are renowned throughout the world; several prominent families show their tapestries at galleries from Belgium to Los Angeles. The finest pieces cost thousands of dollars, and many are commissioned by folk art museums and collectors. The weavers in this war-torn region have taken to depicting scenes of battles and peace in their work; some are so full of emotion you can feel the artist's passion without ever meeting him or her in person. Others are filled with light and color, depicting snowcapped mountains, flowing rivers, and angels flying above serene scenes. Abstract designs reminiscent of Escher mazes are prevalent as well; you can lose yourself for hours staring at their patterns.

The eagle-eyed shopper can find less expensive, high-quality works of art outside the masters' showrooms. No design lasts for long without being

copied. Students and apprentices work frantically during their off hours creating their own distinct styles; their works can be found in Ayacucho's main market and a few shops. One needn't spend hundreds or thousands of dollars to obtain an impressive tapestry.

Markets and shops from Lima to Cusco, Puno, Arequipa, Huancayo, and Cajamarca are filled with irresistible wall hangings (*tapices*), rugs (*alfombras*), and blankets (*colchas*). The most common pieces are made of wool, sometimes combined with acrylic. Aniline dyes are used to produce bright blue, pink, and yellow designs featuring llama, cats, horses, butterflies, and geometric patterns. The small pieces make great throw rugs and pillow covers. Natural brown and white patterns feature Inca gods and warriors. Weavers in Hualhuas near Huancayo produce alpaca blankets so cuddly you want to snatch one up and wrap it around your shivering body instantly.

Pottery, though harder to carry home, is equally enticing. I became particularly enamored with the terra-cotta bulls (*toros*) made in Pucara, between Cusco and Puno. The bulls, ranging from a few inches in height to a few feet or more, are used to hold flowers or money. But they

LEFT: *Mantas* woven in brilliant colors are used as baby carriers and shopping bags in the High Andes. ABOVE: Huancayo's artisans create miniature scenes on dried gourds.

have other roles as well. Throughout the country the figures are placed atop roofs and in the rafters of homes. They face construction sites, symbolizing good fortune as a house is raised or a new bedroom completed, becoming a protector when construction is finished. Shops in Puno, Cusco, Lima, and Arequipa carry these sweet-faced totems, often decorated with shiny green paint.

Quinua, near Ayacucho, is famous for its small ceramic churches (*iglesias*) which sit atop homes and businesses. Another totem for protection, they have tiny steeples and domes, often painted bright white. Quinua artisans also produced clay figurines depicting musicians and nativity scenes. Potters in the Sacred Valley near Cusco create lovely plates, trays, and bowls with hand-painted scenes. The finest ceramic wares are found at the Pisac market and in Cusco's shops. Ceramic beads and buttons are also good buys in this region, and far easier to pack than a large fragile bowl.

Retablos are wooden boxes holding tiny painted ceramic figures depicting Andean scenes. The most elaborate *retablos* come from Ayacucho; historically, they were used as small altars depicting religious scenes. The art form has grown to impressive dimensions in recent decades; one-and-a-half-meter (five-foot)-high *retablos* with several platforms and multiple scenes are on display at Ayacucho's folk art museum and in some hotels. More manageable for the traveling shopper are the smaller red and white boxes housing nativity scenes, small triptychs of sheepherders, and amusing depictions of barber shops, cantinas, and markets. Buy *retablos* when you see them; they're not found everywhere. The best ones are found in Ayacucho and Huancayo.

Jewelry made of fine gold and silver from Peru's mines is an art form as well. The most valuable pieces replicate the designs of the Nazca Lines. Sometimes it seems like every traveler is wearing a pin or necklace in the uniquely angular shape of Nazca's fish and birds. The fine Inca

gold jewelry one sees in Lima's Museo de Oro (Gold Museum) is also reproduced throughout the country; filigreed gold designs are favored by jewelers in Piura and Huancayo. The best shops are in Lima, Arequipa, and Cusco; H. Stern, with branches in most major cities, is considered quite reputable. Those on tight budgets can find silver amulets, earrings, bracelets, and necklaces at any market. The silver is sometimes combined with nickel or other alloys that can turn your skin green. Check out the good stuff first so you can spot the fakes.

Amazonian crafts are a bit harder to come by; the best can only be found in Lima's markets and shops or in jungle towns. Blowguns and darts, necklaces

made from seeds of rainforest plants, crude wood carvings, garish masks, and fine textiles can be found in a few shops in Iquitos and Puerto Maldonado and at the mock Indian villages set up for tourists along the rivers.

You can do all your shopping in a day at the markets and boutiques in Lima, Arequipa, and Cusco, and come up with a haul guaranteed to stuff every inch of your luggage. But you'll miss out on much of the fun and fascination of Peruvian crafts. Far better buys are found at regional markets (see MAKE IT TO MARKET DAY, page 22 in TOP SPOTS) scattered throughout the country. When traveling about, keep in mind the following schedule of market days.

Most are held on weekends; according to Lynn Meisch, author of the valuable art-oriented *Traveler's Guide to El Dorado & the Inca Empire*, markets are not held on Tuesdays and Fridays because Peruvians consider these days to be unlucky.

Daily Markets: Ayacucho, Cajamarca, Cusco, Trujillo, Lima, Puno.

Sunday: Huancayo, Huancavelica, Huaraz, Huánuco, Pisac, Chinchero (Sacred Valley), Juliaca, Sicuani.

Monday: Juliaca.

Wednesday: San Jeronimo de Tunan (near Huancayo).

Thursday: Pisac.

Simple cloth dolls and painted clay jugs tempt visitors at the Chinchero market.

Short Breaks

Lima is a perfect base for long weekends or short vacations at many of Peru's leading attractions. Regional airlines make it possible to visit other parts of the country on short jaunts at very reasonable prices. Both AeroPeru and AeroContinente offer frequent service to leading domestic destinations, with flight times usually from one to two hours.

The most obvious choices are the country's other big cities — Cusco, Arequipa, Trujillo, Iquitos, Ayacucho, and Chiclayo — which offer a wide variety of inducements at every price range. Three days is an almost ideal amount of time to explore Cusco and environs; five days

gives you enough time to throw in Machu Picchu. A long weekend in Iquitos is perfect for a short cruise along the Amazon or several days in a secluded jungle camp. Three days in Trujillo gives you enough time to sample the Spanish colonial flavor around the Plaza de Armas, the sprawling ruins of Chan Chan, the towering Pyramids of the Sun and Moon, and the beachside buzz at Huanchaco. Three days is also a good duration for Arequipa, with enough time for Santa Catalina Monastery, the city's baroque churches, and a day trip to Colca Canyon.

Driving is another option. Anyone with their own vehicle can choose from half a dozen spots within a short drive from Lima including beach resorts, nature preserves, and archeological sites. The ruined city of Pachacamac makes for an excellent day trip south of the capital. A three-hour drive south of the capital via the Pan-American Highway is the Pisco-Paracas area with its fine beach resort and a coastal national park that features pristine beaches, deep-sea fishing, and abundant wildlife.

Heading north from Lima you could spend a whole weekend hiking the nature trails of the Lomas de Lachay National Reserve with its unusual coastal ecosystem or the various archeological sites around Casma. Five hours drive north of the capital is the exquisite Callejón de Huaylas and the Cordillera Blanca, an outdoor adventure paradise that offers quick access to camping, hiking, mountain biking, and rock climbing.

Another alternative is creating your own special-interest tour that can be accomplished over a weekend or holiday period. For instance, you could spend two or three days touring the various wineries of the Ica Valley where most of the country's *pisco* brandy is produced. You might want to fly into Iquitos or Puerto Maldonado for a weekend of bird-watching in the Amazon rainforest. Or a brief jaunt to Puno for several days of trout fishing on Lake Titicaca. Indeed, Peru presents plenty of options for short breaks, areas and activities that render a memorable and extraordinary escape from the routine of everyday life.

Festive Flings

Organized itineraries can quickly disintegrate when one stumbles upon a Peruvian festival. Since there's a fiesta in some part of the country on at least 100 days of the year, chances are good you'll see at least one. The Roman Catholic feast-day calendar is followed with liberal interpretation; saint's days are often celebrated with a combination of religious processions, Inca rituals, and plenty of music, food, and alcohol. Agricultural events are also celebrated with great fervor; historic and political milestones are less important. Most of the major cities have a week of cultural events as well.

Carnaval is one of the most unifying holidays, creating an excuse for days and weeks of wild and exuberant celebration throughout the country. In Iquitos, there are Carnaval celebrations almost every weekend in February leading up to Ash Wednesday and the beginning of Lent. Parades, dances, and plenty of fireworks are traditional in all Carnaval parties, as is the disconcerting local habit of throwing water balloons and even buckets of water on unsuspecting victims. Some of the best spots for

OPPOSITE: Desert marvels await in both north and south of Lima TOP. The Amazon jungle surrounds Puerto Maldonado BELOW. Garish and bizarre masks ABOVE are the hallmark of all religious fiestas.

Carnaval are Puno, Cusco, Callejón de Huaylas, and Cajamarca.

Holy week, or **Semana Santa**, beginning the Friday before Easter, is a very important holiday in Peru. If you can visit Ayacucho at this time, you will be privy to a week's worth of processions, parades, and parties. During Semana Santa, each day's rituals compete in splendor with those of the day before. One on Good Friday, known as the procession of the holy sepulcher, recreates the scene of Christ in the tomb. The lights of the city are dimmed; the only glow comes from the glass-and-wood case in which Christ lies on a bed of white roses. A cortege dressed in black accompanies him, carrying thousands of burning candles. Musicians play a soulful and melancholy melody. Before the procession, devotees and visitors alike crowd into Santo Domingo Church, where the body of Christ is placed on a white shroud in the central nave. Many towns and cities offer spectacular parades, but those of Ayacucho, Cusco, and Puno are generally considered to be the best.

Exactly nine weeks after Maundy Thursday, Peruvians celebrate **Corpus Christi**. The exact date usually falls in mid-June, and the most elaborate processions and parties are held in the region around Cusco. **Inti Raymi**, observing the winter solstice, is the most important Inca holiday and falls on June 24. Cusco, center of Inca history, is the place

to be. Impressive parades and folkloric dance and music performances last all week at the archaeological site of Sacsayhuamán on the city's outskirts. Inti Raymi has become a major tourist attraction; book your rooms months in advance. June 24 is also the feast day for **San Juan Bautista (Saint John the Baptist)**. The combination of Inca and Catholic rituals at a time of astrological importance makes for fascinating spectacles throughout the Andes. June 29 is the **feast of San Pedro and San Pablo (St. Peter and St. Paul)**, a public holiday all over Peru. The proximity to the June 24 pretty much guarantees ongoing partying for over a week. The most jubilant commemorations take place in the fishing

villages along the coast. July 28 to 29 is the celebration of **Independence Day** in Peru, another national holiday.

The feast of **Santa Rosa de Lima** on August 30 is celebrated in villages and towns near the capital city, as is **El Señor de los Milagros (Our Lord of the Miracles)** on October 18. The religious procession to Lima's Plaza de Armas is overwhelming; the saint is credited with saving Lima from earthquakes, and is much revered. Many women wear purple throughout the month to honor him.

As in many parts of Latin America **All Souls Day**, or **Día de los Muertos** (November 2), is an important holiday in Peru. Family members carry food, drink, and flowers to the graves of their departed loved ones. The ambience is festive, though, rather than maudlin. The Inca honored their dead at this time of year as well, and there is a merging of traditions in Andean towns. Many baptisms take place at this time. November 1 to 7 brings the **Puno Festival**, commemorating the legendary emergence of Manco Capac and Mama Ocllo, founders of the Inca empire, from Lake Titicaca. The regional dances presented include the dragon- and devil-oriented *diablada*, which is performed in Bolivia as well. **Christmas** on December 25 is a public holiday, as is half of Christmas Eve.

LEFT AND ABOVE: The faithful don elaborate costumes and dance from dusk to dawn to honor patron saints in villages and cities throughout Peru.

Galloping Gourmets

Some visitors find Peru's cuisine to be utterly boring or odd; others ferret out a few favorites available nearly everywhere. Some basics remain the same. Soups and stews are usually quite good unless they've been watered down. Fish from the ocean and mountain streams and lakes is on nearly every menu. Seafood rules in Lima and the coastal area, while the mountain towns feature wonderful pink trout. Chicken — fried, stewed, roasted, shredded — is ubiquitous. Vegetarians have no problem finding salads, soups, and even meat substitutes in Lima, but their options narrow the farther they wander. Carnivores can sample llama steaks and roasted guinea pig, both considered great delicacies.

To truly enjoy Peruvian cooking you must sample the regional dishes everywhere you go. Peruvians talk dreamily of the *cebiche* (marinated fish) in Lima, *anticuchos* (beef hearts) in Ayacucho, the lamb in Huancayo, and the *mollejitas* (chicken innards) in Arequipa. Granted, some of these are acquired tastes; less adventuresome diners can still sample regional tamales with a wide range of fillings wrapped in corn dough, or a range of potato dishes that stagger the mind. Pasta, the universal comfort food, is readily

available — one traveler stuck with pasta carbonara nearly everywhere he went. Pizza is also common in most cities; some of the international chains are joining the burger joints in strip malls. The major grocery stores offer an abundance of take-away items, from sandwiches and *empanadas* (vegetable or meat stuffed turnovers) to great bread and regional cheese, fruit, and vegetable salads, and hot dishes. Don't miss the produce and meat markets, held daily in many places, where bizarre fruits, oddly shaped potatoes, and buckets of grains offer endless opportunities for experimentation.

BREADS

Wander the streets of Huancayo and you find it hard to imagine how anyone could stay thin amid the proliferation of bakeries. The smell of fresh bread permeates the streets in most cities. *Panaderías* (bakeries) and *pastelerías* (pastry shops) are never hard to find. The flat, somewhat dry rolls served with meals in most restaurants are sad replicas of the truly fresh ones sold in markets. Bakers in Huancayo make great wheat and grain breads (*pan integral*).

CHEESE AND DAIRY PRODUCTS

Given the prevalence of cattle ranches in certain parts of the Sierra, local cheese is a delicacy. Tangy white cow cheese is sold at delicatessens from Lima to Puno; since pasteurization is a concern, stick with high-end markets when buying from a giant round of Ayacucho's famed cheese. Pasteurized milk is sold in cartons at grocery stores; many cooks rely on canned evaporated milk for their recipes. Yogurt is available in most towns; restaurants in Cusco and Arequipa serve wonderful breakfasts of fresh fruit, homemade granola, and yogurt.

VEGETABLES

Over 300 (some say 3,000) varieties of *papas* (potatoes) grow in Peru's mountain gardens; some are as tiny as a baby's fist; others are odd purple, yellow, orange, and brown lumps. Some have bizarre

names, such as the potato *lumchipamundana* that makes the young bride cry. Until the Spanish conquest Europe didn't even have potatoes; they were imported from Peru. Every region has its special potato dishes; sometimes it seems every bowl has at least one potato floating about somewhere. *Papas a la Huancaina* may well be the country's most ubiquitous dish; the recipe originated in Huancayo, where local cooked potatoes are covered with cheese and chilis. *Yacu chupe* is a hearty soup made of potato, cheese, garlic, cilantro, parsley, peppers, eggs, onions, and mint. *Causa* is a cold mashed-potato dish with lemon, pepper, hard-boiled eggs, olives, sweet cooked corn, and an onion sauce.

Corn is the second most prevalent vegetable, sold on the cob (*choclo*) from street stands. *Choclo con queso* (corn on the cob with cheese) is a great quick snack, though you do have to consider the water the corn is boiled in. Corn is also the base of Peru's most common drink, *chicha* (see BEVERAGES, below). *Canchas*, corn kernels fried and sprinkled with salt, are served with drinks and some *cebiches*. They're sold in cellophane bags in most markets, as are deep-fried

lima beans. Corn dough is used to make *tamales*, filled with meat, vegetables or fruit and wrapped in banana leaves. Palm hearts appear in salads in Iquitos.

SPICES, CHILIS, AND HERBS
Aji chilis are the most popular spice in Peru; a chili marinade is placed on the table much like salsa in Mexico. *Aji de Lima*, a small orange or red chili, produces a milder spice than *aji de colorado*, a fiery dried red one. Large *rocoto* chilis appear on menus (especially in Arequipa) as *rocoto relleno*, a spicy pepper stuffed with beef and vegetables. Herbs grow wild and in cultivated patches are used liberally, especially in soups. You'll note the taste of mint, oregano, basil, parsley, and cilantro in clever combinations, most often in soups.

SOUPS AND STEWS
Ingredients are combined, stretched, and cleverly spiced in Peru's soups and stews, which are often sufficient for a full meal. *Hualpa chupe*, a regional soup from

LEFT: The aromas of grilled fava beans and bananas waft from street stands. ABOVE: The dazzling colors of mountain-grown corn are highlighted when displayed on woven cloth.

Huancayo, is a fragrant blend of chicken, *aji* chilis, and *achiote* (a blend of spices). *Chupe verde*, another soup, is an herbal broth filled with potatoes, cheese, and eggs. Corn, hunks of pork, and tripe are blended in the hearty stew called *mondongo*. *Estofado de carne* is a beef stew; *sancochado*, combines meat and vegetables.

Sopa a la criolla is a reliable blend of thin noodles, diced beef heart, potatoes, vegetables, and spices. Recipes vary throughout the country; the best I found was in Iquitos and in the Barranco area of Lima. *Chupe de camarones* is a savory shrimp stew; *parihuela* is a kind of bouillabaisse.

FRUITS

Green, red, and yellow bananas appear in markets in every region; each has a distinct flavor that goes far beyond the imported bananas sold in the North America or Europe. Other fruits appear seasonally; a ripe mango is cause for celebration. Though some of the stranger tropical fruits are an acquired taste, be sure to try *chirimoya* (custard apple), *guanábana* (also called soursop), pomegranates, and *maracuyá* (passionfruit). You needn't even find the fruit; just order a *licuado* (fruit drink) or *helado* (ice cream) from a street stand to capture the essence of the distinct flavors. Papayas the size of watermelons are available year-round. Avocados, called *paltas*, also come in several sizes, shapes and flavors, and are used in sandwiches and salads in the trendier restaurants of Lima and Cusco. Fried plantains appear at nearly every jungle meal; fried plantain and banana chips (called *chifles*) are great snacks.

FISH AND SHELLFISH

The fruits of the sea are served liberally throughout Peru. Check out Costa Verde or one of the other seafood-buffet restaurants in Lima for an introductory overview. *Ceviche* (called *cebiche* in Castilian Spanish) is a popular dish throughout Latin America and Spain. The Latin spelling of the name (*ceviche*)

is typically used for the simplest version of the dish, which consists of fresh fish or shellfish marinated in lime juice. It is served as a "raw" fish cocktail or salad with toasted or cooked corn. The name *cebiche* is normally used for more complicated versions of the dish, in which several varieties of seafood are mixed together along with chilis, cilantro, tomatoes, and onions. *Escabeche* is a more filling combination of raw fish and prawns with *aji* chilis, onions, sliced eggs, olives, and chunks of cheese. Both dishes rate special treatment along the coast and in Lima and most major cities, where you can find *cebecherías* (*cebiche* cafés) and *marisquerías* (seafood restaurants).

Tuna, sea bass, and whatever happens to be fresh appear on menus grilled, baked, or fried. Pricier restaurants use various fancy sauces on their fresh fish, but the simplest preparations always taste the best. Mountain trout, corvina, and bass are prepared in similar fashions. Never pass up a chance to have pink trout, one of the country's finest delicacies. In the northern Amazon area, fish dishes have a distinctive Brazilian flair. *Paiche*, said to be the world's largest freshwater fish, is a local specialty in Iquitos; it's usually served with white rice and fried green plantains.

MEATS

The thick beef steaks one finds readily in Argentina are rarely seen outside Lima. In rural Peru beef is normally stretched to its full potential for feeding many mouths. Steaks are usually skinny and chewy; thus, beef is usually served with a sauce or in stews and soups. *Lomo saltado* (sautéed beef) is a flavorful combination of beef strips, onions, tomatoes garlic, *aji* chilis, and fried potatoes. *Lomo a la huancaina* uses strips of beef with and egg and cheese sauce. Beef hearts, called *anticuchos*, star in brochettes, soups, and stews. The best recipes come from Ayacucho, Huancayo, and Lima. Tripe appears in soups and stews, *caucau* is a dish of tripe, potatoes, peppers, and sliced egg, served with white rice. *Chaqui* (dried meat) is a staple in the Andes, where a slaughtered cow may feed a family for a year. *Olucos con charui* is a hearty dish of vegetables, beans, and dried meat, topped with cheese.

Guinea pigs (*cuy*) are nearly as common as chickens in markets and homes, though restaurants serving *cuy* are most often found in highland cities. The sweet furry critters are sold live in most markets and are not bought as pets. *Cuy* is served whole or butterflied, and can be quite greasy. Rabbits get similar treatment in some mountain villages. Chicken can become tiresome quickly; just the overwhelming prevalence of chicken restaurants and takeouts in most cities becomes a turnoff. Chicken is sliced, diced, shredded and boiled in soups, stews and casseroles; the best way it's served is roasted whole over a wood fire on rotating spits.

Pigs and lambs are reserved for major celebrations; *lechón* (roasted pig) and *pachamanca* (lamb slowly roasted in an underground pit) are served at some country restaurants on Sundays and feature heavily in regional fiestas. Duck (*pato*) and goat (*cabrito*) are served in the north.

SWEETS AND DESSERTS

Sugary snacks and lavish *tortas* (cakes) are part of the daily diet. Candies and sweet treats sold in shops and on the street include *alfajores* (shortbread), *cocadas al horno* (macaroon-like cookies), *ganja blanco* (boiled evaporated or condensed milk and sugar, sometimes mixed with pineapple or peanuts). *Churros*, fried spirals of sweet dough sprinkled with sugar, are irresistible treats sold in plazas and from street stands everywhere. Hardier desserts include *mazamorra morada*, a blend of purple maize, sugar, cinnamon, and milk. Fruits and sweet sauces fill *panqueques* (crêpes); coconut, chocolate, and lemon flavor *tortas*, or cakes.

BEVERAGES

Peru's favorite carbonated beverage is Inka Cola, a yellow-green sugary soda. Other brand-name sodas are available as

well, along with bottled still water (*agua sin gas*) and carbonated water (*con gas*). *Licuados* made with fresh fruit and milk or water are wonderful and can be ordered by the pitcher (*jarra*). There are several good beers, often pegged to a particular region, as with the Cusqueña and Arequipa brands. Cristal, Pilsener, and Malta brown ale are the most common brands. Peruvian wines produced in Ica are sad competition for those from Chile and Argentina. *Chicha*, the national beverage for fiestas and any celebration, is made from fermented corn. It is served in taverns called *chicherias*. Various regions claim to produce the best chicha, though none of it could be called smooth. Beware of the chicha passed around at parties and parades; it may be made with unhealthful water. *Chicha morada*, made of purple corn, is nonalcoholic and refreshing. *Pisco*, a kind of sweet brandy, is powerful stuff, best sampled in a pisco sour — made with beaten eggs whites and sugar. Coffee is served as an infusion along with hot water; cappuccino, espresso and other coffee drinks are served in the main cities. *Mate* (tea) made from coca leaves is served when guests arrive at hotels in high-altitude areas; it relieves many of the symptoms of altitude sickness.

Small potatoes are skewered with chunks of beef for an instant meal served in the street.

Special Interests

Peru offers travelers a wealth of educational experiences combining nature, culture, and history. Though there are a few companies offering structured tours for birders and history buffs, travelers with specific interests are best off choosing a region that best fits their field of study and hooking up with local guides and companies.

ARCHEOLOGY, ANTHROPOLOGY, AND HISTORY

Many of the companies mentioned in TAKING A TOUR, below, offer comprehensive packages that hit the highlights, but you can easily arrange a theme trip on your own. If archeology is your bent, you must see Machu Picchu and the Inca ruins in the Sacred Valley, the Nazca Lines, Chan Chan in the north, and the tomb of Sipán near Chiclayo. If living cultures are of more interest, include Lake Titicaca, the Sacred Valley, Puno, and the Amazon Basin. History buffs should allot plenty of time for Lima's museums, convents, churches, mansions, and Plaza de Armas — do not miss the Museo de Oro (Gold Museum).

BIRDING

Peru is a birder's paradise. Flamingos, seagulls, and sandpipers flock around Paracas and flutter above sea lions, turtles, and penguins at Islas Ballestas. Condors soar above the Colca canyon. Quetzals, oropendula, and hummingbirds favor the high eastern slopes of the Andes; macaws, parrots, and truly exotic species favor the rainforest and lowland jungles. **Field Guides, Inc.** ((512) 327-4953 TOLL-FREE IN THE UNITED STATES (800) 728-4953 FAX (512) 327-9231 E-MAIL fgileader@aol.com WEB SITE www.fieldguides.com, PO Box 160723, Austin, Texas 78716-0723, offers numerous tours in different regions of Peru, including Northern Peru, Machu Picchu, and the fabulous Manú National Park. The guides are knowledgeable and the offering of birds is rich and varied.

LANGUAGE CLASSES

Peru has yet to become a major Spanish-language center like parts of Guatemala or Mexico have become. But there are a few good language schools catering to foreigners. The best are in Cusco and Lima.

RESEARCH AND VOLUNTEERING

Several tour operators including International Expeditions and Wildland Adventures (see TAKING A TOUR, below) offer tours geared toward scientific interests. The most research currently taking place is in Manú, around Iquitos, and at Tambopata; all have research stations that are typically offered in tour packages. The University of California at Berkeley **University Research Expeditions Program (UREP)** ((510) 642-6586 FAX (510) 642-6791 E-MAIL urep@uclink.berkeley.edu WEB SITE www.mip.berkeley.edu/urep, 2223 Fulton Street, Berkeley, California 94720-7050, facilitates partnerships between researchers and members of the general public. Opportunities are provided for students, teachers, and the

LEFT: Quechua ranchers play their flutes while tending alpaca in Andean fields. RIGHT: Llamas and Quechua ladies feel at home amid the stones at Sacsayhuamán ABOVE. Hammered gold collars and other precious artifacts are displayed at the Brüning Museum BELOW.

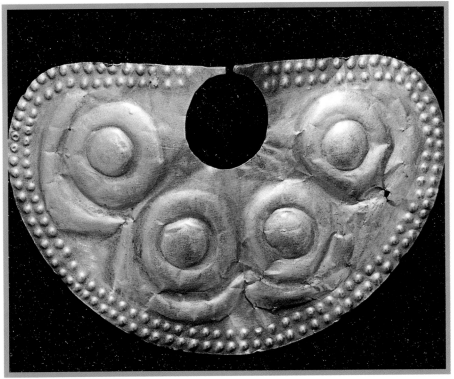

scientifically minded to join university researchers on projects with economic, environmental, and human importance. Projects vary; contact the university for a brochure with the current expeditions.

Taking a Tour

Many travelers rely on guided tours to Peru's most famous attractions, thus reducing the hassles and decisions inherent in traveling through this vast country. The most common tours include Lima, Machu Picchu, the Nazca Lines, and a brief stay in the Amazon Basin. Some combine Machu Picchu with Ecuador's Galápagos Islands. Companies specializing in a particular area such as the Inca Trail are listed in the regional chapters. Those offering an overview of the country are included here.

ADVENTURE

Hiking, river rafting, and mountain climbing are becoming more popular options for travelers to Peru and are offered by the following companies.

Adventure Specialists ((719) 783-2519 FAX (719) 783-2076 (winter (/FAX (719) 630-7687) E-MAIL adventur@rmii.com,

473 Country Road 271, Westcliffe, Colorado 81252, has several expeditions to Peru, including customized climbing expeditions, lost cities expeditions to Chacha Picchu (16 days) and Choquiquirao (18 days), and the New Inca Trail (10 days).

Mountain Travel Sobek TOLL-FREE IN THE UNITED STATES (800) 227-2384 FAX (510) 525-7710 E-MAIL info@mtsobek.com WEB SITE www.mtsobek.com, 6420 Fairmount Avenue, El Cerrito, California 94530, features mountain trekking (six to 15 days) and Amazon adventures (10 days) as well as cultural and rafting adventures. You can contact their European sales office as ((44) 1494-448901 FAX (44) 1494-465526 E-MAIL sales@mtsobekeu.com; and their Australian sales office at ((02) 9-264 5710 FAX (02) 9-267 3047 E-MAIL adventure@africatravel.com.au.

REI TOLL FREE IN THE UNITED STATES (800) 622-2236 FAX (206) 395-4744 E-MAIL travel@rei.com WEB SITE www.rei.com/travel, 6750 South 228th Street, Kent, Washington 98032, has a 10-day trip includes a hike up the Inca Trail to Machu Picchu and a river-rafting trip on the Huambutio-Pisac River.

Wildland Adventures ((206) 365-0686 TOLL-FREE IN THE UNITED STATES (800) 345-4453

FAX (206) 363-6615 E-MAIL info@wildland .com WEB SITE www.wildland.com, 3516 NE 155th Street, Seattle, Washington 98155, presents trips to Peruvian and Bolivian Inca Ruins (with various routes taking from nine to 14 days). Their trips stress contact with natives; the physical requirements vary from easy walking to serious trekking.

Earth River Expeditions ((914) 626-2665 TOLL-FREE IN THE UNITED STATES (800) 643-2784 E-MAIL earthriv@envirolink.org WEB SITE www.earthriver.com, 180 Towpath Road, Accord, New York 12404, offers hardcore experiences. Navigating a remote and challenging class-V river in the Colca Canyon, this trip is recommended for very physically fit individuals only; however, rafting experience is not a requirement.

CRUISING

Some cruise lines offering South America voyages include a stop in Lima and offer side trips to Machu Picchu. Others specialize in sections of the Amazon Basin.

Abercrombie & Kent International ((630) 954-2944 TOLL-FREE IN THE UNITED STATES (800) 323-7308 FAX (630) 954-3324 WEB SITE www.abercrombiekent.com, PO Box 305, Oak Park, Illinois 60303-0305, *YOUR CHOICE*

offers an Amazon Adventure tour: a 10-day river excursion between Iquitos, Peru and Leticia, Columbia. You can also do cruise extensions to Machu Picchu or the Tambopata Jungle Camps. They also have offices in Australia ((03) 9-699 9766, 90 Bridgeport Street, Albert Park, Melbourne, Victoria 3206; and in the United Kingdom ((0171) 730-9600 FAX (0171) 730-9376, Sloane Square House, Holbein Place, London SW1 8NS.

Saga Holidays International, Ltd. ((617) 262-2262 TOLL-FREE IN THE UNITED STATES (800) 432-1432 WEB SITE www .sagaholidays.com, 222 Berkeley Street, Boston, Massachusetts 02116, books Princess Cruises to South America which include four nights in Peru. Lima, Cusco, and Machu Picchu are on the itinerary.

GENERAL INTEREST

Travelers intent on seeing the best of Peru in one journey can combine archaeology, nature, and culture by joining one of the following organized tours. **Questers** TOLL-FREE IN THE UNITED

OPPOSITE: Simple rock shelters blend with the wild surroundings of Huascarán National Park. ABOVE: Trains travel through the Andes under glacier-topped peaks between Cusco and Machu Picchu.

STATES (800) 468-8668 FAX (212) 251-0890 E-MAIL quest1973@aol.com WEB SITE www.questers.com, 381 Park Avenue South, New York, New York 10016. This tour company focuses on ancient civilizations and nature.

Lima Tours ((51-1) 4245110 FAX (51-1) 3304488 E-MAIL inbound@limatours .com.pe WEB SITE www.limatours.com.pe, Belén 1040, PO Box 4340, Lima 1, Peru, offers mostly three-day tours and they can combined to suit your needs. A Best of Peru tour is also available with stops in Lima, Trujillo, Arequipa, Colca, Cusco, Lake Titicaca, Nazca and Machu Picchu. The trip is completed in 17 days.

Overseas Adventure Travel ((617) 876-0533 TOLL-FREE IN THE UNITED STATES (800) 955-1925, 625 Mt. Auburn Street, Cambridge, Massachusetts 02138, provides an 18-day package including a trip up the Amazon River and a stay at the Tambopata Jungle Lodge. An overnight visit to Machu Picchu from Cusco is included, as are three days in the Galápagos.

In the United Kingdom, Peru tours can be arranged through **Journey Latin America** ((0181) 7478315; **Thomas Cook Holidays** ((0173) 3330300; and **Encounter Overland** ((0171) 3706845. In Australia, tours can be booked through **Inco Tours** ((02) 4351-2123; **South American Adventures** ((08) 8272-2102; and **South American Travel Centre** ((02) 9264-6397.

NATURAL HISTORY

Ecotourism is a fairly new concept in Peru; as one Amazonian guide says "It's hard to worry about nature when you don't have enough to eat." A few companies offer complete immersion in Peru's wilderness areas, and travelers who take time to fully explore the highlands and jungles will stumble upon excellent guides during their journeys. To set up nature experiences in advance contact the following companies.

Through **American Wilderness Experience** ((303) 444-2622 or TOLL-FREE IN THE UNITED STATES (800) 444-0099 FAX (303) 444-3999, 2820-A Wilderness Place, Boulder, Colorado 80301, you can book an eight-day ecotour with nature and culture of the Amazon as the emphasis. There is

also a 13-day horseback or walking tour, with camps and lodges in Cusco. **Adventure Center** ((510) 654-1879 TOLL-FREE IN THE UNITED STATES (800) 227-8747 FAX (510) 654-4200 E-MAIL adventctr@aol .com WEB SITE www.adventure-center.com, 1311 63rd Street, Suite 200, Emeryville, California 94608, is a sales agent for quite a few travel companies including Explore Worldwide and Overland Adventures. A myriad of travel opportunities are available through this company and a representative can send you a brochure on the area with emphasis on what you are interested.

International Expeditions ((205) 428-1700 TOLL-FREE IN THE UNITED STATES (800) 633-4734 E-MAIL intlexp@aol.com WEB SITE

www.ietravel.com/intexp, One Environs Park, Helena, Alabama 35080, has eight-day Rainforests of Peru expeditions with an optional five-day Cusco and Machu Picchu extension. Also offered is Rainforests of the Tropical Andes (10 days) and Manú (nine days).

Holbrook Travel, Inc. ((352) 377-7111 TOLL-FREE IN THE UNITED STATES (800) 451-7111 FAX (352) 371-3710 WEB SITE www.holbrooktravel.com, 3540 NW 13th Street, Gainesville, Florida 32609, offers trips including Machu Picchu and the Galápagos (nine nights); Altiplano (eight nights); Peru and Bolivia, from Cusco to Bolivian Pantanal (six nights); Peru's Pre-Columbian civilizations (12 nights). There is also birding to

Manú Wildlife Center and the Tambopata Research Center.

Nature Expeditions International TOLL-FREE IN THE UNITED STATES (800) 869-0639 FAX (520) 721-6719 E-MAIL NaturExp@aol.com WEB SITE www.naturexp.com, 6400 East El Dorado Circle, Suite 210, Tucson, Arizona 85715, invites the traveler to join them on one of several Peru tours, including an eight-day or 17-day upper Amazon adventure, depending on how much time you have, as well as a Peru Discovery tour and an expedition to Machu Picchu.

The countryside around Cusco changes from a dusty brown to verdant green in the rainy season.

YOUR CHOICE

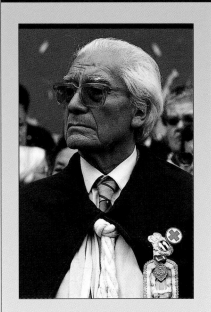

Welcome to Peru

ANDEAN PEAKS, AMAZONIAN TRIBUTARIES, and long stretches of barren desert and sand form the natural landscape of Peru, a country ruled by the gods of wind, earth, water, and sun. Few places encompass such environmental extremes, from glaciers to bubbling hot springs. Earthquakes, volcanoes, mudslides, droughts, and floods rule the nation far more powerfully than any politician (though some have been just as fierce).

Ridges of mountains called *cordilleras* separate the populated coast and the largely deserted jungle, which form the boot-shaped land bordered by Ecuador, Colombia, Brazil, Bolivia, Chile, and the Pacific Ocean. The terrain ripples from beach and desert into the depths of the Colca Canyon, up the foothills of the Andes to the *altiplano*, a moonscape of mountaintops stripped of vegetation by the elements. Land peaks into clouds at Huascarán, the highest mountain in the country at 6,768 m (22,205 ft) above sea level. Ice coats the Cordillera Blanca near Huaraz and shimmers from glaciers above the Sacred Valley. East of the mountaintops cloud-forest gives way to rainforest and *La Selva* (the jungle), home to macaws, parrots, tapir, and capybara — the largest rodent in the world. Though the lumber, oil, and mining industries have left great gashes in nature, condors, mountain bears, jungle monkeys, and jaguars still manage to thrive in isolated outposts.

Peru's natural diversity is matched by its wealth of cultures; the Amazon Basin alone contains hundreds of separate groups speaking different dialects. Quechua is the common language in the Andes, though vocabulary, food, and dress differ vastly from region to region. The mountain people have never been particularly involved with those of the jungle; at times it seems the nation is a series of separate countries. Many people from the coast have never seen the rainforest and rivers that cover much of Peru's land mass; thus, nature often gets second billing after economic development. To see the fires, smoke, and ash from burning forests and agricultural fields during dry season is appalling; one wishes every environmental agency in the world would get involved in Peru.

The country's economy, infrastructure, and tourism industry fell to bits during nearly two decades of internal strife when the Sendero Luminoso movement brought the military out in full force. Travelers were scared away; some days the train to Machu Picchu never left Cusco because no one wanted to take the dangerous ride. Andean highland towns including Ayacucho, Huancayo, and Cusco suffered tremendous losses through death, disappearances, and the outflux of residents looking for safety in coastal cities. Writer and onetime presidential candidate Mario Vargas Llosa chronicled the years of terrorism in *Death in the Andes*, a raw novel I'm glad I didn't read before visiting Peru.

As this book goes to print the entire country is experiencing a rebirth, a resurgence of identity. Throughout the country, Peruvians are counting on peace and prosperity while claiming their individualistic identities. *Limeños*, residents of one of South America's most cosmopolitan cities, deal with robberies, kidnappings, and financial shifts with equanimity, saying their lives are far better and more secure than in the past. Developers have returned to the coast and are building resorts and marinas. As Peru's economy endures global shifts and appears relatively stable, more and more entrepreneurs are investing in small inns and tourism, which continues to rise.

Peru has emerged from decades of isolation with its character and customs intact. All Peruvians seem to welcome tourists with a sense of hope and opportunity. Amazonian teenagers are learning bits of Spanish and English so they can ferry sightseers to clay licks and black lagoons. City slickers are hip to the latest fashions and trends from Europe and Japan. Yet boat builders still weave reeds into canoes at Lake Titicaca, while ranchers in bright wool caps with ear flaps herd llama, alpaca, and sheep in the Sacred Valley. Archeologists continue uncovering mummies and hordes of gold treasures at ruins in the north; astrologers and mystics continue to study the Nazca Lines. Everyone becomes an amateur in some specialty while traveling through the country: some fall for the jungle mystique while others search canyons and mountains for elusive condors, a symbol of all that is beautiful and free. Peru grows on you, offering itself in stark and mesmerizing scenes.

Quechua-speaking woman and child in Ayacucho market.

The Country and Its People

SITUATED IN THE HEART OF THE ANDES mountain range, wedged between the sweltering Amazon Basin and the rich waters of the Pacific Ocean, Peru has always been the linchpin of South America's history, geography, and spiritualism. Civilization first took root here more than six thousand years ago, at about the same time that advanced societies were starting to appear in the other great cradles of human endeavor—Mesopotamia, the Nile Valley, the Indus region, and eastern China. Thanks to a mystical, magical relic called Machu Picchu—and their misfortune at the hands of the Spanish conquistadors — the Incas are the best known of Peru's ancient peoples. But they are far from being the most significant. At least a dozen different civilizations, spread across the length and breadth of country, have contributed to the mosaic that comprises modern Peru.

A LAND OF DAZZLING CONTRAST

The third largest country in South America, Peru covers roughly 1.3 million sq km (496,000 sq miles), an area about the size of France, Spain, and Portugal combined. Situated on the western side of the continent adjacent to the Pacific Ocean, the country is bounded by Ecuador and Colombia in the north, Brazil and Bolivia in the east, and Chile in the south.

Peru comprises three main geographical regions — the coastal plains, the Andes mountains, and the Amazon rainforest. The coastal area (La Costa) runs from the Atacama Desert in the south to the mangrove country around Tumbes in the north. Although primarily composed of uninhabitable desert, the coast is broken by dozens of fertile river valleys, cradles of ancient civilization that today have evolved into rich farming lands and urban areas.

The Pan-American Highway, originally constructed in the 1940s and 1950s, runs the length of the coastal area connecting most of Peru's most populous cities.

Directly east of the coastal plains are the mighty Andes, the second highest mountain range in the world after the Himalayas. Huascarán is Peru's tallest peak — and the highest mountain in all the tropics — soaring 6,768 m (22,205 ft) above sea level. The Andes are slowly growing even higher as

the Nazca tectonic plate burrows beneath the South American plate. This contributes to the region's geological instability, manifested by frequent earthquakes and volcanic activity. The high plains region that separates the various cordillera is called the altiplano, an arid and windswept region that flaunts its own special beauty.

As you travel farther inland, the mountains gradually give way to the jungle (La Selva) and the world's largest tropical rainforest. Although it shrouds more than half the country, the Amazon region is sparsely

populated and barely developed. Enormous rivers water the basin including Río Napo, Río Madre de Dios, Río Ucayali, and Río Amazonas.

THE PRE-COLUMBIAN ERA

Peru is the historical crown jewel of South America, a place where the march of time has left its mark with numerous ruins and countless artifacts. Since the 1870s archaeologists have been attempting to produce a chronological framework of the different pre-Columbian cultures that developed in the high Andes valleys and various fertile river basins along the desert coast. However, this has proved difficult as these civilizations didn't have written language and other remnants of their societies were demolished by the subsequent cultures that displaced them.

The region's first inhabitants were probably nomadic hunters and gatherers who

LEFT: Devotee at the Fiesta de la Virgen del Carmen in Paucartambo. ABOVE: Traditional Indian weaving.

lived in caves. Human remains that date back some 14,000 years have been found in caves. In about 4000 BC, the early Peruvians began planting beans and squash as well as cotton. In such a way they became less nomadic, settling down in villages along Peru's coastal strip and living in simple one-room dwellings. They also fished, using nets and bone hooks as their primary tools. Evidence suggests the potato made its introduction as a staple food from about 3000 BC.

Between 2000 and 1000 BC, tribes of the Lower Formative Period constructed large

era as the country's most important for cultural development during pre-Columbian times, and it was during this period that metallurgy (gold, silver, and copper) and stone carving appeared in Peru for the first time.

Toward the end of this period, the Chavín began to lose their unifying influence. Over the next half century it appears that no one people dominated Peru, with groups like the Salinar culture of the Chicama Valley and the Paracas culture south of Lima generating local rather than regional importance.

ceremonial temples in coastal areas. These people also matured their simple ceramics into sculpted, colored vessels, improved weaving techniques, and developed agricultural terraces in the highlands.

During the Early Horizon Period (1000 to 300 BC) religion evolved into something much more structured under the influence of the Chavín culture in Ancash. The Chavín worshipped a jaguar deity, constructing a number of temples and pyramids where these felines and other gods were worshipped. The most important religious complexes either directly effected by or heavily influenced by Chavín culture were situated at Chavín de Huántar, Sechín, and Kotosh. Some archaeologists view this

The fabulous Classic Period emerged about AD 200 when the people in the Trujillo area began casting pottery from molds and the people in the southern desert developed polychrome techniques. Both groups were so prolific with their ceramics that archaeologists have been able to piece together substantial information about their existence.

The Mochica or Moche culture along the north coast, which peaked in influence around AD 500 to 600, organized the first real urban center of Peru with a well-defined hierarchy. The common people performed agricultural tasks while the upper echelon held both secular and sacred power. People lived in simple structures arranged in clusters around temples and palaces. Spiritually, the Moche focused on nature and ancestors with human sacrifice playing an important role. Opponents in battle were beheaded and offered up to the gods, and there is some evidence that Moche religious, military, and political leaders participated in a human blood cult. The Moche built huge adobe religious platforms like the Pyramids of the Sun and Moon near Trujillo and the pyramids of Sipán near Chiclayo. Sipán also contains a necropolis with treasure-filled royal tombs discovered in 1987, one of the most important archaeological finds in South

beliefs and replaced them with their own values. During this period, their influences spread through much of the Andes and along the coast, laying the foundation for the Inca Empire which would later replace them.

By about 1000, Wari-Tiahuanaco influence was starting to be eclipsed by individual groups as Peru went through a 400-year period of isolated developments. The best known of these cultures was the Chimú in the Trujillo area, with the huge adobe city of Chan Chan as its capital. The Chimú used their knowledge of bronze manufacture to

America since the discovery of Machu Picchu in 1911. It appears the Moche were wiped out by a terrible drought (probably El Niño-inspired) in the late sixth century.

Cultures more or less contemporaneous with the Moche included the Nazca in the southern desert, known mainly for the temple complex at Cahuachi, and the Tiahuanaco on the shores of Lake Titicaca. Although peaceful at the dawn of their influence, the Tiahuanaco took on increasing aggressive tendencies. The period from 650 to 1100 was dominated by what is now called the Wari-Tiahuanaco (also spelled Huari-Tiahuanaco) culture — Peru's first militaristic urban society. Having once conquered another group, the Wari-Tiahuanaco eradicated existing

spread their influence as far as Tumbes in the north and Paramonga in the south.

The ancient culture about which we know the most is that of the Inca, mainly because the Spaniards left a precise written record of what they found when they conquered the region in the early sixteenth century. The Inca were not especially sophisticated from an artistic point of view, but they were master builders and had a highly efficient military that easily vanquished the area's older civilizations. Spreading out from their heartland in Cusco, the Incas dominated Peru for three centuries, extending their empire from

LEFT: Colonial-era engraving of Conibo Indians making oil from turtle eggs. ABOVE: Geometric patterns decorate the ruins of Chan Chan.

present-day Ecuador to central Chile. They insisted that conquered areas adopt their culture and religion, and they forced thousands of people to migrate to other parts of Peru in order to dilute any possible resistance.

CONQUEST AND THE COLONIAL PERIOD

But the Inca were no match for the Spanish conquistadors, who used superior weapons and subterfuge to overcome their shortfall in numbers. During his third expedition to the

proved a good choice as it had a natural harbor nearby, a dependable water supply, and offered quick access to the Andes. It soon became the fulcrum of Spanish domination of the entire western side of South America, seat of the viceroyship of Peru.

Peru developed rapidly during the colonial period into one of the crown jewels of the Spanish realm. Less than two decades after its founding, Lima was a wealthy city with elegant houses and shops lining wide streets. The suburbs of Rimac and the port area of Callao had became the fashionable

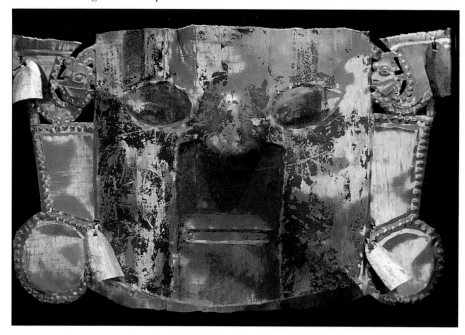

Americas, Francisco Pizarro landed on the Ecuadorian coast and continued on foot to Peru, founding the country's first Spanish town — San Miguel de Piura — in September 1532. In November of the same year, Pizarro captured the Inca emperor Atahualpa at Cajamarca. He held the emperor captive for nearly a year, extracting a vast ransom in return for Atahualpa's release. After collecting a fortune in Inca gold and silver, Pizarro went back on his word: he ordered Atahualpa's execution and then marched on Cusco.

As the Spaniards required a coastal capital for their new dominion, Pizarro chose a location in the Rimac Valley and founded his new city on January 6, 1535 (the Catholic feast of Epiphany or the Day of Kings). Lima

living areas for the very rich who wanted to escape the noise and clamor of the central city. However, turmoil continued in the hinterlands well into the sixteenth century as the Incas fought the Spaniards to regain control of Peru and the conquistadors fought amongst themselves for control of the rich colony. Pizarro was assassinated in 1541. Thirty years later the Inca organized a rebellion that nearly toppled the Spanish. But they were eventually defeated and their leader Túpac Amaru was summarily executed.

The seventeenth century was relatively peaceful and Peru sailed into its heyday as the major economic, political, and cultural center of the Andean colonies. The eighteenth century was marked by a slowdown in growth, exacerbated by a huge earthquake in 1746 which killed 5,000 people in Lima alone (10% of the population). In 1780, the indigenous people again revolted against their exploitation and once again the Spaniards were able to defeat them and execute their leader, Túpac Amaru II.

INDEPENDENCE AND THE REPUBLIC

By the early nineteenth century there was increasing dissatisfaction throughout Latin

were fought in 1824, at Junín on August 6 and at Ayacucho on December 9.

San Martín took over the reigns of power in Lima, but he was soon supplanted by Bolívar — who ruled Peru as a virtual dictator for the next two years. Bolívar retained tight control over the Andean Confederation—Colombia, Venezuela, Ecuador, Peru, and Bolivia—until 1826, when he was finally forced into exile. Within a year of his departure, the Peruvian people had revoked Bolívar's constitution and elected General La Mar as the country's first democratic president.

America with the high taxes imposed by Spain. Peru was no exception. The colony's longing for independence was exasperated by the discovery of large mineral deposits, including vast amounts of guano (seabird droppings), which was used in fertilizer.

In 1821, after liberating Argentina and Chile from Spanish control, José de San Martín landed near Paracas with an invasion force. From a balcony in the tiny seaside town of Huacho, north of Lima, he formally proclaimed Peru's independence. A year later, after liberating Venezuela and Colombia, Simón Bolívar and Field Marshall Sucre continued the emancipation of Peru. Two major battles for Peruvian independence

Despite vanquishing the Spanish, the Republican period was not marked by tranquility. Trouble continued to brew in South America for much of the nineteenth century as the various ex-colonies clashed with one another over border lines and natural resources.

La Mar was overthrown in 1829 by a military junta under the leadership of General Gamarra. Four years later, the people elected General Orbegoso to the presidency and Gamarra was forced into exile. Orbegoso was overthrown by the army just six months later and a new military junta took control. From exile, Gamarra plotted to oust his ri-

LEFT: Golden funeral mask in the Brüning Museum. ABOVE: Indian wedding in Chinchero.

vals and reestablish himself as president — an aim he achieved in 1841.

Following Gamarra's death, Peru entered another period of political upheaval with six presidents in four years. In 1845, the educated and enlightened Ramón Castilla came into power, perhaps the first man of any integrity to rule Peru since independence. During Castilla's presidency a new moderate constitution was introduced and the country experienced rapid economic growth based on exports of guano fertilizer, sugar, and cotton. Slavery was abolished

forced to sign the humiliating Treaty of Anco. Bolivia lost all of her Pacific coast; Peru lost the area around Tacna until 1929 when it was finally ceded back.

By 1890, General Caceres was in power and Peru was facing bankruptcy. The guano reserves were virtually exhausted and the nitrates lost to Chile. An international plan to bail out the country was put into effect with the formulation of the Peruvian Corporation in London, which assumed Peru's US$50 million foreign debt in return for control of the national economy. The corpora-

during this period and there was virtually no social unrest.

But after Castilla's two terms in office, political chaos soon returned. Corruption and overspending on public programs left the country on the verge of economic collapse. In the 1872 elections, Peru's first civilian president was voted into office — capitalist Manuel Pardo.

The nadir of post-colonial Peruvian history was the War of the Pacific (1879–1883). Bolivia and Chile were the first combatants, fighting over rich nitrate deposits in the Atacama Desert. Peru came to Bolivia's aid and was promptly invaded by a superior Chilean army that occupied Lima for two years. In the end, both Bolivia and Peru were

tion soon came to dominate Peru's major infrastructural components and most of its natural resources.

THE TWENTIETH CENTURY

The era of Modern Peru is said to have begun in 1895 with the forced resignation of General Caceres. By early 1900s, the bulk of the country's wealth was in the hands of a few wealthy landowners, big businessmen, and foreign investors. The lot of the ordinary man was deteriorating rapidly.

Augusto Leguía was elected president in 1908, the first member of the bourgeoisie to attain this office. Under his autocratic rule Lima was modernized and foreign investment from North America increased rapidly, outstripping that of Britain. But Leguía did little for the peasant class and it was during his tenure that the first labor movement took root. After changing the constitution to allow himself to remain in office for four terms, Leguía was ousted by a military coup in 1930 — a year after his fourth term began.

The worldwide depression in the 1930s badly affected Peru, as demand for its exports crashed. In 1932, Trujillo's middle class led an uprising against local plantation owners over the primitive conditions on the haciendas. Brutally suppressed by the army, it's estimated that about 5,000 rebels lost their lives during the revolt. Social unrest continued for the next two decades.

Fernando Belaúnde was elected to power in 1963 with a reform agenda. He tried to introduce sweeping social, economic, and agrarian changes — including a dissolution of the haciendas that had dominated rural Peru since Spanish colonial times. Belaúnde was deposed in 1968 by General Juan Velasco, who went on a rampage of industrial nationalization that alienated the United States and many Western European countries. Civilian rule finally returned in 1980 with the reelection of Belaúnde as president after 12 years in exile. Since then all Peruvian presidents have been elected democratically and all have served their full term of office.

In May of 1971 an earthquake devastated much of northern Peru. The 7.7-magnitude tremor killed about 70,000 people and has been called the most deadly disaster ever to occur in the western hemisphere. Poverty was already rampant in many rural areas at the time of the quake, but the natural disaster amplified the huge disparity between the European-based population in coastal cities and Indian people living mostly in the highlands. This disparity flared into virtual civil war during the 1980s and early 1990s, a period that has come to be called the Terror Years. An estimated 25,000 lives were lost as guerrilla groups like *Sendero Luminoso* (Shining Path) and *Movimiento Revolucionario Túpac Amaru* (MRTA) waged war against the government and business community. Both sides were responsible for civilian massacres and flagrant atrocities.

The late 1980s and early 1990s were also marked by severe economic problems, which exacerbated the guerrilla problem. Inflation was at runaway levels, at one point reaching the 10,000% mark. Foreign debt spiraled out of control, reaching US$24 billion.

RECENT EVENTS

Then came Alberto Fujimori. The ambitious son of Japanese immigrants, Fujimori was elected president in 1990 and took office on Peru's Independence day, July 28. To get a

grip on the economic chaos and terrorism he had inherited from his predecessors, Fujimori introduced many unconventional measures. His most controversial move came in 1992 when he dissolved congress, a move that pundits called the *auto-golpe* (self-coup). Although this led to the suspension of most foreign aid, Fujimori retained popular support and the country's economic situation gradually improved. Guerrilla activity collapsed after Sendero Luminoso commander Abimael Guzmán was captured in 1992 and the MRTA leadership was decimated in the Japanese Embassy siege of 1996.

Under Fujimori's leadership, inflation has dropped to a manageable 20%. Pegging the Peruvian *sole* to the United States dollar helped the local currency into a much needed period of stability. The easing of taxes and import laws, plus the privatization of many state enterprises and the elimination of monopolies, led to renewed confidence from the international business community. Fujimori's

LEFT: Inca ruins at Pisac in the Sacred Valley.
ABOVE: Shanty towns sprout on the outskirts of Lima.

other great accomplishment was ending the terrorist threat: forcing the Sendero Luminoso and MRTA into virtual oblivion.

However, some of Fujimori's moves met with increasing criticism both at home and abroad, especially his penchant for changing the law to fit his whims. A new constitution adopted in 1993 included a change of law which allowed presidents to run for two consecutive terms of office — specifically so Fujimori could run for another term. He began his second term on July 28, 1995, continuing the period of stability and economic

health. In 1998, when the nation's top constitutional court rule that Fujimori could not run for a third term (in 2000), he merely disbanded it, ushering in the latest round of student demonstrations and media vitriol.

Fujimori defends his radical policies by advertising his economic accomplishments: Peru's inflation was just 5.3% during the first half of 1998, better than in many Western industrial nations.

Despite recent economic growth, poverty is still rampant, with malnutrition and diseases a huge problem in shanty towns around the major cities and in much of the countryside. Fujimori wants to tackle this problem with family planning and birth control, but this puts him at odds with the powerful

Catholic Church. Peru's population reached 23.4 million in 1994, a figure that is predicted to double by 2022. Migration from countryside to city is epidemic, putting immense strain on infrastructure and fueling an urban crime wave that is already legend. Poverty-stricken communities were hit hard during the 1997–1998 El Niño storms. Thousands of lives were lost, much of the Pan-American Highway was washed away and billions of dollars in property damage was inflicted on communities that were already eking out nothing but a bare-bone existence.

Peru's other festering wound is an ongoing border conflict with Ecuador. The two neighbors first went to war over disputed territory in the Amazon region in 1941. Even though the Rio de Janeiro of 1942 gave Peru jurisdiction over what are now the departments of Amazonas and Loreto, Ecuador has never accepted defeat. Scuffles break out every few years between the two countries, including a 1995 flare up that took 40 lives on both sides of the frontier. As this book went to press, other Latin American governments were brokering talks between Lima and Quito in the hope of resolving the border issue once and for all.

TODAY'S PERU

About three-quarters of Peru's 23 million inhabitants live in urban areas, largely along the coast. With an estimated 7.2 million people in the metropolitan area, Lima is the country's largest city. Other large urban areas include Arequipa (1.5 million), Trujillo (900,000), Chiclayo (400,000), Chimbote (300,000), and Cusco (300,000).

Spanish and Quechua are the official languages, but there are also regional languages like Aymara (around Lake Titicaca) and various Amazon Indian dialects. Indians comprise the largest ethnic group (45%) followed by *mestizos* (37%) and Europeans (15%). Smaller ethnic groups include Japanese, Chinese, and Blacks. More than 90% of the population follows the Roman Catholic faith, but Protestant missionary groups have made significant inroads in recent years, especially in the Amazon region.

ABOVE: Public affection is part of Peru's Latin heritage. RIGHT: Turn-of-the-century façade in Iquitos.

The Country and Its People

Lima

LIMA IS ONE OF THE GRAND OLD CITIES OF THE AMERICAS, founded roughly 40 years after Christopher Columbus's first landfall in the western hemisphere. There are times when it seems five centuries old — tired and worn and ready for a change — and other times when it seems as fresh as a boomtown. It all depends on the neighborhood, the season, your own particular mood. Because if Lima is anything, she is eclectic.

One of the most cosmopolitan and complex urban areas in South America, Lima is actually three or four cities in one. A bustling, clamorous Spanish colonial city that crowds around the Plaza de Armas and other downtown squares. A modern, elegant European city that flourishes along the tree-lined avenues in San Isidro and Miraflores. A cheerful seaside resort that perches on the mighty cliffs of Barranco and the Costa Verde. The hardcore third-world funk that dominates Callao, Rimac, and other poverty-stricken zones. Lima is all of these things and more.

The city harbors a thriving middle and upper class, people who are very much in tune with what's going on in the rest of the world. Their children are most likely educated in the United States and Europe. They probably have a condo in Miami or an apartment in Madrid. In fact, you often find that residents of posh suburbs like San Isidro and Miraflores go for months, even years, without venturing into central Lima.

At the opposite end of the Lima spectrum are the dozens of crowded *barriadas* or *pueblos jovenes* ("young towns"), shanty towns in which the majority of the city's most recent immigrants live. A population boom in the Andes, sparked by modern medicine and lack of birth control, together with the bloody "Terror Years" of the late 1980s and early 1990s, prompted a massive exodus from the Andes to the capital, as millions of farmers and herders came searching for security and prosperity in Lima. From a relatively small base of 300,000 in 1930, Lima's population had spiraled to three and a half million by the late 1970s. Over the last two decades it has doubled again, reaching 7.2 million — one-third of Peru's population. But it's this mix of rich and poor, Indian and European cultures, that makes Lima such a cosmopolitan and fascinating city.

Most of Lima's ills can be attributed to this massive, uncontrolled growth in the latter half of the twentieth century, the same "population bomb" that threatens other third-world capitals like Mexico City, New Delhi, Jakarta, and Nairobi. Lima is overwhelmed by noise, pollution, and traffic. There are myriad pickpockets and muggers, beggars and con men. And then there's the weather: thick coastal fog, gray overcast or drizzle for much of the year (December and January are the only genuinely sunny months).

Travelers often pass right through Lima on their way to the country's more famous attractions such as Cusco, Machu Picchu, and the Amazon. Even *Limeños* are apt to gripe about the sorry state of their metropolis. But that doesn't mean there aren't worthwhile sights and attractions. Lima offers more museums than just about any other Latin American city, including the fabulous Museo de Oro (Gold Museum) and Museo de la Nación (Museum of the Nation), two of the world's most important collections of pre-Columbian artifacts. Its baroque churches are the stuff of legend, especially the enchant-

LEFT: Spanish-style architecture graces much of seaside Barranco. ABOVE: Engraving of conquistadors and Indians at the Museum of the Nation.

ing Santo Domingo and the eerie San Francisco with its bone-filled catacombs. Lima's restaurants are excellent, particularly the seafood palaces. And the shopping isn't bad either, if you know where to look.

While the traffic and pollution continue as major headaches, the petty crime situation has improved greatly in recent years. With the election of a new municipal government in 1996 and the easing of the terrorist threat after the Japanese Embassy siege, Lima has undergone major changes.

For better or worse, beggars and street peddlers (*ambulantes*) have been banished from the city center, especially the area around the Plaza de Armas. Street sweepers comb the area for litter and gardeners preen the public lawns and flower beds. Funds have gone into the restoration of historical buildings that were previously crumbling. The police presence in this neighborhood is also more obvious (an armed cop on nearly every corner) resulting in a drastic plunge in pickpocketing and petty thievery. Whether or not these trends will outlast the present administration remains to be seen. Lima is now a much more pleasant, and safer, city to explore.

BACKGROUND

For at least three thousand years advanced civilizations have occupied the coastal plain that embraces modern Lima. The famous Temple of Pachacamac 30 km (just under 19 miles) south of the modern city center may have developed as a religious hub and spiritual node as early as AD 500. The first true urban area that arose near the banks of the Río Rimac was Cajamarquilla, a vast adobe city developed by the Cuismancu people around 1200. By the time the Spanish conquistadors arrived in 1533, the entire area had fallen under the sway of the powerful Incas. Although this was a rather minor part of the empire, the Rimac river valley embraced three Inca cities (Maranga, Carabayllo, and Surco) and more than four hundred pyramid temples.

It didn't take long for the Spanish to leave their mark on the area. The modern city of Lima was founded by conquistador leader Francisco Pizarro on the Feast Day of the

Epiphany (January 6) in 1535. He had a number of reasons for choosing this site: fresh water from the Rimac, quick access to a deepwater port at Callao (a distinct military and commercial advantage), a much milder climate than the Andes, and sufficient distance from the Inca heartland around Cusco — in case of civil war.

Originally dubbed Cuidad de los Reyes (City of the Kings), Lima very quickly grew into the most prosperous Spanish settlement in the New World, a city of Renaissance palaces, churches, mansions, cobblestone

plazas and courtyards that nearly rivaled the grand cities of Europe. Lima was also an early center of learning, boasting the New World's oldest university (founded in 1551). But there was also a dark side to its fortune: from 1570 it was the South American bastion of the bloody Spanish Inquisition. It's thought that thousands of people were tortured and murdered inside the Archbishop's Palace and other religious strongholds, the bodies conveyed through secret underground passages to the catacombs beneath San Francisco Convent.

Lima continued to prosper until 1746 when a massive earthquake ravaged most of the old colonial center. The number of dead is estimated at more than five thousand. But the city was quickly rebuilt, mostly in the baroque style popular at that time, a profusion of intricate "wedding cake" façades on churches and public buildings and mansions decorated with lush courtyards and ornate wooden balconies. Soon Lima regained its prominence in politics and commerce, especially under the reign of Viceroy Amat (1761–1776) who introduced many progressive ideas in government and society.

The South American wars of independence in the early nineteenth century accomplished what no natural disaster could do:

while outlying villages like San Isidro, Miraflores, and Barranco developed into stylish suburbs for Lima's upper class.

GENERAL INFORMATION

There are two places in Lima where you can obtain free-of-charge facts, figures, and maps. The best is **Infotur Peru Tourist Information** ((1) 4310117 FAX (1) 3305412, Jirón de la Unión (Belén) 1066, Office E-2. Run as a nonprofit public service, Infotur offers information on almost anything you could want

they ended Lima's status as the preeminent city of the continent by breaking the huge Spanish domain into eight separate countries, each with their own bustling capital. Lima's darkest hour came during the War of the Pacific (1879–1883), when the city was occupied for two years by Chilean forces who looted much of her public and private art, carting everything back to Santiago, where it remains to this day.

Lima didn't blossom again until the 1920s, when a general economic boom across Latin America and the leadership of President Leguía sparked a new era of construction and population growth. Many of the magnificent buildings around the Plaza San Martín and Plaza Grau were constructed at this time, and

to know about Lima in specific or Peru in general including opening hours, transportation options, shopping recommendations and safety tips. Ask for Lily or Laura, both of whom used to work for the government's walk-in tourist office before it closed.

The **Lima Municipal Tourist Office** is an information desk located just inside the front door at the Oficina de Catastro ((1) 4274848 or (1) 4276080, Jirón Conde de Superunda 177 (between the Plaza de Armas and Artesanía Santo Domingo). The staff is friendly but not very proficient in English. This is a good source of information on tourist attractions

Among exhibits in the National Museum of Anthropology and Archeology are displays on Chancay pottery LEFT and Indian corn ABOVE.

CENTRAL LIMA

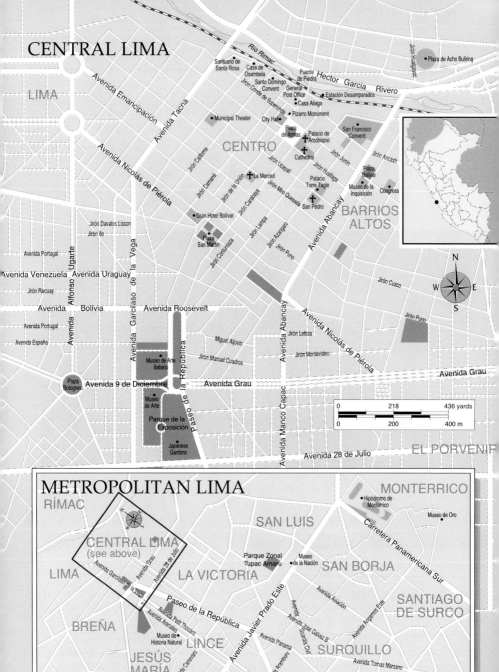

LIMA

Avenida Emancipación

Avenida Tacna

Avenida Nicolas de Piérola

Rio Rímac

Santuario de Santa Rosa
Casa de Osambela
Santo Domingo Convent
General Post Office
Casa Aliaga
Pizarro Monument

Puente de Piedra

Puente Hector Garcia Rivero

Estación Desamparados

Municipal Theater
City Hall

Jirón Conde de Superunda

Plaza de Armas

Palacio de Arzobispal

San Francisco Convent

Jirón Junín

Jirón Ancash

CENTRO

Jirón California

Jirón Camaná

Jirón de la Unión

Jirón Ucayali

Jirón Carabaya

La Merced

Cathedral

Palacio Torre Tagle

San Pedro

Jirón Miró Quesada

Jirón Huallaga

Plaza Bolívar

Museo de la Inquisición

Congress

BARRIOS ALTOS

Gran Hotel Bolívar

Jirón Davalos Lisson
Jirón Ilo

Plaza San Martín

Jirón Conjumaza

Jirón Lampa

Jirón Puno

Jirón Azángaro

Jirón Cusco

Avenida Abancay

Avenida Portugal
Avenida Venezuela
Jirón Récuay

Avenida Uruguay

Avenida Garcilaso de la Vega

Alfonso Ugarte

Avenida Bolivia

Avenida Roosevelt

Avenida Portugal
Avenida España

Museo de Arte Italiano

Miguel Aljovin

Jirón Manuel Cuadros

Paseo de la República

Jirón Leticia

Jirón Montevideo

Avenida Nicolás de Piérola

Avenida Abancay

Jirón Puno

Avenida Grau

Plaza Bolognesi

Avenida 9 de Diciembre

Museo de Arte

Parque de la Exposición

Japanese Gardens

Avenida Grau

Avenida Manco Capac

Avenida 28 de Julio

EL PORVENIR

Plaza de Acho Bullring

Jirón Huánuco

N
W — E
S

| 0 | | 218 | | 436 yards |
| 0 | 200 | | 400 m | |

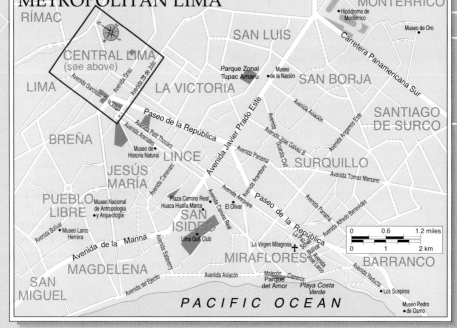

METROPOLITAN LIMA

RÍMAC

CENTRAL LIMA
(see above)

Avenida Garcilaso de la Vega

Avenida Grau

Avenida 28 de Julio

LIMA

SAN LUIS

MONTERRICO

Hipódromo de Monterrico

Museo de Oro

LA VICTORIA

Parque Zonal Tupac Amaru

Museo de la Nación

SAN BORJA

Carretera Panamericana Sur

SANTIAGO DE SURCO

Paseo de la República

BREÑA

Avenida Petit Thouars

Avenida Arenales

Museo de Historia Natural

LINCE

Avenida Javier Prado Este

Avenida Aviación

Avenida Arequipa

Avenida José Gálvez B.

Avenida Panama

Avenida Panama

SURQUILLO

Avenida Tomas Marsano

Avenida Aviación

Avenida Argamos Este

JESÚS MARÍA

Avenida Cervanci

PUEBLO LIBRE

Museo Nacional de Antropologia y Arqueologia

Avenida Bolívar
Museo Larco Herrera

Avenida de la Marina

MAGDALENA

SAN MIGUEL

Plaza Camino Real
Huaca Hualla Marca

El Olivar

SAN ISIDRO

Lima Golf Club

Avenida Salaverry

Avenida Canada Real

Avenida Arequipa

Avenida Aramburu

Paseo de la República

Avenida Alfredo Benavides

Avenida La Salle

Avenida Bolívar

Avenida José Larco

La Virgen Milagrosa

MIRAFLORES

BARRANCO

Avenida Reducta

Avenida del Ejercito

Avenida Aviación

Malecón
Parque del Amor

Cisneros

Playa Costa Verde

Los Suspiros

Museo Pedro de Osmo

PACIFIC OCEAN

| 0 | 0.6 | | 1.2 miles |
| 0 | 1 | | 2 km |

in central Lima. It is open Monday to Friday from 9 AM to 6 PM and Saturday from 10 AM to 4 PM.

The best source of information in all of Peru, indeed the entire continent, is the **South American Explorer's Club (SAEC)** (/FAX (1) 4250142 E-MAIL montague@amauta.rcp.net WEB SITE www.samexplo.org, Avenida Portugal 146 (near Alfonso Ugarte) in the Breña district. The catch is that you have to join the club to use its copious reference library and Internet connection. Most people think the annual fee is a bargain considering what you get: books on all aspects of Peruvian culture, history, and geography; various tourist guides and maps; helpful "trip reports" on each province and all major tourist destinations submitted by club members and meticulously stored in binders. Founded by Don Montague and Linda Rojas in 1977, the SAEC is a priceless source of information and a great place to meet other travelers. Annual membership costs US$40 for one person or US$60 for a couple, including use of SAEC facilities in Lima, Quito, and Ithaca, New York, as well as the club's quarterly magazine. Other membership privileges include luggage storage and mail forwarding. SAEC-branded souvenirs, as well as guide books and maps, are sold at the Lima location.

WHAT TO SEE AND DO

At the very heart of ancient Lima is the **Plaza de Armas**, where the Incas built their royal city and the conquistadors their early Spanish settlement. The ornate bronze fountain is its oldest relic, erected in 1650. The Cathedral is the oldest structure, rebuilt in 1746 after the previous church was devastated by an earthquake.

Dominating the plaza's northern flank is the **Palacio de Gobierno (Government Palace)**, built in 1938. Local Indian chieftain Tauli Chusco ruled from a stone palace on this site. Francisco Pizarro tore it down and used the rubble to construct his own mansion, where he fell victim to an assassin's blade in 1541. The **changing of the guard**, with all its pomp and circumstance, takes place at noon (Monday to Saturday): 30 minutes of scarlet-and-blue uniforms and marching music reminiscent of the Big Ten football game.

Lima's mammoth **cathedral** (built on the site of an ancient Inca temple dedicated to the puma god) is not a stunning beauty, and there is nothing especially interesting about the architecture, designed by Francisco Becerra and fashioned after Jaén Cathedral in Spain. Construction began shortly after Lima was founded (1535) but was not completed until the 1640s. Devastated by several earthquakes over the years, the structure is largely a reconstruction—although it retains its original Renaissance style.

Despite its architectural homeliness, the "mother church" of Peru has many curious little sideshows. A wonderful mosaic covers the walls of Pizarro's Tomb, on the right as you first enter, although no one is quite sure if those are really Pizarro's bones in the sepulcher. The **Cathedral Museum** ((1) 4275980, extension 254, offers numerous treasures, both sacred and secular. These include ivory crucifixes, clothing once worn by Pope John XXIII, and an enormous painting called *The Dynasty of the Incas* (1746) which depicts Peru's Inca and Spanish rulers from Atahualpa through Carlos V. "El Zodiaco de los Bassano" is a bizarre collection of nonreligious paintings rendered in the sixteenth and seventeenth centuries. The museum is open daily and the admission fee includes a guided tour in Spanish and English.

Adjacent to the Cathedral is the wonderful **Palacio de Arzobispal (Archbishop's Residence)**, built in 1924 and one of the city's finest examples of Spanish colonial revival. Unfortunately it's not open to the public except by special appointment. On the opposite side of the plaza is the harvest-gold façade of Lima's **Palacio Municipal (City Hall)**, another twentieth-century reproduction of the old colonial style. Inside is a small art collection and around the side on Pasaje Santa Rosa is a monument to Inca leader **Tauli Chusco**. The museum is open Monday to Friday and admission is free.

WEST FROM PLAZA DE ARMAS

A narrow avenue called Jirón Conde de Superunda runs west from the plaza through a district rife with ancient architecture. At the edge of the square is the impressive **Pizarro Monument**, the conquistador astride

a bronze stallion. A little farther along is Lima's **Central Post Office** with its lovely central arcade where you can purchase stamps, envelopes, writing pads, postcards, maps, and small souvenirs. Inside is a small **Museo Filatélico (Post and Stamp Museum)** ((1) 4287931 which celebrated its 100th birthday in 1997. Local stamp collectors have an informal gathering here every Sunday morning. Admission is free. Also in this area is **Casa Aliaga** ((1) 4276624, Jirón de la Unión 224, built in 1535 and supposedly the oldest private house in South America. Members of the Aliaga family still reside here and it can only be visited with prior permission from the owners or as part of a private tour.

One of the capital's most underrated sights is **Santo Domingo Church and Con-** vent ((1) 4276793, Jirón Conde de Superunda 200, erected between 1540 and 1599 with some later additions. The convent's central courtyard is simply gorgeous, decorated with Spanish tiles and murals that depict the life of Saint Dominic, lavish rose bushes, Moorish-style arches, and wooden balconies. Check out the nativity scene with its life-sized wooden figures at the northwest corner of the courtyard. Elsewhere in the convent are the Library, with its eerie golden light, and the underground chapel where Saint Rose of Lima is buried. Outside the Chapel of San Martín de Porres are huge paintings depicting his miracles including a 1948 incident in Paraguay which assured his canonization. Saint Martin, who lived from 1579 to 1639, is one of the Catholic Church's few black saints.

day it's said that you can see the port of Callao from its rooftop.

Another local curiosity is the **Sanctuario de Santa Rosa de Lima**, near the corner of Jirón Conde Superunda and Avenida Tacna. This small seventeenth-century church is dedicated to western hemisphere's first native saint. Adjacent to the shrine is Santa Rosa's hermitage, a tiny mudbrick room where she once prayed. Also part of the complex is a small ethnographic museum with weapons, jewelry, and other artifacts collected by Catholic missionaries in the Amazon jungle. The museum is open daily and entrance is free.

The ancient *barrio* across the **Puente de Piedra** bridge is called **Rimac**, after the nearby river. Although few tourists venture this way, the neighborhood is part and parcel of Lima's heritage and culture. Originally populated by black African slaves, Rimac is still a rough-and-tumble area that isn't especially safe at night. But within its confines are **Plaza de Acho Bullring** and the adjacent **Bullfight Museum (** (1) 4823360, Jirón Hualgayoc 332, which contains numerous matador artifacts and toreador paintings by notable artists including Goya. The museum is closed Sunday and there is an entrance fee. The local bullfight season runs October to November.

EAST FROM PLAZA DE ARMAS

Behind the Government Palace is Lima's central **Train Station (Estación Desamparados) (** (1) 4287929 or (1) 4289440. It's been a rather dismal and lonely place since trains stopped running across the Andes. But there is still action on weekends when a new tourist train called the "Rumbo al Sol" takes daytrippers to San Bartolomé in the foothills east of Lima (see AROUND LIMA, page 92). Running east of the station is a busy little street called **Jirón Ancash** which was Lima's backpacker mecca until the train service into the Andes went belly-up in 1991.

One block east of the station is **San Francisco Church and Convent (** (1) 4271381, erected between 1620 and 1687. The ochre façade and gray domes are menacing, betray-

His personal symbols — broomstick, dog, and cat — appear in many of the paintings in the chapel. The museum is open daily and there is an entrance fee.

Directly opposite Santo Domingo and Basilica Vera Cruz is a pleasant little square with trees and benches. Adjacent is the **Artesanía Santo Domingo** arts and craft market (see SHOPPING, page 93). Farther west along Jirón Conde de Superunda is an unusual blue building called **Casa de Osambela (** (1) 4277987 with Turkish-style domes and extravagant wooden balconies. Home of the Garcilaso de la Vega Inca Culture Center, this nineteenth-century masterpiece is currently undergoing extensive renovations. Once the mansion of wealthy merchant Marqués Martín Osambela, on a clear

Lima's annual Festival of the Lord of the Miracles runs through much of October.

ing the fact that San Francisco houses catacombs where many victims of the Inquisition were probably buried. The catacombs weren't discovered until 1943. Subsequent research determined that the underground passages beneath the convent were a burial place until 1808, when the first city cemetery was inaugurated. There are an estimated 25,000 sets of human remains. Researchers now think there were secret passageways between the catacombs and the Tribunal of the Sacred Office (Inquisition) on Plaza Bolívar. The convent boasts many architectural treasures including a Moorish-style wooden copula made from cedar beams, the intricately carved bishop's seating area in the balcony of the main chapel, and the cloisters, with huge paintings depicting the life of Saint Francis. The catacombs and convent can only be viewed as part of a guided tour. They are open daily and entrance is free.

This neighborhood also harbors some of Lima's most important colonial mansions. **Casa Pilatos** ((1) 4275814, Jirón Ancash 390, was built in 1590 and is one of Lima's oldest houses. Its current tenant is the National Cultural Institute. Especially noteworthy are the central courtyard and main staircase, which can usually be viewed without an appointment. The house is open Monday to Friday during regular office hours and admission is free. Nearby is the fabulous **Torre Tagle Palace** ((1) 4273860, Jirón Ucayali and Jirón Azangaro. Erected in 1735 by the wealthy Torre Tagle family, it's a typical example of Spanish colonial architecture with intricate wooden balconies in the Moorish style imported from southern Spain. Although it now houses the Ministry of Foreign Affairs, you can tour the building by private appointment.

On the opposite side of the Ucayali/Azangaro intersection is the intriguing **Church and Convent of San Pedro** ((1) 4283010. The Jesuits inaugurated this baroque compound in 1638 with murals in the sacristy depicting the life of Jesuit founder Saint Ignatius of Loyola. The high altar with its lavish gilt is one of the most spectacular in Peru. San Pedro is open daily and there is an entrance fee to the convent.

The area around **Plaza Bolívar** is called the Barrios Altos or "Old Town" because it's

one of the oldest parts of Lima. Holding forth in the square is liberator Simón Bolívar on horseback with the stark white façade of the national **Congress Building** as a backdrop. The square was once called the Plaza de la Inquisición because the Tribunal of the Sacred Office was situated here from 1570 to 1820. Memories of that dreadful era endure at the **Museo de la Inquisición (Museum of the Inquisition)** ((1) 4287980 or (1) 4270365, Jirón Junín 548, on the plaza's south side. Among its gruesome features are the original tribunal room with its mahogany ceiling, as well as dungeons and torture chambers in the basement. The museum is open daily and entrance is free. Guided tours are in Spanish.

SOUTH FROM PLAZA DE ARMAS

A bustling pedestrian street called Jirón de la Unión runs due south, connecting Plaza de Armas with another flamboyant square called the Plaza San Martín. This five-block promenade could easily be dubbed "Chicken Alley" because of the proliferation of barbecued chicken outlets. There are plenty of other fast-food outlets as well as jewelry and clothing stores, cinemas, and bookshops. The street is a hangout for local students, lottery-ticket peddlers, pickpockets, and money changers.

One structure of note along Jirón de la Unión is the **Fotografía Building** with its flamboyant Gaudí-style façade, built in 1856. Also along this stretch is **La Merced Church**, on the site where the first Roman Catholic mass in Lima was celebrated in 1534. Parts of the current church date from the early seventeenth century, but it's mostly an eighteenth-century affair with an elaborate chancel and attractive cloister. Currently undergoing extensive renovation, the church often bustles with worshippers during the middle of the day. The church is open daily and entrance is free.

Nearby is **Casa de Riva-Aguero** ((1) 4279275, Jirón Camaná 459, a small Peruvian folk-art museum situated in a splendid Spanish colonial mansion. The house is closed Sunday and admission is free. Opposite is **San Agustín Church**, at the corner of Jirón Ica and Jirón Camaná. This is a typical ex ample of the Churrigueresque school of Spanish colonial architecture, with an elaborate eighteenth-century façade that combines baroque and Moorish influences. Two blocks farther west along Jirón Ica is Lima's lovely **Municipal Theater**, which was recently rebuilt after a devastating fire.

Plaza **San Martín** was laid out in 1921 to commemorate the centenary of Peruvian independence from Spain. At center stage is a bronze equestrian statue of liberator José de San Martín while on the west side of the square sits the **Gran Hotel Bolívar** with its exquisite Belle Époque decoration. Two blocks farther south is a large, rectangular open space called the **Paseo de la República**, flanked by disagreeable modern buildings such as the Lima Sheraton and several government monstrosities.

Off to one side of the avenue is a pleasant green space called **Parque Neptuno**, which harbors the **Museo de Arte Italiano (Museum of Italian Art)** ((1) 4239932, Paseo de la República 250, housed in a fascinating neo-Renaissance building that looks completely out of place among the colorless highrises. The exhibits are a mixed bag of contemporary Mediterranean painters, twentieth-century Peruvian art, and reproductions of Italian masters donated by the Italian government. The museum is open Monday to Friday and there is an entrance fee.

Within a stone's throw is the impressive **Museo de Arte (National Museum of Art)** ((1) 4234732 or (1) 4236332, Paseo Colón 125. A magnificent showcase of four centuries of Peruvian art, the collection runs the gamut from baroque religious paintings to Spanish colonial furniture to pre-Columbian pottery. In addition to the vast permanent collection, the museum also offers interesting temporary shows. There is an ongoing film program as well as public classes or workshops in various Peruvian arts including sculpture, puppets, *retablos*, and *cajon* — traditional decorative boxwork. The museum is closed Monday and there is an entrance fee.

If you're still in the mood for walking, continue southward into the large **Parque de la Exposición**, about all that remains of a world's fair staged here in 1868. The park is somewhat scruffy these days, but it boasts a pleasant **Japanese Garden**.

SAN ISIDRO AND PUEBLO LIBRE

San Isidro was once a tranquil farming community on the outskirts of Lima, but during the twentieth century it has evolved into a wealthy residential enclave, shopping mecca, and business hub with numerous steel-and-glass towers along **Avenida Javier Prado**, which bisects the district from east to west. There are lots of places to shop but the most popular for *Limeños* is the ritzy **Plaza Camino Real**, a modern American-style mall that sprawls along one entire block of Avenida Camino Real between Paz Soldan and José Domingo Choquehuanca. Directly opposite is a small handicraft market called **Centro Artesanal San Isidro**. The surrounding streets are chock-a-block with restaurants, clubs, and outdoor cafés, making San Isidro a pleasant place to while away an afternoon.

In centuries past, San Isidro's raison d'être was olive cultivation, a tradition reflected today in the myriad olive trees of **Parque de Olivar**, a block east of the shopping mall. This is all that remains of an olive plantation started more than 450 years ago by the area's first Spanish settlers. Among the trees are a few displays of old olive-making equipment, as well as benches, lawns, and fountains.

West of the mall is **Huaca Huallamarca** ((1) 2224124 or (1) 4402145, Avenida Nicolás de Rivera 201, the most central of the 400 mudbrick pyramids that marked the Lima area at the time of the Spanish conquest. It was erected by the Maranga people between AD 200 and 500 but largely reconstructed in modern times. You can clamber over the *huaca* or tour a small museum with artifacts found at the site. The site is closed Monday and there is an entrance fee.

Likewise, **Pueblo Libre** is a onetime agrarian community that was transformed by twentieth-century urbanization into one of Lima's most crowded suburbs. But among the many houses and apartment blocks you can find two interesting collections. The **Museo Nacional de Antropología y Arqueología (National Museum of Anthropology and Archeology)** ((1) 4635070 or (1) 4632009, Plaza Bolívar, highlights Peruvian culture from the Stone Age through the arrival of the Spaniards. Among the museum treasures are Chavín obelisks and stelae. There are also scale models of Machu Picchu and other famous ruins. The museum is closed Monday and there is an entrance fee.

The largest ceramic collection in Latin America is housed within the stout colonial walls of the **Museo Rafael Larco Herrera (** (1) 4611312, Avenida Bolívar 1515. Named after a former vice-president who amassed this collection during the 1920s and 1930s, the museum contains more than 45,000 items including pottery, mummies, textiles, gold artifacts, and a cactus garden. The museum is open daily and there is an entrance fee. Guided tours are available in Spanish and English.

Wedged between San Isidro and Pueblo Libre is the **Museo de Historia Natural (Museum of Natural History) (** (1) 4710117, Avenida Arenales 1256 in Jesús María district. This is a small and somewhat depressing collection of stuffed animals and other zoological artifacts typical of the Amazon, Andes, and other Peruvian ecosystems. The museum is open daily and there is an entrance fee.

MIRAFLORES

Both in body and spirit, Miraflores is like a breath of fresh air, a sharp contrast to the "mean streets" that dominate so much of the Peruvian capital. This breezy, seaside suburb perches on cliffs above the deep-blue Pacific, the haunt of surfers and sunseekers. But it's more than just a beach town. Miraflores also throbs with Lima's best nightlife, the vast majority of its top restaurants, and profuse shopping. Peruvians flock here at night and on weekends, and many overseas visitors choose to base themselves in Miraflores despite its distance from the central city.

Playa Costa Verde is the wide white-sand beach that sprawls at the base of the Miraflores cliffs. Perching atop the cliff are a twisting road called **Malecón Cisneros** and half a dozen green spaces with magnificent views including Parque Salazar, Parque Neicochea, and the famous **Parque del Amor (Lover's Park)** with its erotic statue of two lovers entwined in a passionate kiss. Along this stretch are wide lawns, playgrounds, flower

gardens, and a towering blue-and-white striped lighthouse called the **Faro la Marina** that is operated by the Peruvian Navy.

Avenida José Larco leads from the clifftop parks into the heart of Miraflores, culminating in a leafy precinct called **Parque Kennedy** surrounded by outdoor cafés and punctuated by the spires of **La Virgen Milagrosa** church. A lively **flea market** takes shape in the park on Friday and Saturday nights, about the only place in Miraflores where you can snatch a bargain. Nearby is a small amphitheater which offers poetry readings, guitar solos, and Latin bands in weekend evenings.

The area's prime street for souvenir shopping is the **Avenida La Paz** between Schell and Bolívar, where nearly every shop sells

antiques, jewelry, silver, alpaca, or other handicrafts. It's along here that you will find **Pasaje el Suche**, a cozy alley lined by white-washed cottages with green-tiled roofs, where you can partake of a pisco sour or purchase Peruvian arts and crafts.

Miraflores offers several private art and artifact collections. **Museo Amano** ((1) 4412909, Calle Retiro 160 (off Avenida Angamos), is an assortment of pre-Columbian textiles and pottery with particular emphasis on the little-known Chancay culture. The museum is open Monday to Friday afternoons by appointment only and entrance is free. The **Enrico Poli Collection** ((1) 4222437, Lord Cochrane 466, offers an extensive hoard of both pre-Columbian and Spanish colonial treasures including priceless Sipán gold

pieces. The museum is open daily by appointment only and there is an entrance fee. Miraflores also boasts its own ancient monument in the **Huaca Pucllana** ((1) 4458695, Calle General Borgono 800, a recently excavated pre-Inca pyramid. Archaeologists have dated the structure to the fourth century AD and believe it's built in the shape of a sacred toad or frog. The site is closed Tuesday and there is an entrance free.

Beyond Miraflores is another pleasant seaside suburb called **Barranco**, which also perches on cliffs above the Pacific. In many respects this is Lima's answer to Greenwich Village or Soho: a neighborhood of artists, writers and musicians, a place that seems to

Roman Catholic pilgrims flood the Plaza de Armas during the Festival of the Lord of the Miracles.

Lima

run at a much slower speed (and much higher intellect) than the rest of Lima. Peruvian college students and singles flock to Barranco after dark to catch *peña* folk music performances and dance in the various clubs along Avenida Grau and the central plaza.

Barranco's most engaging structure is the **Puente de los Suspiros**, an old wooden bridge across a wooded ravine that attracts both sightseers and young lovers. Tucked away in a quiet residential area is the **Pedro de Osma Colonial Art Museum (** (1) 4670937 or (1) 4670915, Avenida Pedro de Osma 421, an engaging and well-maintained collection that includes Spanish colonial painting, sculpture, furniture, and silver as well as temporary shows on various themes. The museum is closed Monday and there is an entrance fee.

EASTERN SUBURBS

San Borja and **Monterrico** are bastions of Lima's middle and upper classes, with many large homes surrounded by walls and gardens. The area also boasts a horseracing oval, golf course, and two of Peru's best museums.

The expansive **Museo de la Nación (Museum of the Nation) (** (1) 4377822 or (1) 4769879, Avenida Javier Prado Este 2466, is an excellent place to scrutinize the nation's archeological and cultural heritage with scale models, lifesize replicas, and diagrams spanning 2,000 years of history covering every province. Somehow this exhaustive museum manages to represent every major Peruvian culture. Among its treasures are Chavín stone carvings, Nazca pottery, Paracas weavings and Inca stonework, as well as traditional folk dress from all over Peru. It also contains a fascinating exhibit on traditional Peruvian medicine and health science including a display of pre-Columbian and colonial surgery equipment which looks more like a gallery of torture implements. The museum is closed Monday and there is an entrance fee.

Even more comprehensive is the **Museo de Oro (Gold Museum) (** (1) 4352917 or (1) 4350791, Avenida Alonso de Molina 1100, in Monterrico. This is one of the world's most stunning museums, a collection that leaves you awestruck by its sheer magnitude. Even more amazing is the fact that all of this gold

was amassed by a single man — tycoon Miguel Mujica Gallo — who started the hoard in 1938 with 50 gold pieces. He established the museum in 1970 on the grounds of his private estate and at last count there were more than 40,000 pieces in total. Señor Mujica recently turned 87 years old and is still adding something new to the collection every day.

The collection is dominated by pre-Inca cultures, because most of the Inca gold was melted down by the Spanish and shipped back to Europe. The conquistadors never uncovered the tombs and temples of civilizations that flourished in Peru before the advent of the Inca Empire. In fact, many of the most astounding discoveries (like the Sipán tombs) were not made until the last

decade. Every major epoch is represented including Chavín, Paracas, Nazca, and Moche. Everywhere you look there's shimmering gold: ceremonial daggers and funeral masks, huge nose plugs and earrings, jaguar and puma effigies, even wallpaper and chain mail uniforms forged from solid gold. In addition to gold artifacts, the museum boasts numerous other treasures including mummies, hats and cloaks made from Amazon bird feathers, beaded coca leaf bags, and erotic pottery.

On the upper floor is Señor Mujica's other collection, a vast **Arms Museum** that contains weapons, uniforms, and other military paraphernalia from all over the world. Among the most-prized items are samurai swords and armor from Japan, Oliver Crom-

well's ivory dagger, a sword that once belonged to Czar Alexander I of Russia and a uniform worn by Generalissimo Francisco Franco of Spain. Both museums are open daily and there is a combined entrance fee.

AROUND LIMA

The **Rimac Valley** cuts a giant slash through the Andes foothills east of Lima providing a perfect path for the main road and rail routes into the *altiplano* region. The highway is busy but unfortunately the train service was suspended in 1991 because of lack of funds to keep the track in good repair and terrorist activity.

Rimac is an ancient *barrio* in the heart of modern Lima.

Partial rail service was restored in 1998 with the inauguration of the **"Rumbo al Sol"** train service which takes visitors from downtown Lima to San Bartolomé in the Andes foothills. The trains run only on Saturday and Sunday, departing Lima at 8:30 AM with a 10:45 AM arrival in San Bartolomé. The return trip departs at 4 PM with a 6:15 PM arrival back in Lima. The fare is S/13 round trip. You can purchase tickets at the station Monday to Saturday 8 AM to 4 PM. For information call ((1) 4289440 or (1) 4276620.

The foothills boast several attractions of both the natural and historic variety. **Puruchuco** is a pre-Inca palace with a good museum, only about a half-hour drive east of downtown Lima. **Marcuhuasi** is perhaps the closest area that escapes the overcast gloom that covers Lima for most of the year, a marvelous highland area with deep blue skies that features hiking trails, campsites and weird rock formations.

The most important archeological site in the Lima region is **Pachacamac** on the coastal plain about 30 km (20 miles) south of the city center and close to the beach at Playa San Pedro. Thought to have been first developed around AD 500, like many ancient sites it was taken over and assimiliated into the Inca realm. Some of the more recent structures were built by the Incas. The heart of Pachacamac features large mudbrick pyramids in various states of disrepair. The Pyramid of the Sun is the largest, perched on bluff overlooking the sea. The Pyramid of the Moon and the Convent of the Sun Virgins have both been partially restored. There is a small museum, souvenir stall, and café near the entrance, plus an enclosure with llamas. The temples are spread across a wide area and it takes several hours to explore the whole complex on foot. As an alternative you can join a guided excursion offered by Lima Tours (see TAKING A TOUR, page 58) or other travel agencies. The ruins are open daily and there is an entrance fee.

SPORTS

Like people all around the world, many Peruvians are into **jogging**. One of the most popular spots is Miraflores, where you can dash through the clifftop parks above the Pacific and around the leafy confines of Parque Kennedy. Another hot jogging spot is Parque el Olivar in San Isidro with its broad lawns and olive tree-shaded walkways.

Tennis is one of the few sports (other than soccer) where Peru has produced world quality players, and it's not surprising given the number of tennis clubs around Lima. Las Terrazas ((1) 4452265 or (1) 4452997 in Miraflores was founded in 1918 and is Peru's oldest and most prestigious tennis facility. It offers clay and cement play at four different facilities including the clifftop Malecón Cisneros courts and the beachfront Club Waikiki. Courts are available to nonmembers during daylight hours (S/15 per hour) or you can purchase a transient membership for S/600 per month. Also open to nonmembers is Lawn Tennis Club ((1) 4330907 or (1) 4338743, Avenida 28 de Julio on the Campo de Marte in Jesús María.

Golf is gradually growing in popularity but space limitations mean there are few places to tee off. The plush Lima Golf Club lies in the heart of San Isidro while the Los Incas Golf Club is on the eastern edge of town in Monterrico district.

Like most big Latin American cities, Lima also has a **horseracing** facility, the Hipódromo de Monterrico. Races are held throughout the year on Tuesday and Thursday nights (6 PM) and Saturday and Sunday afternoons (2 PM). The Jockey Club gallery is open to nonmembers for a nominal fee that includes use of the club's excellent restaurant. For a whole different type of equestrian sport try to catch a chukka at the **Lima Polo Club** ((1) 4365712, Avenida El Cortijo 700 in Monterrico.

Traditional Latin American sports are also popular. **Bullfights** are staged at the Plaza de Acho ((1) 4823360, Avenida Hualgayoc 332 in Rimac, on Saturday and Sunday afternoons in October and November. **Cockfighting** takes place at the Coliseo de Gallos ((1) 4770934 or (1) 4418718, Paseo de la República 6500 in Barranco.

One of the city's havens for sports enthusiasts is the **Lima Cricket & Football Club** ((1) 2640027 or (1) 2640028, Calle Justo Vigil 200 in Orrantia del Mar, which offers tennis and squash courts, swimming pool, lawn bowling, and a gymnasium. Temporary membership is available for singles and couples.

Lima is a certified beach town with its own **surfing** cult. Even in foul weather you can usually see a couple of surfers bobbing up and down in the swell along the Costa Verde, waiting for the perfect wave. Waikiki Beach is probably the most popular for surfing, but any of the strands along Miraflores or Barranco will do.

If you haven't brought your own surf gear hop into Big Wave next to Bohemie Café (see page 98) in San Isidro where you can purchase or rent wetsuits and boards. General sports and recreation equipment (golf clubs,

I think the best selection of arts and crafts in the central area is at **Artesanía Santo Domingo** on Jirón Conde de Superunda opposite Santo Domingo Convent. This two-story complex sports several dozen shops selling gold and silver items, alpaca sweaters and blankets, ponchos, shirts, and backpacks. One of the shops, Artesanía Tito at No. 215, specializes in traditional Andean musical instruments.

Another block up the same street toward the Plaza de Armas is the historic **Post Office Arcade** where you can purchase stamps,

tennis rackets, soccer balls, sports shoes, etc.) can be purchased at two sporting goods shops at Plaza Camino Real in San Isidro.

Anyone who wants to explore the open ocean off Lima should call Expediciones Viento Sur ((1) 9617994 or (1) 9614867, Avenida Grau 855 in Callao. The company offers **maritime ecological tours** to offshore islands as well as **sailboat charters** by the day or week.

SHOPPING

At first glance Lima appears to offer fairly slim pickings when it comes to shopping. As locals will tell you, the trick is knowing where to look.

envelopes, writing pads, postcards, and maps in addition to small souvenirs.

In terms of atmosphere — pleasant shops, English-speaking sales people, wide range of merchandize, relative lack of pickpockets — the chic **Miraflores** district is probably the best place to shop in all of Lima. But you can expect to pay higher prices than in downtown shops or the artisan markets. **Avenida La Paz** between Bolívar and Schell boasts a large concentration of antique, artisan, and jewelry shops catering to both the tourist market and wealthy Peruvians. Among the shops along this stretch are **Artesanías Migue** ((1) 2411145 at No. 344

The back streets of Lima are ripe for exploration.

and **La Casa de la Alpaca** ((1) 4476271 at No. 665.

The quaint and cozy **Pasaje el Suche** runs between Avenida La Paz and Avenida Alcanfores, an alley lined with whitewashed cottages with green tiled roofs. Tenants include restaurants, bars, and shops selling typical Peruvian arts and crafts including alpaca sweaters, pottery, and paintings. One of the best is **El Arcon** ((1) 4476149, which peddles handicrafts and antique silverware.

Slightly off the beaten path in Miraflores is an excellent shop called **Kuntur Huasi** ((1)

woodwork and leather items, jewelry and beads, as well as key chains fashioned from real ants and scorpions.

Plaza Camino Real in San Isidro is one of Lima's largest and most popular modern shopping centers, with many European and American shops including Samsonite luggage, Hushpuppy shoes, Giorgio's, Ferraro, and Valente. Several stores specialize in maternity clothing, baby accessories, and kids clothes. In addition there are two sporting goods stores and a Citibank branch for changing money.

4440557, Avenida Ocharan 182, with handicraft items from all over Peru. Those who venture down to Barranco should make a point of visiting **Las Pallas** ((1) 4774629, Avenida Cajamarca 212, which sells collector's items from the Andes including amulets, textiles, and masks.

Miraflores has two *artesanía* shopping markets with numerous small stalls — **Artesanía Gran Chimú** and **Mercado Artesanal** — both along Avenida Petit Thouars north of the Ovalo traffic circle. But the only place in this neighborhood where you can really find a deal is the **flea market** that sets up every Friday and Saturday night in Parque Kennedy. There's all kinds of stuff including old books, stamps, and record albums,

Across street is the **Centro Artesanal San Isidro** ((1) 4217318, a small collection of arts and craft shops. For sterling silver dinnerware and other ornaments try **Ilaria** ((1) 2218575, Avenida Dos de Mayo 308, San Isidro. Another place to buy fine silver is **Camusso** ((1) 4420340 or (1) 2211594, Avenida Ricardo Rivera Navarrete 788, San Isidro. Or you can visit the showroom at the Camusso silver factory ((1) 4250260 or (1) 4239913, Avenida Colonial 679. The factory is open Monday to Friday 8:30 AM to 5:30 PM.

Pueblo Libre district has evolved into a minor shopping mecca in recent years, with the appearance of large warehouse-size artisan markets along Avenida de la Marina. Foremost among these is the **Gran Mercado**

Inka ((1) 4610550, at No. 884, which hawks stuff from all over Peru at reasonable prices. Elsewhere in Pueblo Libre is a fine little arts and crafts shop called **Casa de la Mujer Artesana** ((1) 4238840, Avenida Peru 1550.

WHERE TO STAY

Lima offers a wider array of accommodation than any other Peruvian city, ranging from international luxury hotels to modest bed-and-breakfast inns.

VERY EXPENSIVE

Perhaps the best place to stay in all of Peru is the **Hotel el Olivar** ((1) 2212120 FAX (1) 2212141 E-MAIL reservas@el-olivar.com.pe, Pancho Fierro 194 in San Isidro. This ultra-modern luxury hotel overlooks the tranquil confines of the famous Olive Grove Park and the posh mansions of San Isidro. Guest rooms are elegantly trimmed in earth tones like maroon, lavender, and olive, and outfitted with all the latest gadgets including mini-bar, safe-deposit box, cable television, video cassette recorder, and fax/modem connection. If you're in the mood for romance, try the honeymoon suite with its massive Jacuzzi. Nearly all rooms offer expansive views, as does the rooftop swimming pool.

Another stylish choice is the **Hotel Oro Verde** ((1) 4214400 FAX (1) 4214422 E-MAIL peovl@ibm.net WEB SITE www.ascinsa.com/hoteloroverdelima, Via Central 150, Centro Empresarial Real, San Isidro. With more than 240 rooms, this is one of Lima's largest hotels, a modern 18-story highrise that overlooks the San Isidro country club. Guest rooms are impeccably decorated, although not as original as the nearby Olivar. The tropical garden features a swimming pool and there's also a well-equipped fitness center.

EXPENSIVE

One of Lima's best new offerings (and one of my personal favorites) is **Posada del Inca** ((1) 2212121 or (1) 2224373 FAX (1) 4224345 or (1) 2224370 E-MAIL posada_ventas@el-olivar.com.pe WEB SITE www.posadas.com.pe, Avenida Libertadores 490 in San Isidro. Owned and operated by the same

people who run the posh Hotel el Olivar, this intimate hotel (only 50 rooms) offers comfortable rooms and a super-friendly staff at nearly half the price of its big brother. The decor is sort of a modern take on ancient Inca motifs, festive colors like ochre and crimson that you won't find in many hotels. The only drawback is a lack of recreation facilities (such as a swimming pool or a health club). Posada's daily breakfast buffet is one of the best in Lima.

The seaside Miraflores district offers a number of solid choices including the popular **Maria Angola** ((1) 4441280 FAX (1) 4462860 E-MAIL postmast@m-angola.com.pe WEB SITE www.rcp.net.pe/M-ANGOLA, Avenida La Paz 610, Miraflores. Rooms are decorated in pseudo-Iberian style but feature all the modern conveniences you could possibly want. Downstairs are several excellent restaurants and Peru's largest casino. Nearby is the low-key **El Condado Hotel** ((1) 4443614 FAX (1) 4441981 E-MAIL condado@condado.com.pe WEB SITE www.condado.com.pe, Alcanfores 425-465, Miraflores. A favorite of visiting businessmen, this hotel offers 50 guest rooms and 48 serviced apartments with special weekly or monthly rates. Right next door is the charming little pedestrian street called Pasaje el Suche with some of Lima's best arts and craft shops.

If you're into "grande dame" hotels then check out the **Gran Hotel Bolívar** ((1) 4272305 FAX (1) 4287674, Jirón de la Unión 958, on Plaza San Martín in downtown Lima. Built during an age when marble floors, brass plumbing, and crystal chandeliers were requisites of any luxury hotel, the Bolívar has seen its fair share of history and is often used as a backdrop for local television productions. Fifty years ago this was *the* place to stay in the Peruvian capital, but like much of Latin America it fell into disrepair after the 1950s. After languishing for years, the hotel underwent major renovations in 1998, bringing the guest rooms and public areas up to scratch with current international standards. Afternoon tea is served beneath the glass rotunda in the lobby, breakfast and lunch on an open-air terrace that overlooks a busy downtown street.

San Isidro district is filled with chic boutiques and elegant mansions.

There are several large, modern hotels in the central area that cater mostly to the business crowd. **Hotel Crillon** ((1) 4283290 FAX (1) 4265920, Avenida Nicolás de Piérola 589, sports a penthouse restaurant and bar with great views of the old city. The **Lima Sheraton** ((1) 4333320 or (1) 4336367 FAX (1) 4335844, Paseo de la República 170, has everything you would expect of an international chain hotel including two restaurants, a fitness center, a business center, a swimming pool, and a shopping arcade. But this has to be one of the most unfriendly locations in Lima, an island of gray concrete surrounded by busy avenues.

MODERATE

Built in 1918 as the mansion of a wealthy Peruvian, bygone charm prevails at the **Hotel Antigua Miraflores** ((1) 2416116 FAX (1) 2416115 E-MAIL hantigua@amauta.rcp.net.pe, Avenida Grau 350 in Miraflores. Owner David Wroughton has done a superb job of restoring the old residence into a modern hotel without losing any of its oldfashioned enchantment. The place is filled with antique furnishings, wooden fixtures fashioned from Oregon pine, and modern Peruvian artwork, while the tiny central courtyard is a haven of tranquility. Guest rooms come with private bath, hot water, minibar, and cable television. Suites feature Jacuzzis and kitchenettes with microwave. The Antigua is within short walking distance of many good restaurants in this quiet Miraflores neighborhood. This is my choice as the best value-for-money hotel in all of Lima.

Another great little hotel is the seafront **Miramar Ischia** ((1) 4466969 FAX (1) 4450851, Malecón Cisneros 1244, Miraflores. Perched on a cliff above the deep blue Pacific, the three-story Miramar is an Art Deco mansion converted into a charming boutique hotel. The spacious guest rooms feature antique furnishings and some have balconies overlooking the coast. All offer private bath, cable television, and telephone. Behind the house is a garden with sundeck and lawn; inside is a small bar dedicated to the memory of Marilyn Monroe.

For a complete change of pace try **Suites Eucaliptus** ((1) 4452840 or (1) 4458594 FAX (1) 4443071, San Martín 511 (at Avenida Larco). Situated in the heart of downtown Miraflores, perhaps I would best describe the Eucalyptus as a bizarre cross between a medieval monastery and the Addams Family mansion. The place is a real trip, decorated with religious icons, taxidermed animals, surrealist art, Persian carpets, and heavy wooden furniture. All rooms have private bath with hot water, plus cable television. Suites feature Jacuzzi and kitchen.

Hostal El Patio ((1) 4442107 or (1) 4444884 FAX (1) 4441663, Diez Canseco 341-A, is another strange little place in Miraflores. Reminiscent of an Arizona desert motel, El Patio offers a dozen rooms with a funky 1950s decor set around a Spanish-style courtyard with gurgling fountains. Suites feature cable television and kitchen. All rooms have private bath with hot water. The place is clean, the price is right.

Two other moderate abodes in the Miraflores area are the **Hostal Inca Palace** ((1) 4443714 FAX (1) 4441858, Calle Schell 547; and the **Hostal Residencial Alemana** ((1) 4456999 FAX (1) 4473950, Avenida Arequipa 4704.

INEXPENSIVE

Downtown Lima offers half a dozen budget abodes within a two-block radius of the Plaza de Armas. One of the best is the **Wiracocha Hotel** ((1) 4271178 or (1) 4274406, Jirón Junín 284 (half a block east of Plaza de Armas). The Art Deco decor has seen better days, but the rooms are clean and feature private bath (some with hot water). Around the right side of the Government Palace is **Hostal Lima** ((1) 4285782, Jirón Carabaya 145, with 20 modestly furnished rooms and a rather gloomy central courtyard. In addition to a shared bath and no hot water, the manager doesn't speak much English. But it's hard to beat the price or location.

Situated in this same area is the **Hotel Europa** ((1) 4273351, Jirón Ancash 376 (opposite San Francisco church), which sports a wonderful two-story lobby. This is a favorite with the young backpacker crowd. There are shared baths and hot water is available in the morning and evening. Another old favorite in central Lima is the **Pension de**

Familia Rodriguez ((1) 4236465 FAX (1) 4241606, Avenida Nicolás de Piérola 730. Rooms come with bath, breakfast, and lots of hot water. Slightly more upmarket in the downtown area is the **Hostal la Estrella de Belén** ((1) 4286462, Jirón de la Unión (Belén) 1051. The proprietors speak English; rooms are modest but are clean and come with bath and hot water.

The posh San Isidro district doesn't offer much in the way of cheap accommodation, but a welcome exception to the rule is the **Youth Hostel Malka** ((1) 4420162 FAX (1) 2225589, Los Lirios 165 (between Las Camelias and Paseo Parodi). Proprietor Henry Kleinberg keeps a tidy eight rooms including a dormitory that sleeps six. The bath is shared, but there's hot water in the shower. The rate does not include breakfast. Another choice is the **Miraflores Youth Hostal** ((1) 4465488, Casimiro Ulloa 328, which features dormitory accommodation and communal bathrooms with hot water.

WHERE TO EAT

VERY EXPENSIVE

Lima's largest and most famous restaurant is the glorious **Costa Verde** ((1) 4772172 or (1) 4772424, on Barranquito Beach in Barranco. Don't let anybody tell you that size doesn't matter because it definitely does at this establishment. The main dining room is enormous, almost as large as an airplane hanger, with massive picture windows that look out onto the Pacific. And while you can choose from various à la carte items like lobster thermidor, *corvina* (sea bass), vichyssoise, oysters, smoked salmon, and stone crab, nearly everyone dines at the grand buffet— 478 different dishes, most of them seafood related, everything absolutely fresh and delicious. In fact, Costa Verde is listed in the *Guinness Book of Records* as the world's largest buffet spread. The cost is also colossal: US$60 per person; US$30 for children. That includes house wine and entrance to the after-dinner disco that unfolds around 10 PM each night. I guarantee that you will never forget your night at this place.

Rincon Gaucho ((1) 4474778 or (1) 2540052, Parque Salazar in Miraflores, is a

meat-eaters paradise as well as a shrine to Argentina's bygone gaucho culture. The mixed grill offers various carnivore treats or you can choose from main courses like filet mignon, beef cordon blue or spicy chorizo sausages. Rincon once had a sweeping view of the Pacific, but a new shopping plaza currently under construction will soon block out most of the panorama.

EXPENSIVE

One of Lima's most romantic new restaurants is **Posada del Marqués** ((1) 4474838, Avenida Grau 498, situated in a lovely Moorish-style villa in Miraflores. The house specialty is paella, six different types including *valenciana antigua* with chicken and rabbit, and *fidena de gandia* with shellfish. Another taste treat is *rueda de lomos a la francesa*: three medallions of beef prepared in three different ways covered in a sauce of pepper, mustard, and Roquefort cheese. The paella dining room in back features a glass wall so that you can see the chef do his thing.

Another gourmet choice is **Brujas de Cachiche** ((1) 4471883 or (1) 4466536, Avenida Bolognesi 460, Miraflores. The place is named after Cachiche village in the Nazca Desert which is famous for witches, folk healers, and sorcerers and many of the dishes have mystic themes. *El gran bruja* ("the great witch") is sautéed tenderloin beef with hot chilis, olive oil, and black beans; *cabrito a la nortena* is baby goat stew, popular in northern Peru; *causa rellena* is a savory first course that features crab meat stuffed into yellow Andean potatoes. The decor is pretty wild too, especially the huge modern mural over the main dining room. Reservations are recommended.

The creation of expatriate Swiss chef Urs Schaerer, **Giuseppe Verdi** ((1) 2410094, Avenida Grau 1721, is a special treat in the heart of Miraflores. True to its name, this European-style café offers live classical music every evening as well as copious Impressionist-style artwork produced by the eclectic Schaerer. The gourmet Italian menu offers a number of pasta dishes in addition to heartier fare like veal scaloppini and saltimbocca. The interior has a cave-like ambience, or you can dine al fresco on the front patio. Even if you don't eat, the tiny piano bar offers comfortable seats and sweet music.

Down on the waterfront in Miraflores is the popular **Punta Sal ℂ** (1) 2424524, Malecón Cisneros Cuadra 3, which offers fantastic ocean views with its vast array of Peruvian-style seafood. Among the signature dishes of award-winning chef Adolfo Perret Bermudez are sea bass and lobster in curry sauce, octopus with lemon and olives, and lobster cannelloni. There's also plenty of *ceviche* to choose from, as well as Chinese dishes and a children's menu. Punta Sal has another branch in San Isidro district ℂ (1) 4417431, Avenida Conquistadores 948.

My vote for the best French food in Lima is **Le Bistrot de Mes Fils** ℂ (1) 4226308, Avenida Conquistadores 510, San Isidro. Chef de cuisine Sandra Tuss Freire has created a mouthwatering selection: swordfish with an eggplant purée, shrimp ravioli, roast duck with foie gras, cannelloni stuffed with sole and crab, ricotta cheese pasta with asparagus, as well as more traditional French dishes like escargots. The wine list is nearly as impressive and the waiters come *à la Parisienne*, with long white aprons and a bit of attitude. The café decor features lots of fresh flowers, arty black and white photos, and a tree growing up through the middle of the wooden roof.

Likewise, the city's best Italian cuisine is probably served up at **La Trattoria di Mambrino** ℂ (1) 4467002, Manuel Bonilla 106, Miraflores, which offers creative takes on spaghetti, ravioli, tagliatelle, lasagna, and gnocchi. Pasta sauces vary from night to night but the seafood recipes are especially good. Two dishes you might want to try are the gnocchi with ricotta cheese and spinach in a cream sauce, and the veal ravioli in a champagne and tomato sauce. And you get wonderful homemade bread as a starter. My only problem with La Trattoria is the service, which tends to run somewhere between snooty and downright rude.

Restaurants in the trendy Barranco district seem to come and go with all the whim of youthful fashion. But one place that's been around for awhile is **Manos Morenas** ℂ (1) 4674902, Avenida Pedro de Osma 409, which specializes in Peruvian Creole-style food including *chicharrones* (deep-fried pork skins), *anticuchos* (shish-kebabs), *papas rellena*

(stuffed fried potatoes), *tamalitos verde* (corn-flour roll with green sauce), and *sangresitas* (blood sausage). Many of these dishes are included in a Creole sampler called the *Piqueo Manos Morenos*. The menu also includes seafood dishes like sea bass and *pulpo al olivo* (boiled octopus), as well as tasty *tacu-tacu* (navy bean and white rice pancakes). The venue is equally charming: an old seaside mansion filled with antiques and surrounded by leafy trees. I prefer to eat outside on the breezy front terrace. There is live Creole music on weekends.

MODERATE

Nearly every restaurant in Miraflores has *ceviche* on the menu, but the only place that specializes in that seafood treat is **Don Beta Cebichería** ℂ (1) 4469465, José Galvez 667. Vincenzol Romano Vasile, the Brazilian-born chef and owner, serves up 19 different types of *ceviche* including dishes prepared squid, octopus, sea bass, scallops, crab, mussels, and sea snails. There's also a tempura and sushi bar. Or you can choose from various other dishes on the expansive menu including stuffed crab in a white sauce and seafood risotto with langoustines and shrimp. Don Beta is bright, cheerful and noisy, with good service and a friendly staff. This is my choice for best *ceviche* along the entire Peruvian coast.

Miraflores also harbors a trendy café-bar called **El Suche** ℂ (1) 2427090, Avenida La Paz 646, situated on a narrow alley called Pasaje el Suche behind the Hotel El Condado. It's hard to decide what's more interesting here: the funky decor or a tasty menu that includes things like crêpes, tapas, or hot chicken, ham and mozzarella sandwiches. An extensive drinks list includes various fruit juices, cocktails, and coffees. Happy hour for both food and drinks is 4 PM to 7 PM daily. This is one of the few places in the neighborhood that stays open late, until 2 AM.

If you want to check out the trendy young Lima scene duck into **Bohemie Café & Mas** ℂ (1) 4465240 or (1) 4450889, Avenida Santa Cruz 805 on the border between San Isidro and Miraflores districts. This is basically a Peruvian version of Hard Rock Café with guitars and other musical mementos perched on the walls. The menu features a number of tasty sandwiches and salads (lobster, Thai, chicken Caesar) as well as seafood risotto and Indonesian satay. The dessert menu is to die for: crème brûlée, profiteroles, and cheesecake with white chocolate. And don't feel out of place just because you left your portable telephone at home.

Another San Isidro hangout is **Café Ole** ((1) 4401186, Pancho Fierro 115, which serves up burgers, soups, salads, and desserts to the well-healed office and late-night crowd that frequents this area. The front patio affords

to Lima circa 1920. About all they have to serve are sandwiches and drinks.

In my opinion **Los Heraldos** ((1) 4274044, Jirón Ancash 306, is the best of the budget cafés in central Lima. The menu is eclectic to say the least: *carne adobo* (barbecued beef), fried fish, chicken cooked in beer, shrimp with rice, potato salad, fish soup, *tortilla* omelets, and various Chinese dishes like wanton soup, fried rice, and pineapple chicken. The beer comes ice cold, the Chinese owners and their staff are *mucho* friendly and there's live music Friday and Saturday nights.

good people watching. Right up the street is another trendy little placed called the **News Café** ((1) 4216278 or (1) 4416985, Santa Luisa 110. Burgers, salads, pizza, and pasta are the hallmarks here. There's a rack of magazines and newspapers to read while you're eating (or waiting for that tardy date), mostly Latin press.

INEXPENSIVE

The area around the Plaza de Armas is the fulcrum for cheap eats in Lima. Perhaps the oldest establishment is **El Cordano**, an ancient bar and café opposite the train station. The decor is a little scruffy and the waiters a bit slow but this place will transport you back

A favorite with civil servants who work in the Plaza de Armas area are the two little cafés in the **Post Office Arcade** which serve up simple dishes like hot roast beef sandwiches and fish filet with beans and rice. Set lunches run as little as S/3.50.

There aren't a lot of cheap eats in San Isidro. But one place where a meal won't cost you an arm and a leg is **La Baguette** ((1) 4419431, Avenida Libertadores 300. This little neighborhood snack bar features pizza, sandwiches, and freshly baked pastries and bread.

Miraflores used to feature a number of budget restaurants, but they have faded away in recent years to an onslaught of upmarket

Many of Lima's street vendors have been moved to new quarters in the suburbs.

eateries. One of the holdouts is **Govinda** ((1) 4442871, Calle Schell 634, a combination vegetarian restaurant and healthfood store. The selection runs the gamut from whole-wheat sandwiches, stir-fried rice, and pasta dishes to *lomo saltado* (made with soy meal), yogurt shakes, and fruit juices. Govinda also has tasty desserts — try the *arroz bengali*, an Indian treat made from rice, yogurt, figs, honey, and fruit. The adjacent shop sells herbs, ginseng, bee pollen, and other New Age delights.

In keeping with its trendy image, Mira-flores offers a number of pleasant sidewalk cafés, especially around Parque Kennedy. **El Tigre Café**, at Calle Lima 359, offers an eclectic selection including chorizo sausages, Hawaiian burgers, giant hot dogs, *tamalitos verde* with Creole sauce, salads, and omelets as well as cheesecake, ice cream, and fruit pies. Next door is a similar sidewalk estab-lishment called **Café de la Paz** ((1) 2416043, Calle Lima 351.

Lima students head for Barranco district on Friday and Saturday night to drink and listen to music. But there are also a number of inexpensive places to eat like **El Hornito Pizzeria** on the main square, which offers al fresco dining and great people watching.

NIGHTLIFE

Don't expect to find a *zona rosa* with a huge concentration of nightlife. Lima's after-dark scene is spread far and wide with each dis-trict displaying an entirely different atmo-sphere.

The young and trendy with cash to burn flock to glitzy nightclubs along **Avenida de la Marina** in San Miguel and Pueblo Libre that feature music, dance, dinner, gambling and live shows. These places are easily iden-tified by their garish neon signs, funny names, and the flotillas of Mercedes and BMWs parked out front. You won't find very many foreigners in these places, but it's a fascinat-ing glimpse into the lifestyle of Lima's middle- and upper-class youth. Cover charges usually run around S/100 on week nights and S/500 on Friday and Saturday. One of anchors of this strip is **Texas Station** ((1) 5611050 or (1) 4642540, Avenida de la Marina 2430.

Disco is definitely alive and well in other parts of Lima. One of the city's biggest dance floors is **Svago Beach** ((1) 4772424 at the popular Costa Verde restaurant in Barranco which rocks from 10 PM to 5 AM on Thurs-day, Friday, and Saturday nights. **Noctambul Discoteca** ((1) 2470044, Avenida Grau 627 in Barranco is another popular dance spot. As an alternative you can salsa the night away at **Boleros**, Calle Santa Luisa 156, a popular Cuban restaurant and bar in San Isidro.

Traditional Peruvian music clubs are called *peñas*, although you might also find jazz, folk, blues, reggae, or rock at these places. Bar-ranco is famed for its lively *peñas* including **La Estación** ((1) 2470344 or (1) 4775030, Ave-nida Pedro de Osma 112, which offers a wide range of live acts in a cozy atmosphere. Far-ther up the street is the breezy **Manos Morenas** ((1) 4674902, Avenida Pedro de Osma 409, which offers live Creole music on weekends. Closer to the town square is **La Vieja Taberna** ((1) 2473741, Avenida Grau 268, which offers a wide range of musical acts from Peruvian folk to Latin jazz. Nearby is **El Ekeko** ((1) 2473148, Avenida Grau 266, with acts that tend more towards tropical and Latin sounds. In the downtown area near the Plaza de Armas, **Los Heraldos** ((1) 4274044, Jirón Ancash 306, features cheap drinks and live bands on Friday and Saturday nights.

When I'm in the mood for a quiet drink I duck into the **Orient Express Bar** in the Pasaje el Suche, Miraflores. Modeled after the ac-claimed train, it sports half a dozen stools and four booths paneled in dark, rich wood. Barranco's **Kachibache Pub** ((1) 4770756, Avenida San Martín 141, is a cozy place with funky decor where you can actually have a conversation over a cold beer. **Parque Ken-nedy** in Miraflores offers pleasant outdoor cafés like El Tigre and Café de la Paz, a flea market that unfolds on weekend nights, plus a small amphitheater which offers poetry readings, guitar solos, and Latin bands on weekend evenings.

Classical entertainment also has its place in Lima society. The **Philharmonic Society** ((1) 2426396, Porta 170, Office No. 301 in Miraflores, stages concerts at various ven-ues around the capital featuring visiting European, Asian, and North American art-ists. Information on performances is also available at the Teleticket windows in Wong supermarkets. The **Ballet Municipal** ((1) 4280157 continues stages performances at the Municipal Theater in central Lima.

Instituto Cultural Peruano-Norteamericano ((1) 2411940 or (1) 2417687, Avenida Arequipa 4798 in Miraflores, offers a wide range of music and dance performances including piano recitals, jazz concerts, and folk dancing. **Sala Alzedo** ((1) 4267206, Jirón Huancavelica 265 in central Lima, also has an eclectic slate including chamber music, chorale, and classic guitar. Finally, the **Centro**

Pacific coastline. The city's Jorge Chavez International Airport is served by more than two dozen international carriers with daily flights from Europe and North America as well as large South American cities like Quito, Bogota, Santiago, La Paz, Buenos Aires, and Sao Paulo.

In days gone by Lima was an important rail terminus, but there is no longer passenger rail service to other major cities. The fastest way to reach other major Peruvian destinations is air service from the domestic terminal at Jorge Chavez. There are daily

Cultural Universidad Católica ((1) 4223221 or (1) 4223305, Avenida Camino Real 1075 in San Isidro, offers a year-round menu of classical music and dance.

Movie fans flock to the **Filmoteca de Lima** at the National Museum of Art ((1) 4234732 or (1) 4251101, Paseo Colón 125 in central Lima, to see an ongoing selection of international films including various film festival winners from Cannes, Venice, Berlin, and Sundance.

HOW TO GET THERE

Lima is one of the most centrally located capital cities in South America, situated at about the midpoint of the country's long

flights to and from Cuzco, Iquitos, Arequipa, Trujillo, Chiclayo, Ayacucho, Piura, and other cities.

Lima is connected to other coastal cities by the Pan-American Highway, which is in excellent condition along most of its length. Running north from the capital, the highway stretches to Trujillo, Chiclayo, Piura, and Tumbes near the Ecuadorian frontier. Running south from Lima the highway runs through Pisco, Ica, Nazca, Arequipa, and Tacna near the Chilean frontier. There is frequent bus service from Lima to all of these cities, as well as popular destinations in the interior like Cuzco, Ayacucho, and Huánuco.

Lima's central station offers excursion trains into the Andes foothills.

High Andes

NARROW HIGHWAYS AND DILAPIDATED RAILROAD tracks climb the hillsides east of Lima into the Andes, where few casual travelers venture. Yet for me, the Andean mountain towns are among Peru's most fascinating destinations. In a way, I much prefer these cities to Cusco, long overrun by tourists. In the less popular towns visitors are treated as guests and embraced by locals eager to share their regional foods and folk arts.

Peru's most famous train line, known as the highest railroad in the world, runs from the capital city high into the mountains at Huancayo, 3,240 m (10,731 ft) above sea level. Unfortunately, the train doesn't go there anymore, and hasn't since the 1980s. It used to be one of the premier journeys in Peru, as desirable as the trek to Machu Picchu. There is always talk of restoring this line, but until that time buses are the vehicle of choice for tourists and business travelers. Filled with markets, artisans' workshops and some of the friendliest people in Peru, Huancayo is one those places you long to call home, at least temporarily. In fact, many of the gringos I met in the city were there on extended stays; I watched one, upon her departure, burst into tears every time she hugged a Quechua *mama* (woman) selling jewelry or weavings.

The same feelings capture travelers who spend any time in Ayacucho, south of Lima. Home of the Sendero Luminoso (Shining Path) movement from the 1970s to 1990s, Ayacucho is a captivating, soulful place still recovering from decades of insurgent violence. I was the only gringo in town during my latest stay and was treated to impromptu meals and tours nearly every time I started conversing with a local hotelier or entrepreneur. It's the one place I long to return for a month or more.

Both cities are surrounded by fascinating villages, archaeological sites, and natural wonders. Northwest of Huancayo, roads and rail lines lead through vast mining regions and tiny market towns to Cerro de Pasco, center of the mining industry above the Amazon basin. Southeast of Huancayo far more primitive roads lead to remote settlements, the Indian city of Huancavelica and on to Ayacucho. The entire region is filled with the sort of scenery one envisions before visiting the Andes, from rivers rushing

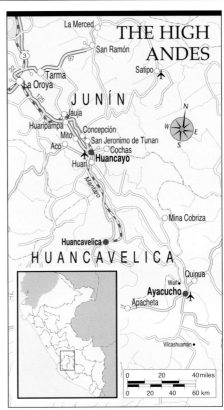

through forests to children in bright red costumes tending sheep in vast pastures. Altitude sickness can be a problem when you first arrive; take at least a day to adjust if you're coming from sea level.

HUANCAYO

The ride to Huancayo is one of the prettiest drives in the country, following a steep ascent from the coastline and Lima into the Andes. The road parallels the train tracks for much of the way, and passes through several impressive tunnels blasted into formidable mountains. The main highway northeast from Lima branches at the mining town of La Oroya, with the southern stretch heading past market towns and ranches to the city of Huancayo, capital of the department of Junín. With a population of 849,000, the city is large and commercial. Yet it has remained rich in talented artisans, fascinating markets, and engaging parks.

Vivid red woolen shawls and scarves keep Quechua women warm in chilly Chinchero.

The city sits in the Valle del Mantaro river valley, 3,272 m (10,731 ft) above sea level in a rich agricultural region. It was capital of the pre-Incan Huanca (also spelled Wanka) civilization, whose members solidly resisted invasion by the Inca and the Spanish conquistadors. In fact, Peru's independence from Spain was declared in the Huancayo region in 1820. The city remained isolated until 1908, when the railroad was built from Lima. It soon became an important agricultural region for the country, producing vast quantities of wheat. The Valle del Mantaro is one of the richest agricultural and cultural regions in the Andes, dotted with villages with distinct styles of dress, music, and dance. Though it's not considered one of Peru's main tourist attractions, the region is filled with fascinating sights and is well worth visiting for more than a few days.

GENERAL INFORMATION

There is a **Tourist Information Office (** (64) 233251, located by the Plaza Constitución at Calle Real 481 in the back of the Casa de Artesana. It's open Monday through Friday 8 AM to 1 PM and 2:30 PM to 6:30 PM. The most reputable companies offering tours of the area include **Wanka Tours (** (64) 231743 FAX (64) 231778 at Calle Real 565; **Murakami Tours (** (64) 234745 at Jirón Lima 354; and **Agencia Alfonso Velit (** (64) 231743 in the same office as Wanka Tours at Calle Real 565. The tours are all similar, offering stops at artisan villages and small archeological sites.

The agencies will change traveler's checks as well as set up tours.

Lucho Hurtado, owner of La Cabaña restaurant (see WHERE TO EAT, page 112) and **Incas del Peru** travel information center (also at the restaurant), is the city's unofficial ambassador, dispensing information to anyone who happens by his office. He has a book exchange there, and a language school on the property. Students are treated to visits to the market for classes in local food, flowers, and products used for healing; Hurtado's market tour is an astonishing education in itself. He also offers tours around the region and into the high and low jungle and mountains. Hurtado is immensely knowledgeable in all aspects of the region; ask to see his folk art collection, the finest in the city.

WHAT TO SEE AND DO

First impressions don't do justice to Huancayo, which looked like an ugly big city to me as I rode from the bus station to my hotel. The four-lane Calle Real, running through the center of the city, is jam-packed with buses and cars and lined with an unsightly jumble of shops and restaurants. Once I started walking, however, the city slowly revealed its soul.

The **Plaza Huamanmarca**, on Calle Real between Prolongación Ica and Jirón Piura, was the center of the city when it was founded by the Spaniards in 1572, and was once a vibrant place that held the weekly Feria Dominical (Sunday market), which has been relocated to the west side of town. Now, the concrete square is home to the Municipal Hall and the telephone and post offices, and underwent a much-needed beautification project in 1998.

Plaza Constitución (or **Plaza de Armas**) also on Calle Real, is the heart of the city, though it lacks the flowers, trees, and collection of local characters that enliven most Andean plazas. It is so indistinguishable I never even took time to have my boots shined there — my usual approach to grasping a city's local scene. The **Capilla de la Merced** at the Plaza de Armas is the chapel where the Constitutional Congress gathered in 1830, and is a national monument. Inside is a collection of Cusqueño-style paintings (see BACKGROUND, page 128 under CUSCO).

The **Parque del Cerro de la Libertad** (also called Torre-Torre) at the end of Avenida Giráldez one kilometer (slightly over half a mile) east of downtown, has a small zoo, a public swimming pool, and a restaurant that serves regional dishes. It's a popular spot with locals on the weekends, when plays and folkloric dance performances are held in the open amphitheater.

The **Parque de la Identidad Wanka**, northeast of downtown in the San Antonio neighborhood on the outskirts of the city, was constructed in the late 1990s and is one of the country's finest public parks. The park was designed to highlight the indigenous

The landscape grows barren and dry along the road from Ayacucho to Huanta.

cultures, plants, and traditions of the Wanka Indians, a small regional group who predated the Inca and left few edifices for exploration. Walkways and bridges are made of thousands of stones set in rippling patterns; a sculpture of a giant gourd represents the *mates burilados* (carved gourds) made by local artisans. Rock and cement benches are hidden amid cactus and flower gardens filled with marigolds in September. Children climb about on a rock castle set beside swings. Across the street from the main park is an area devoted to regional cuisine, with sev-

eral restaurants clustered around a courtyard. This is the perfect place to sample *pachamanca*, lamb roasted in an underground rock pit. The meal takes so long to cook it's usually only served on weekends, when brass bands called *cachimbos* blast away while the meat roasts for several hours. During the week, locals gather at the restaurants in the evening for coffee and fresh *picarones* (sweet fried donuts).

The traditions of local shamans and Andean mystics are preserved at **Wasi Wasi**, off Avenida Los Angeles, behind the cemetery. Located in a busy residential area near the city, the center is home to artist Pedro Marticorena, a wizened, hard-living man who creates bizarre masks, sculptures, and paintings depicting mystical visions. Marticorena's home-cum-gallery is a gathering spot for local artists and shamans who sometimes conduct private ceremonies in the dirt yard, which is overflowing with the artist's odd works. His three-foot-high masks carved from tree bark and trunks evidence a strong interest in hallucinatory images; I

found them quite scary. Drop-in guests are discouraged — you probably wouldn't be able to find the place anyway. Ask at local galleries, tour offices, and La Cabaña for a guide who knows Marticorena and can arrange a visit.

Fiestas dominate the annual calendar in the entire Huancayo region, and you're bound to witness at least one religious procession while staying in the area. Carnaval, Holy Week, and Christmas are all celebrated with fervor, but the biggest celebrations take place during May for the **Fiesta de las Cruces**. Parties, parades, and fireworks dominate the scene throughout the month.

SHOPPING

The weekend **Mercado**, held along Avenida Huancavelica, is the offshoot of Huancayo's traditional Feria Dominical. It's best on Sundays when artisans from the Mantaro Valley descend upon the city to sell their wares. Schedule your visit to coincide with the market; it's the one place where you can completely immerse yourself in local customs. Ladies dressed in multiple layers of skirts all have a *manta* (vivid, striped cloth) wrapped around their shoulders and long braids hanging beneath black felt hats. The men, on the other hand, tend to favor polyester shirts and slacks. The market stretches along several streets; certain areas are devoted to household items including plastic pails, brooms, and mops, while others feature rows of "modern" clothing — an unattractive mix of bland dresses, blouses, and nylon underpants.

A few streets are home to the artisans, who display straw baskets, *mantas,* felt hats, leather bags, *retablos* (miniature scenes framed in painted wooden boxes), and woven bags and belts. Of particular importance are the dried gourds carved with intricate scenes depicting religious processions, historical events, and village lifestyle. The art, called *mate burilado*, is immensely time consuming, and the resulting creations true treasures. Huancayo's weavers are also very talented; be sure to purchase at least one of their exquisite belts with pictures of the local train woven into the design.

Other than the market, the best selection of handicrafts is displayed at the **Casa de Artesana** at Calle Real 495. Individual artisans rent space in the large building and sit weaving, carving, and spinning wool as shoppers mill about. The **Centro Commercial Artesanal El Manatial** at Jirón Ancash 475 is packed with shops and stands.

The **Mercado Mayorista** food market on Prolongación Ica by the train station is also fascinating. The market spreads for several blocks, with stands displaying snake skins and roots for healers, dozens of varieties of

the **Hotel Turismo Huancayo** ((64) 231072 at Jirón Ancash 729. The colonial-style building sits on a small quiet section of the street and has an impressive lobby. The rooms are decent, with televisions, phones, and 24-hour hot water. The **Hotel Olímpico** ((64) 214555 FAX 215700, at Jirón Ancash 408, is also fairly modern and is located close to the plaza.

Inexpensive

La Casa de La Abuela ((64) 238224 FAX (64) 222395, Avenida Giráldez 691, is one of the nicest hotels in town, with rooms in a con-

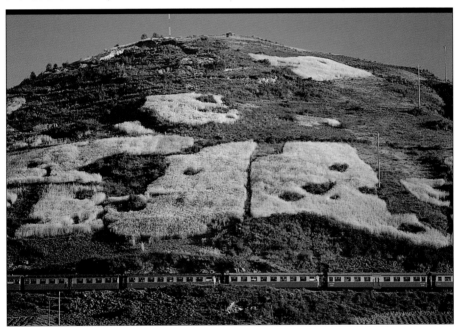

Andean potatoes, pumpkins and squash, cages of furry guinea pigs, and heaps of fresh trout.

WHERE TO STAY

For the most part, Huancayo's hotels are simple and comfortable, offering few frills. There are no first-class hotels in town.

Moderate

The **Hotel Presidente** ((064) 231275, at Calle Real 1138, may well be the most modern place in town, with an elevator, televisions, and phones in each room, which have private baths. Street noise can be a problem. The architecture is more pleasing to the eye at

verted mansion. Some rooms are dormitory-style while others are private; currently most have shared baths, though private baths are under construction. The backyard is a nice gathering spot where guests feast on continental breakfast included in the rate. The hotel is across the street from La Cabaña restaurant and often houses students from the restaurant's language school. The **Hostal Plaza** ((64) 210509, Jirón Ancash 171, has 22 rooms with private baths, and is a quiet, friendly place. Close to the plaza, the **Hotel Confort** ((64) 233601, Jirón Ancash 231, has

LEFT: Exotic produce, such as these cactus fruit, abound in Andean markets. ABOVE: Few roads and towns appear along the remote railway to Machu Picchu. OVERLEAF: Mines such as this one near Arcata have forever transformed the Andean countryside.

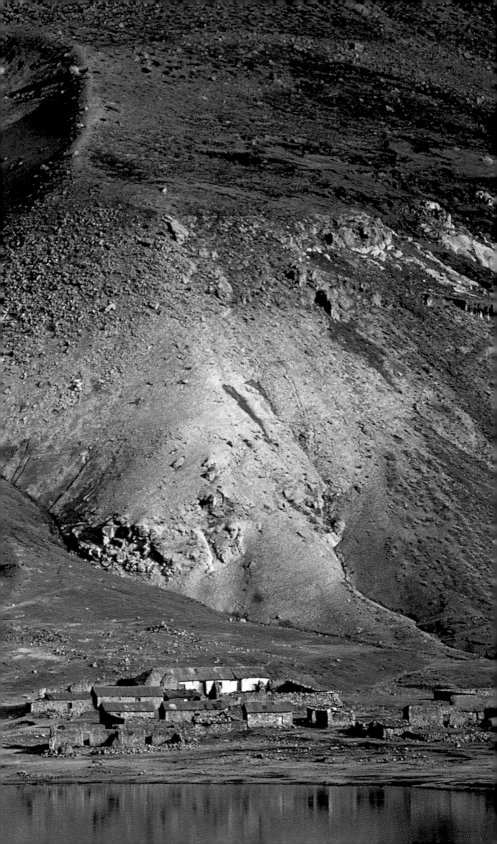

clean rooms with private baths. Also recommended in this price range are the **Hotel Baldeón (** (64) 231634, at Calle Amazonas 543, and the **Hotel Kiya (** (64) 231432, at Avenida Giráldez 107.

WHERE TO EAT

Rich in fresh produce, seafood and meat, Huancayo has an abundance of regional dishes worth sampling. Be sure to try *papas a la huancaina* (potatoes with cheese sauce and sliced egg), *chicharrón* (roasted pork),

Moderate

As much a central meeting area as a restaurant, **La Cabaña (** (64) 223303, at Avenida Giráldez 652, is packed nearly every night. Diners stop by for great wood-oven pizzas, lively music, and a few *calientitos*, a soothing hot herbal drink with a dash of pisco. There are several rooms and a courtyard. The best tables are at the front by the fireplace and stage.

Antojitos ((64) 237950, Jirón Puno 599, is another lively spot packed with diners feasting on pizzas and platters of grilled meats to

machca (a mix of toasted grain used for porridge), and local fruits including red bananas and *granabilla*, a type of passionfruit. *Hualpa chupe*, a regional soup, is a fragrant blend of chicken, *aji* chilis, and *achiote* (a blend of spices). *Chupe verde*, another soup, is an herbal broth filled with potatoes, cheese, and eggs. Corn, hunks of pork and tripe are blended in the hearty stew called *mondongo*, which makes a savory, filling inexpensive meal. As in all Andean towns, *cuy* (guinea pig) is a local treat. Here it's fried and served with a *salsa colorado*, a red sauce made with chilis, onion, and *achiote*. You can eat extremely inexpensively by shopping at the market for breads, vegetables, roasted meats, and fruit.

the sounds of live romantic tunes. Jammed with downtown workers at lunch, **El Olímpico (** (64) 234181, Avenida Giráldez 199, is a good place to try local dishes including fried *cuy*. **Restaurant El Padrino**, at Avenida Giráldez 133, also serves regional dishes.

Inexpensive

Huancayans must have an incredible fondness for sweets, given the constant aroma of baking pastries, breads, and cookies wafting through the streets. *Panaderías* (bakeries) can be found in nearly every block. **Panadería Koky (** (64) 234707, at Jirón Puno 298, is the prettiest place in town, with small linen-covered tables scattered about a large, quiet dining room. The restaurant specializes in elaborate pastries but also serves pizzas and sandwiches, and has a delicatessen counter and liquor shop. **Las Gaviotas** ((64) 235290, Jirón Lima 279, specializes in seafood including grilled mountain trout and *ceviche*. Vitamins, yogurt, soy milk, and vegetarian meals are available at **Restaurant Vegetariano** at Jirón Cajamarca 379. Of the dozens of chicken restaurants in downtown, **Pollos a la Leña** ((64) 234362, Calle Real 549, stands out for its smoky-flavored chicken, fresh salads, and family ambience.

car, or *colectivos*. Travel time is six to eight hours. If you decide to drive, limit your travel to daytime hours. The scenery is sensational as you leave Lima and head up into the Andes. In approximately five hours you will reach La Oroya; from there head east to Tarma or south to Huancayo. First-class bus service to and from Lima is available on the Cruz del Sur, Mariscal Caceres, and Etusca lines. There is also bus service between Huancayo and Ayacucho, though the ride lasts eight to 12 hours over a miserable road.

NIGHTLIFE

Huancayo's nightlife is as varied as its music and folk arts, with *peñas*, discos, and bars opening after 10 PM. **La Chiminea**, Jirón Lima 253, is a small club with live 1960s rock-and-roll; the band offers a menu of songs so patrons can choose their favorite Beatles' tunes. **Marisquería** on Avenida Giráldez by the plaza has a second-story dance club complete with rotating mirrored ball and large dance floor.

HOW TO GET THERE

There is currently no train service from Lima to Huancayo. Your choices are bus,

VALLE DEL MANTARO

The entire river valley around Huancayo is filled with incredible sights, including artisan villages, archaeological sites, mountain trails, streams, and lakes. You could easily spend two or three days concentrating on just one aspect of the valley, which is divided into several provinces.

Traveling northeast from Huancayo one reaches **Cochas Chicas** and **Cochas Grandes**, 11 km (nearly seven miles) from downtown. Headquarters for the master gourd-carvers of the area, the two towns offer travelers the

LEFT: Dazzling minerals catch the eye in Huancarani markets. RIGHT: Potatoes are a far more valuable staple.

opportunity to visit with the artists and purchase original works. Elaborate gourd carvings can cost upwards from US$100, but the uninitiated are pleased with less intricate souvenirs purchased in the artisan's home. **Hualhuas**, on the east side of the river 12 km (just under eight miles) from Huancayo, is a weaver's town where ponchos, blankets, and sweaters are woven from hand-spun alpaca and lamb's wool tinted with dyes from chilca-chilca, cochineal, and nogal plants. **San Jeronimo de Tunan**, 16 km (about 10 miles) from Huancayo, holds a Wednes-

sans. Archaeology tours cover the major sites scattered through the region, including the ruins of **Warivilca** near **Huari**, ten minutes drive from the city. The center of the Huanca (Wanka) culture two centuries before the Inca arrived, the site includes a museum with some artifacts and bones.

Other attractions include the town of **Ingenio**, 30 km (16.6 miles) northeast of Huancayo, where mountain trout are bred and farmed. Spiky artichoke plants fill fields around the streams in this region. **Huayao**, 17 km (10.6 miles) northwest of Huancayo,

VALLE DEL MANTARO

| 0 | 11 | 20 miles |
| 0 | 10 | 20 | 30 km |

Jauja
Huaripampa
JUNÍN
Concepción
Mito San Jeronimo de Tunan
Río Mantaro 45
LIMA Aco
Hualhuas
Cochas
Huancayo
Huari

day market featuring fine silver and gold jewelry and ornaments, usually designed in a filigree style.

Historical sights include the **Convento de Santa Rosa de Ocopa**, located 25 km (15 miles) northeast of Huancayo in **Concepción**. The convent was built in the eighteenth century as part of a Franciscan mission to evangelize the Amazon people. The library holds over 25,000 volumes, some dating back to the fifteenth century. There is also a Museum of Natural History and a church, reconstructed in 1905, that houses carved wooden altar pieces. Across the river from the town of Concepción is **Mito**, where the regional folk dance called *La Huaconada* originated. **Aco**, located near Mito, is home to excellent ceramic arti-

is home to the **Observatorio Geofísico** where meteorological and seismic tests are conducted.

HOW TO GET THERE

The easiest way to explore the valley is with a guide or group tour from one of the operators mentioned above. You can explore on your own if time permits by taking mini-buses from the Plaza Constitución.

HUANCAVELICA

Fortunately for train buffs, cars still run from Huancayo south past rivers and waterfalls to Huancavelica, a traditional Andean town at 3,680 m (12,070 ft) above sea level. It's possible to visit the town in a day by taking the early morning train from Huancayo, though you'll spend at least eight hours traveling back and forth. The town was important to the Spaniards for its mercury deposits in the surrounding mountains, and long after the conquest Spanish entrepreneurs were building mansions from their mining profits. The population is nearing 400,000, and the town remains an important mining center. Fortunately, its colonial architecture and indigenous lifestyle have remained fairly intact.

towns congregate in the city for the **Feria Dominical** or Sunday market, well worth checking out.

Where to Stay and Eat

There are not a lot of hotels in this town. The best is probably the **Hotel Presidente (** (064) 952760, located on the Plaza de Armas. The rooms are comfortable and it offers private and shared bathrooms. The **Restaurant Olla** on Avenida Gamarra serves international and Peruvian meals at reasonable prices.

Though there are few tourist services, it's a great untrammeled place to learn about indigenous culture and wander mountainside trails.

What to See and Do

Along the **Plaza de Armas** are the **cathedral**, the **Iglesia de San Sebastián** and **Iglesia de San Francisco**. The cathedral has two white towers and a doorway of carved red stone. Construction was begun in 1673 and completed in 1733. The **San Cristóbal Thermal Baths**, north of the Río Huancavelica, are said to have therapeutic properties and draw people from all over to cure their ailments. Artisans from surrounding

How to Get There

A primary reason for visiting Huancavelica is to take the train, one of the few scenic, pleasurable train rides left in the country. It's not comfortable, necessarily, but the ride lasts only four to six hours each way and is gorgeous. The local train, called the *Train Extra*, runs Monday through Saturday; the trip takes about five hours. The *Train Expreso* also runs Monday through Saturday; this train takes approximately four hours. From Huancavelica to Lima your best bet is the bus by way of Huancayo.

LEFT: Herbal potions to cure all worries are mixed at Huancayo's market. ABOVE: Charms and coins produce instant music on a dancer's hat.

THE HIGH JUNGLE

North of Huancayo and east of the mining region around La Oroya, the mountains give way to steep canyons into the Amazon basin. **Tarma**, the first major town on the east road, has 155,000 residents, many of whom are employed in the surrounding fields where flowers are grown for export. The town is a pretty spot, with a plaza and colonial churches set against the mountains. Smaller towns in the area are known for their weav-

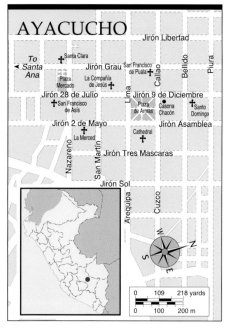

ing and agriculture; many of the hundreds of types of Andean potatoes are grown here.

The road drops down the mountains to **San Ramón**, 80 km (50 miles) east of Tarma, and **La Merced**, 90 km (56 miles) east of Tarma, which mark the beginning of the high jungle, at 760 m (about 2,000 ft) above sea level. Coffee plantations and tropical fruit orchards fill the hills leading down to multiple rivers and tributaries feeding into the Amazon Basin. This remote area, rarely visited by travelers, is one of the most scenic in the country, dotted with indigenous communities with distinct languages, dress, and customs.

Buses and small charter planes venture farther southeast to **Satipo**, home to the Ashaninka Indians. Somewhat seedy, yet fascinating, the town was developed as a base for Spanish missionaries and for the rubber industry. From Satipo one can explore the remote Cutivireni National Park, a natural reserve with a few small indigenous communities.

AYACUCHO

A beautiful colonial city filled with gorgeous architecture and talented artists, Ayacucho is one of the most rewarding destinations in Peru. Visitors encounter the spirit of the region the moment they enter the airport, where a weaving by local artist Edwin Sulca hangs alongside the following poem:

> *I want to be like the wind*
> *that runs over continents*
> *and drags all evils*
> *and dashes them against the rocks.*
> *I want to be the brother*
> *and give his hand to the fallen one*
> *and strongly embraced*
> *look for the peace of the world.*

Ayacuchanos are just beginning to trust the peace that has settled over their treasured city since 1992. Center of the Sendero Luminoso (Shining Path) movement from the late 1970s to early 1990s, Ayacucho suffered enormously during the *epoca de terrorismo*, the era of terrorism, when thousands of Ayacuchanos and military personnel were killed in open and subversive warfare. The capture of the movement's leader Abimael Guzmán in September 1992 brought peace to the region, which is gradually recovering its infrastructure and characteristically warm and hospitable spirit.

Travelers, long missing from one of the most culturally wealthy destinations in the Andes, have begun to return and are welcomed with enthusiasm. Today, Ayacucho is an amazingly peaceful place, where sentimental Ayacuchanos are eager to embrace strangers and show off their city's charms. And lovely it is, settled amid Andean hills, filled with colonial mansions and churches and natural beauty. Quechua is the first language of many of the residents, though Spanish is spoken in the city. Foreigners are still a novelty and are greeted with all the curiosity and affection of a people long cut off from the rest of the world. Children stop and ask the time of day simply to have a chance to speak with someone from outside. Adults are anxious to ask your impressions of their city and describe the beauty of the countryside.

The population of 120,000 is gradually increasing as Ayacuchanos who fled to Lima during the years of terror return home and rebuild their family compounds. Many of those who left were Quechua Indians who fared poorly in the city.

Some of the country's most famous artists are Ayacuchanos who endured horrible hardships while pouring their emotions into incredible woven tapestries and elaborate *retablos*, multitiered displays of plaster characters reenacting the city's famed religious processions and historic battles. The city hosts some of the most elaborate fiestas in the country; thousands of Peruvians descend upon Ayacucho during *Semana Santa*, or Holy Week, beginning the Friday before Easter. Known as a *fiesta pomposa* (a large, important festival), Ayacucho's celebration lasts for a week's worth of processions, parades, and parties (see FESTIVE FLINGS, page 48) famed for their spirit and pageantry. Carnaval is also spectacular here, and less elaborate celebra-

tions are held nearly every month — with so many churches, there's always a patron saint to honor.

BACKGROUND

Ayacucho, also known by its pre-Hispanic name of Huamanga, may have been inhabited as long ago as twenty thousand years, as evidenced by archaeological digs at the nearby caves of Piquimachay. The valley was the center of the Wari (also spelled Huari) culture around AD 700; ruins from the period can be found at the archaeological site of Wari, 22 km (13.7 miles) from Ayacucho. The Inca later moved into the area, centering their administration of the region at Vilcashuamán. Fierce battles between the Inca and Spanish conquistadors resulted in the conquest of the indigenous peoples and the founding of the city of Huamanga in 1540 by Francisco Pizarro.

The region was the center of the independence movement in the 1800s; in 1824 the last Spanish army was finally defeated and sent packing from Peru in Quinua, just 37 km (23 miles) from the city's center. The name was changed from Huamanga to Ayacucho in 1825, and many locals still refer to it by the older name. The most recent horrors of Ayacucho's often violent history began in 1977, when like-minded souls started organizing and talking of revolution. In 1980, the *Lucha Armada* (Army of Light) was formed, mostly with students rebelling against a repressive government. The first truly violent attack by the revolutionaries occurred on March 3, 1982, when bombs rocked the city and dozens of people were killed in gunfire battles. The violence continued for years, through the 1980s and into the 1990s, until the Shining Path's leader was captured in Lima. Peace finally settled over the worn-out populace in 1996, when the bombed-out infrastructure and wounded spirits of the inhabitants began the process of rehabilitation. The city's basic services are still under repair; many businesses do not have phones; water and electricity are unreliable; and the sounds of construction are constant.

Ayacucho's artists create fanciful clay churches replete with worshippers.

High Andes

Although there is still a strong military presence in Ayacucho, it is less visible than in the past. Travelers can safely roam about without encountering problems. It's best to stay away from political discussions, however, and to avoid traveling alone in the countryside, where some military checkpoints still exist. Do not wear camouflage-type clothing, and carry a copy of your passport at all times.

GENERAL INFORMATION

Ayacucho can be a bit confusing, since street signs are virtually nonexistent. You may find the name of the street on plaques over businesses. Located at 2,761 m (9,000 ft), Ayacucho's climate is mild and dry, with an average temperature of 17.5°C (63.5°F). The rainy season lasts from November through March. The **tourist office** in Ayacucho ((64) 812580 is located at Portal Municipal 44 by the Plaza de Armas and is open Monday through Friday, 8 AM to 3 PM. The **Tourism Police Office** ((64) 812179 is at Jirón Arequipa 100. Internet access is available at the **Instituto Pacifico** ((64) 814299 at Callao 106. **Wari Tours Ayacucho** ((64) 811414 FAX (64) 811415, at Portal Independencia 70, and **Morochucos Tours** ((64) 818908 FAX 818674, at Portal Constitución 14, offer tours of the city and outlying sights.

WHAT TO SEE AND DO

I tend to begin and end every day at the **Plaza de Armas**, where all the town seems to descend in the evening. Couples flirt and kiss on wrought iron benches under laurel trees; gardeners work constantly on flower beds packed with perfect perennials. Most of the city's major attractions are within easy walking distance of the plaza; several face it from surrounding streets.

The **Palacio de Marqués de Mozobamba**, at Portal Unión 37, is the oldest mansion in the city, built in 1550. Like most of the colonial-era buildings, it is fronted with stone arches, called *portales*. The baroque-style palace now houses the **Escuela de Bellas Artes (School of Fine Arts)**. Sightseers can wander through during school hours.

The **Universidad Nacional de San Cristóbal de Huamanga**, at Portal Independencia 57, was founded in 1677 and is one of the oldest universities in the Americas. It is one of the more liberal schools in the country; Abimael Guzmán, founder of the Sendero Luminoso, taught here in the 1970s. The university has always attracted national intellectuals and artists; it was, in many ways, the logical place to begin a rebellion. Ayacucho's history of major battles between the indigenous peoples, the Inca, and the Spaniards gives its populace a sense of independence and thoughtfulness. Many of its most talented residents remained in the city throughout the years of terror, enduring the watchful eyes and probing actions of both the military and the rebels. The university still attracts liberals, and suspicion is as common as friendliness. Again, visitors can wander through when the building is open for classes.

Several *casonas* or colonial mansions built in the sixteenth century by wealthy mine owners surround the plaza and have been adapted for commercial use. **Casona de la Municipalidad**, at Portal Municipal 44, is used as the City Hall. **Casona Chacón** at Portal Unión 28 on the Plaza de Armas now houses the Banco de Credito and is open to the public during banking hours. The mansion is the best preserved colonial edifice by the plaza, and has two large interior patios framed by stone arches. Several of the smaller rooms around the first plaza fronting the bank's offices house the **Museo de Arte Popular Joaquín López Antay (museum of regional art)**. The museum houses a valuable overview of the best work of local artisans, including silver filigree work by Don Victor Flores Gutiérrez, *retablos* by Jesús Urbano Rojas and Don Heraclio Nuñez Jiménez, and clay sculptures by Leoncio Tineo Ochoa. The exhibits include photos of the artists and examples of the types of looms used for local weaving. Staff at the offices on the second floor are extremely helpful, and can provide information on visiting the artists' workshops. Admission is free; the museum is open Monday through Friday during banking hours.

An ornate colonial-era archway straddles Jirón 28 de Julio at the beginning of the city's vast market area. The **Mercado Andrés Vivanco** central market, housed in a pale blue one-story building, is filled with tempting purchases along with all the necessities of daily life. The market sprawls for several streets behind the building, and is a wonderful place to observe the Quechua ladies wearing flat brimmed felt hats carrying their babies in brightly colored *mantas* (long cloths) wrapped around their backs. I found myself sitting at the front steps of the market building for hours, watching stylish office workers, shy Quechua children cling-

Known as the city of churches, Ayacucho has at least 33 major churches and several smaller evangelical houses of worship. Unfortunately, many of the churches are locked during the day, but are usually open for mass at 6 AM and 6 PM. The **catedral** (cathedral) on Jirón Asemblea facing the Plaza de Armas was built between 1612 and 1671 by Bishop Don Cristóbal de Castilla y Zamora. The church is noteworthy for its spectacular baroque altarpiece made of wood and goldleaf ornamentation with extraordinary carvings and its altars to the virgins of the conception

ing to their mother's skirts, and hip teenage boys pass by. The main produce and meat stands are housed in the building; two stairways lead up to the entrance from the street, providing space for shoppers to sit and sample their purchases. Flower sellers pile bundles of pink gladiolus, white mums and papery yellow statice under cobalt blue plastic awnings in front of the building. At the back, red- and yellow-striped beach umbrellas shade rounds of homemade cheese — despite worries over pasteurization, I finally bought a chunk of the pungent cheese (with a feta-like taste) and a few hard crusty rolls for my room. I wasn't sick, but then my body is filled with Latin American amoebas.

and the Asunción. Pope John Paul II visited Ayacucho in 1985 in the midst of the revolution; a plaque inside the entrance to the church includes part of his sermon, in which he said he visited Ayacucho to bring a message of love, peace, justice, and reconciliation to the troubled region.

Though rather simple in design, **Iglesia de Santo Domingo**, on Jirón 9 de Diciembre at Jirón Bellido, is a national monument. Also of interest are **Iglesia de La Merced**, on Jirón 2 de Mayo at Jirón San Martín; **Compañía de Jesús**, on Jirón 28 de Julio at Jirón Lima; **San Francisco de Asís**, on Jirón 28 de Julio;

Semana Santa is Ayacucho's most famous celebration, attended by onlookers from throughout the world.

and **Santa Clara**, on Jirón Grau. Built in a variety of baroque and Churrigueresque styles, the churches were constructed in the sixteenth century and have remained some of the finest and best preserved examples of colonial architecture in the country. The churches and mansions are best seen on city tours; ask in advance if the buildings will be open for viewing.

The **Hipolito Unánue Anthropological and Archeological Museum** ((64) 812360, on Avenida Independencia, houses an impressive display of artifacts from the Canka,

women from the country find a name on a blurred wooden plaque.

Outside the city, the town of **Quinua**, 37 km (23 miles) north, is the site of the battle of liberation from Spain. The small town is known for its pottery and silver work. **Vilca-shuamán**, 120 km (74.6 miles) southeast of Ayacucho, was a major Incan outpost. **Wari**, 22 km (13.7 miles) north of Ayacucho, was the capital of the pre-Incan Wari civilization and is believed to have been home to some 60,000 residents. It contains a few ruined walls, plazas and cemeteries. The caves of

Wari, Chavín, Huarpa, Nazca, Ica, and other cultures. The museum is open Monday through Saturday, 9 AM to noon and 2 PM to 6 PM.

Though it may sound a bit macabre, one of the most moving locales in Ayacucho is the **Cemeterio Municipal (municipal cemetery)** located at the end of the airport runway outside town. The cemetery is enormous for such a small city, filled with wall after wall of crypts that look from afar like a huge condominium complex. The number of headstones and plaques from the 1980s is staggering; one can track the major battles during the *epoca de terrorismo* simply by reading the dates. I spent several hours here, at times trying to help older

Piquimachay, 24 km (14.9 miles) west of Ayacucho, are important for their remnants of human and animal bones.

SHOPPING

Ayacucho is one of Peru's major art centers, known for its weavers, painters, potters, and stone carvers. Though city officials are hoping to create an artisans' market, for now, true aficionados are best off visiting the homes of various artists. The tourism offices and tour companies can provide information on the best places to visit. **Santa Ana**, just outside downtown, is a small neighborhood housing some of the country's most famous weavers. Travelers are welcome to visit **Las Voces del Tapiz**, the workshop of Edwin Sulca Lagos ((64) 914242 at Plazuela Santa Ana 82, and **Galería Latina**, the workshop of Alejandro Gallardo ((64) 818616 at Plazuela Santa Ana 105. Both are masters of the art whose weavings have been shown in galleries around the world. Both use natural fibers and dyes from plants found in the area, creating gorgeous, intricate *tejidos* (weavings) using pre-Hispanic and modern designs. Their works run into the hundreds of dollars, and typically take months to design and execute.

Ayacuchano artisans are also famous for their *retablos*, small, finely carved wooden boxes housing three-dimensional religious and political scenes. There are several artisans' workshops in Barrio La Libertad; among the finest *retablos* artists are the Urbano family, who have workshops at Avenida Peru 308 and Avenida Peru 330. Carvings in *piedra de Huamanga* (a hard white stone found around Ayacucho) also depict religious and Andean scenes. A good selection of regional art is available at **Artesanías Huamanguina Pascualito** ((64) 811013 at Jirón Cusco 136, **Ohalateria Artesanías** at the Plaza de Armas, and **Artesanías Helme** at Jirón Bellido 463.

WHERE TO STAY

Ayacucho has an abundance of inexpensive rooms and no luxury hotels. The most expensive places have telephones, televisions, and a fairly consistent water supply. Some places have their own water tanks and generators because public services are unreliable. Inexpensive *hostals* often lack toilet seats and paper, and water is heated by electric devices in the showers. Ask about the water supply when you check in, as you may need to plan your showers accordingly. Advance reservations are necessary around Easter week and in July, when tourism is heaviest.

Moderate

The city's most expensive hotel is the **Ayacucho Hotel Plaza** ((64) 812202 FAX (64) 812314, at Jirón 9 de Diciembre 184. The façade and lobby are lovely and have an arty, colonial feeling which doesn't carry through

to the rooms. Most could use a new coat of paint and upgraded amenities; the best rooms are on the second floor overlooking red tile roofs over the courtyard. A few rooms face the Plaza de Armas and have small balconies, but street noise is a minus. The fancy restaurant with floral linen tablecloths and brass chandeliers is easily the most expensive in town.

The **Hostal El Marqués de Valdefirios** (/FAX (64) 814014, at Alameda Bolognesi 720, appears to be a restored *casona*, but was actually built in the 1940s. The 14-room inn

sits across the street from a tree-lined park in a quiet neighborhood. Handcarved wood cornices and lace spreads on the beds give the house an old-world feeling; not only do the toilets have seats, but the seats have ruffled lace covers. Meals are served in a formal dining room, and the hotel's courtyard is a popular place for parties and receptions.

Inexpensive

The **San Francisco Hotel** ((64) 812959 FAX (64) 814501, at Callao 290, is a charming place loaded with art and antiques. There are several small meeting rooms and lounges on the first floor; one has stone arches typical of Ayacucho's *casonas*. The 45 guest rooms on three floors all have refrigerators and televisions, and some have tiny balconies overlooking the street and separate seating areas. The best part is the superb collection of folk art displayed throughout the property; check out the bug-eyed mask from Puno in

Quechua and Spanish ancestry is evident in the faces of Ayacucho's cowboys.

the stairway. Another major plus is the rooftop cafeteria with a few outdoor tables shaded by umbrellas.

The hospitality of Conrad and Paola Manco creates a warm ambience at the **Hotel San Blas (** (64) 810552, at Jirón Chorro 161. Room rates are incredibly low and include kitchen and laundry facilities. Some of the immaculately clean rooms have private baths and hot water. The rooms and hallways are decorated with locally made pottery and weavings, and the courtyard dining area is a congenial gathering spot.

Florida ((64) 812565, Jirón Cusco 310, is similar in price but cleaner, and has 11 simple rooms facing a center garden. The **Hotel Santa Rosa (** (64) 814614 FAX (64) 812083, Jirón Lima 166, is near the Plaza de Armas and has 26 clean rooms with televisions and phones.

WHERE TO EAT

Ayacucho's cuisine relies heavily on beef, *cuy* (guinea pig), and potatoes. Most restaurants offer inexpensive meals in a friendly setting;

Even less expensive are the simple rooms at the **Hotel Crillonesa (** (64) 812350 at Nazareno 165 in the midst of the market neighborhood. The 43 simple rooms are popular with business travelers who appreciate the low rates and artful decor. Rooms with shared baths are amazingly inexpensive, yet the hotel has its own water tanks with hot water available all day and night.

Hostal Tres Mascaras ((64) 914107 or (64) 912921, Jirón Tres Mascaras 194, is more expensive than the competition. A rambling complex set around lawns and an empty pool, the hotel is popular with European tourists who fill the guest book with favorable reviews. Rooms have fluorescent lights and hot water in the mornings. The **Hostal**

many are closed on Sundays. Jirón San Martín is restaurant row, lined with informal places that are packed for inexpensive set-menu lunches.

Moderate

The loveliest restaurant in town is **La Casona (** (64) 812733 at Jirón Bellido 463. Housed in an old mansion, the restaurant is quiet and pretty, with murals and weavings on the walls above glass-topped tables. This is the place to try *puca picante*, a regional dish combining pork, and potatoes in a mildly spicy red sauce topped by slices of hardboiled egg. The **Plaza Ayacucho Restaurant (** (64) 812202, in the Ayacucho Plaza Hotel at Jirón 9 de Diciembre 184, is easily the fanciest place in town. A peaceful spot with brass chandeliers and floral table linens, the restaurant offers a set menu and à la carte dishes; try the *rocoto relleno* (stuffed pepper).

Inexpensive

A wood-burning oven produces savory pizzas at **Mia Pizza** ((64) 815407, Jirón San Martín 420. Open for dinner only, the restaurant is a friendly spot where diners sit at long picnic tables devouring pizzas, pastas, and great spinach stuffed cannelloni. Alicia and Jorge Aedo de López has been

the courtyard tables at **Los Portales**, just off the plaza. The food is only average, but this is a nice spot to regroup by the plaza. **Max Max** ((64) 817567, at Jirón 9 de Diciembre 139, is a good locale for coffee and *tortas* (cakes) or inexpensive sandwiches.

How to Get There

Air travel between Lima and Ayacucho's Alfredo Mendivil Airport is available on AeroContinente and AeroPeru. The flight takes about 35 minutes. Air service from

presiding over **Restaurant Tradición**, Jirón San Martín 406, since 1967, offering friendly hospitality to their regular customers and travelers. Two inexpensive menus are offered each day along with a long list of main courses including *tallarin* (spaghetti), fried *cuy* (guinea pig), grilled beef, and hearty soups.

Urpicha, Jirón Londres 272, is also a good place to try local specialties. **El Retablo** ((64) 812141, Jirón San Martín 446, offers the same selection as other local restaurants along with a decent vegetable-filled Spanish tortilla. **Imperio Wari** ((64) 815427, also on Jirón San Martín, is open daily for dinner and is a pretty place with carnations on the tables, but the service can be indifferent. Umbrellas shade

Cusco was canceled in the 1980s, but may be revived by the time you visit. Travelers are asked to present their passports when arriving at the airport. Buses from Huancayo, Pisco, Ica, and Lima arrive at one of the terminals on Jirón Francisco or Jirón Carlos Zavala, both within walking distance of the Plaza de Armas. The express-bus station is at Jirón Libertad 257.

LEFT: Quechua ladies dress in their best *mantas* and hats when gathering at markets and fiestas.
ABOVE: Huancayo's carved gourds
entrance folk-art collectors.

Cusco
and the
Sacred
Valley

CENTER OF THE INCA WORLD, THE COLONIAL EMPIRE, and the modern Peruvian Andes, Cusco is fascinating, mysterious, and endearing. In fact, many travelers extend their stays here, ignoring vast portions of their overall itineraries in favor of setting up housekeeping in the Inca's "Navel of the World." Located at 3,415 m (about 11,210 ft) above sea level, Cusco is the entry point for many of Peru's most meaningful attractions. The famed ruins of Machu Picchu, the Sacred Valley, and several rivers, small towns, and archaeological sites lie within a few hours of the city. Expeditions to the southern Amazon Basin often begin here as well.

Outside Lima, Cusco is the most cosmopolitan city in the nation, thanks to the thousands of international tourists arriving each year. Many have stayed, opening restaurants, hotels, travel agencies and shops catering to the diverse tastes of world travelers. Dutch, Hebrew, English, and Italian conversations can be overheard from the terraces of Machu Picchu to the rapids on the Río Urubamba. Pizza and burgers are as common as guinea pig (a local delicacy) in tourist restaurants. You could easily spend two weeks in this region and wish for more.

CUSCO

Narrow *callejones*, or alleyways, lined with granite walls built by Incan laborers in the fourteenth century lead to trendy espresso bars in the modern city of Cusco. Girls in broad felt hats and layered skirts pose for

in one place, Cusco is where you're destined to be.

Over 300,000 *Cusqueños* live in the immediate area of the city; many are indigenous Indians who have retained their lifestyle, dress and beliefs. Rural residents who work with travelers have a grasp of the Spanish and English phrases necessary for dealing with foreigners, but speak Quechua among themselves. It is always fascinating to sit in the central Plaza de Armas and watch ladies wrapped in shawls barter in English then giggle with their friends and gossip in their native tongue. Many still refer to the city as Qosqo.

BACKGROUND

Cusco was first settled by the Inca in AD 1200 and became the capital of the Inca empire and its largest city. Built around the Huacapata ceremonial plaza (in the same location as today's Plaza de Armas), the city was constructed between the Saphi and Tullumayo rivers. Buildings of hard volcanic stone radiated out from the plaza along narrow streets lined with rock culverts for draining water. The city is said to have been designed in the shape of a puma, with the fortress of Sacsayhuamán as the head and the merging of the two rivers as the tail

By the time Pizarro and his conquistadors arrived in 1533 Cusco was a thriving commercial and ceremonial center with temples and shrines filled with gold ornaments. Naturally, the Spanish lost little time in plundering the wealth of the city and subjugating its residents. In 1536, the Inca rulers who had fled to the Sacred Valley launched a mighty attack on the city, only to lose once more. Further skirmishes proved the Spaniards had gained control of the city, and the Inca Emperor Manco and his followers retreated to their remote hideaway at Vilcabamba, the true lost city of the Incas, now known as Espíritu Pampa.

The Spaniards built their colonial city from the ruins of the Inca capital, retaining many of the original stone walls and the basic layout. Much of the center was destroyed by an

snapshots in the city's main plaza; llama and alpaca stroll down the cobblestone streets. Baroque bell towers rise above a skyline of clay-tiled roofs; roses bloom in plazas and gardens year round.

Cusco is a beautiful city. Built from the ruins of Inca temples in a narrow, fertile valley, it seems shrouded in shadows until the sun rises high above the surrounding mountains. Roosters crow from behind pricey hotels and street vendors sell fragrant tamales and steaming hot chocolate to workers hustling to their jobs. By 10 AM, much of the beauty is covered by a haze of smog and cars clog all major arteries. After visiting smaller Andean cities Cusco can seem overwhelming and disappointingly crowded. Yet, if you can only sample the mountain lifestyle

Cosmopolitan Cusco was built from Inca ruins in a fertile valley ringed by the Andes.

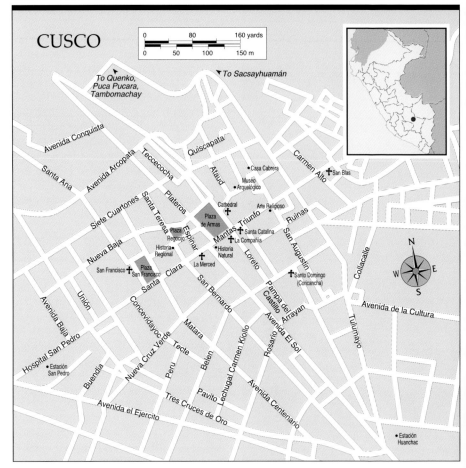

CUSCO

0   80   160 yards
0   50   100   150 m

To Quenko,
Puca Pucara,
Tambomachay

To Sacsayhuamán

Avenida Conquista

Santa Ana

Avenida Arcopata

Teccecocha

Quiscapata

Carmen Alto

San Blas

Casa Cabrera

Ataud

Museo
Arqueológico

Siete Cuartones

Platteros

Cathedral

Arte Religioso

Ruinas

Santa Teresa

Plaza
de Armas

Triunfo

Mantas

Santa Catalina

San Agustin

Plaza
Regocijo

Espinar

La Compañia

Nueva Baja

Historia
Regional

Historia
Natural

Loreto

Pampa del
Castillo

San Francisco

Plaza
San Francisco

Santa Clara

La Merced

Santo Domingo
(Coricancha)

Collacalle

Avenida de la Cultura

Unión

Concevidayoc

San Bernardo

Avenida Arrayan

Avenida Baja

Matara

Tecte

Belen

Avenida El Sol

Tulumayo

Hospital San Pedro

Nueva Cruz Verde

Peru

Lechugal Carmen Kiollo

Rosario

Estación
San Pedro

Buendia

Pavito

Avenida Centenario

Tres Cruces de Oro

Avenida el Ejercito

Estación
Huanchac

N
W   E
S

earthquake in 1650, but the palaces and churches were quickly rebuilt. Paintings and sculptures in the cathedral and other buildings show the growth of the Cusqueña school of painting, under the direction of Bishop Mollinedo. Largely due to his influence, Cusco became a center of the arts, with indigenous and *mestizo* painters adorning many of the city's most famous buildings with their murals depicting the mix of Christian and Andean symbols.

In the following centuries Cusco thrived as the cultural and commercial center of the Andes, rather left-wing in its politics. The city benefited greatly from the attention focused upon the discovery and reconstruction of Machu Picchu, and has since become Peru's most important tourism center. But, like most Andean cities, Cusco suffered mightily during the 1980s, when the Sendero Luminoso maintained a forceful presence in the region. Battles and bombings were far too frequent for comfort, and tourists abandoned the region. The collapse of the national economy further decimated Cusco's prosperity, which only began to recover in the early 1990s. Today, the travelers have returned by the thousands, and the city is experiencing a healthy revival.

GENERAL INFORMATION

Cusco's climate is temperate year round, with heavy rains from January through March. The altitude can be a problem, and many travelers suffer symptoms of *soroche* (altitude sickness) including nausea, headache, aching joints, and extreme fatigue. See TRAVELERS TIPS, page 271, for suggestions on reducing these symptoms. The **Tourist Information Office** ((84) 263176 is located at Portal Espinar 180, near the Plaza de Armas, and is open from

9 AM to noon and 3 PM to 7 PM, Monday through Saturday. There is an information desk at the airport as well, open when flights arrive. The administration offices for government tourism department **(**/FAX (84) 252987 is at Avenida de la Cultura 732.

The **Tourist Protection Bureau (** (84) 252974 on Calle Mantas at Loreto is open daily from 8 AM to 8 PM and also has a desk at the airport open when flights arrive and depart. This valuable service offers tourists assistance with complaints against tour operators, airlines and their services, and helps travelers deal with lost passports and credit cards. The office is staffed by highly professional personnel who are adept at negotiating solutions between tourists and tour operators, the most common of difficulties encountered (see TOURS, below). Note that both this office and the information center are being merged into one at an as yet unknown location. Check at the airport desks for current information.

Should you be a victim of a crime, the **Tourist Police (** (84) 223626 are located at Calle Matara 274.

Internet access is available at **Internet Cusco (** (84) 238173, on Avenida el Sol next to the Banco de Credito, a half-block from the plaza. The **Banco de Credito** is the best place to change traveler's checks without paying a commission; it is open weekdays and Saturday mornings.

The **Cusco Tourist Ticket** is a worthwhile pass that allows entry to most of the city's churches, archaeological sites, and museums for a single fee. The pass is good for five or ten days. The ticket is sometimes available at the tourist information office; if not, check at the Santa Catalina Museum. Many of Cusco's churches and museums are locked when tours are not scheduled and few provide telephone numbers for information. You may find it easiest to join a group tour of the city to gain access to all the prominent buildings. Many museums are closed on Sunday.

Spanish language classes are available at **Amauta (** (84)241422 E-MAIL amautaa@mail .cosapidata.com.pe at Calle Procuradores 50. The school offers a variety of room-and-board programs and intensive Spanish-language immersion.

Holidays attract large crowds to Cusco, for good reason (see FESTIVE FLINGS, page 48, in YOUR CHOICE). Rooms should be booked far in advance during dry season (June through September), Christmas, Holy Week, Inti Raymi (the festival to the Sun held in late June), and All Saints Day.

Getting Around

Cusco's street plan can be immensely confusing. Street names change every few blocks and are often posted with names in Quechua rather than Spanish. Fortunately, most of your wandering will take place within a dozen blocks of the main plaza, and you'll quickly get a grasp of the necessary routes. Taxis in Cusco are very inexpensive and the drivers are endearingly friendly; if you're lost they'll quickly lead you out of the maze to your destination.

TOURS

From the moment you arrive in Cusco you'll be accosted by guides and tour operators eager to accept cash for their questionable services. There are at least 50 agencies in town, most funneling their business to a dozen or so that actually run the tours. Before handing over your money make sure to get an itemized receipt listing all the services of the tour, including departure and arrival times and places, the qualifications of the guide (especially if you're paying for one who speaks English or another foreign language), the type of equipment supplied and, if it's a multi-day tour, the type of hotels and meals included. Problems with tour companies are the main complaint of

Statues of Inca warriors mark roadways and historical sights in Cusco.

most travelers who visit the Tourist Protection Bureau (see above), which helps negotiate solutions. You can also ask at the Bureau if the company you're thinking of hiring has had complaints registered against it.

Unless you have a lot of free time in Cusco you're best off joining a City Tour early in your stay. You'll get a good overview of the city's complex layout and a chance to visit most of the important churches, museums, and archaeological sites with a guide. Most last three to four hours; you should be able to arrange for a guide who speaks your language. Full-day **Sacred Valley** tours include visits to several small towns, markets, and archaeological sites.

Adventure tours including trekking and horseback riding at the ruins, Inca Trail treks, and river rafting and kayaking on the Urubamba and Apurimac rivers are immensely popular and fraught with opportunities for disappointment. In all cases ask to see the equipment being used and obtain a detailed receipt listing all services provided.

Agencies providing a full range of services from airport transfers to Amazon explorations include: **Explorandes** ((84) 238380 on Jirón Sucre; **Lima Tours** (tours and services) ((84) 223874 at Portal Harinas 177; **Condor Travel** ((84) 225961 at Portal Carrizos 205; **Loreto Tour** ((84) 236331 at Calle de Medio 111; **Kantu** ((84) 221381 at Portal Carrizos 258; **Kontiki Tour** ((84) 237043 at Portal de Panes 101; and **Peruvian Odyssey** ((84) 222105 at Avenida el Sol 612.

Adventure tour operators with good reputations include: **Eric Adventures** ((84) 232244 FAX (84) 239772 E-MAIL ericadv@net .cosapidata.com.pe, at Calle Plateros 324; **Instinct Back to Nature** ((84) 238366 FAX (84) 233451 E-MAIL instinct@protelsa.com.pe at Calle Procuradores 50; **Southern Cross Adventures** ((84) 237649 at Portal de Panes 123; **Treck Peru** ((84) 239988 at Avenida el Sol 603; and **Andean Adventure** ((84) 236201 at Calle Heladeros 157.

Helicopter flights to Machu Picchu and the Nazca Lines are available through **HeliCusco** (/FAX (84) 227283 or (84) 243555.

Many of the tour companies offering trips to Manú and Tambopata in the Amazon basin are headquartered in Cusco (see SOUTHERN AMAZON, page 254).

WHAT TO SEE AND DO

Sightseeing in Cusco involves a considerable amount of climbing hills and steep stairways, and can quickly exhaust those not acclimated to the altitude. The most important sites are clustered around a series of plazas, and you can easily spend several hours in one small area checking out the museums, churches, shops, and restaurants without rushing in several directions in confusion.

Around the Plaza de Armas

Give your body a rest upon arrival and concentrate your efforts on the central **Plaza de Armas**, built upon the ruins of the **Huacapata**, center of the Incan city of **Qosqo**. The plaza is bisected by wide sidewalks lined with

yellow metal benches with green wooden slates. All paths lead to the double-tiered stone fountain, the province of children and pigeons. Stake out your own bench beside a patch of alyssum or pansies and take in the scenes. Quechua ladies spin lambswool on handheld shuttles while softly calling attention to their baskets of inexpensive hats and gloves. Shoeshine boys cart their boxes from bench to bench, offering cheap polishes and cleaning for everything from boots to cotton sandals. Cusco's street sellers are the most aggressive in the country; a firm and constant "No, *gracias*" helps drive them away, though it's always a pleasure to sit for a while and chat with one of the ladies who have carted their wares from some rural outpost to tourism central.

The plaza is framed by streets and sidewalks and stone and cement arches called *portales*. Vendors display blankets, shawls, rugs, and other souvenirs along these streets, making walking a bit hazardous and distracting. Colonial-era buildings along the sidewalks have been remodeled and subdivided time and time again into small storefronts housing travel agencies, restaurants, shops, and hotel lobbies. Most buildings are far more attractive on the second floor, where the original living, dining and bedrooms have been transformed into cafés. Most of the buildings have intricately carved wooden *balcones* (balconies) that were all the fashion among European residents in the eighteenth century.

Cusco's baroque cathedral towers above the Plaza de Armas.

Cusco and the Sacred Valley

The balconies usually have a Moorish theme, with spindle railings and arabesque relief carvings. A few are included in second-story cafés — the perfect spot for your morning coffee.

Dominating the plaza at the northeast is the **cathedral**, the largest of several baroque colonial-era churches in the city. The cathedral was built from the ruins of the Inca Viracocha's palace, and sits above street level atop a series of stairs. The church, begun in 1550 and completed in 1654, is one of the most magnificent Spanish colonial churches in South America. The huge main altar is made of solid silver, and several fine murals and paintings hang by side altars. One tower holds the 1659 Maria Angola bell, purportedly one of the largest church bells in the world. The seats and pulpit are of carved cedar. Mass is held every morning in one of the side chapels; the rest of the magnificent building is left in the dark. There are set hours for tours; photography is prohibited. Admission is charged and included in the tourist ticket.

Up a slight hill above the cathedral is the **Museo Arqueológico** ((84) 223245, at the corner of calles Córdoba de Tucumán and Ataud, open Monday through Friday from 8 AM to 7 PM, with a small entry fee. Housed in the colonial **El Palacio del Almirante (The Admiral's Palace)**, this museum displays pre-Inca and Inca objects, including the puzzling *khipukuna*, a system of record-keeping using a series of knots on a rope.

The **Museo de Arte Religioso (Museum of Religious Art)** ((84) 222781 is located one block east of the cathedral at the corner of calles Hatunrumiyoc and Herejes. The building was first the palace of the Inca Roca and was then used as the foundation for the home of the Marquis of Buenavista. In later years it became the Archbishop's Palace and it is still referred to as that today. The mansion was donated by the Church to house a collection of religious art.

The somewhat smaller church of **La Compañía** on the southeast side of the plaza is often confused with the cathedral due to its location and ornate façade. The church was built by the Jesuits, starting in 1571, but was destroyed by the 1650 earthquake. Work began again and the current building was

completed in 1668. The **Lourdes Chapel** to the side of the church is used for exhibitions of arts and crafts. The narrow, unmarked Callejón Loreto beside la Compañía leads past the stone walls of the Inca *Acclahuasi*, **Temple of the Sun Virgins**, now housing the Convent of Santa Catalina. Inside, the **Museo de Santa Catalina**, at Loreto and Arequipa, displays a large collection of paintings from the seventeenth- and eighteenth-century Cusqueña school of painting. The paintings combine Spanish and Incan imagery and were used to help convert the Inca to Catholi-

cism. The **Museo de Historia Natural**, near La Compañía on the first block of Avenida el Sol, contains a collection of stuffed animals, birds, and reptiles indigenous to the various regions of the country.

Around Santo Domingo

Southeast of the Plaza de Armas, at Pampa del Castillo and Santo Domingo, is the **Coricancha** complex, dominated by the seventeenth-century colonial church of **Santo Domingo**. The best view of this church built atop Inca ruins is from its base on Avenida el Sol, where remnants of the Inca Temple of the Sun lie scattered on a broad lawn used as a playground for local children. Rocks the size of dining tables once carved to angular precision have been worn into curves by the weather and human hands over the centuries and now lie amid green lawns. The walls of the Inca temple rise up a hillside, giving viewers a sense of the majesty of what was once the richest temple in the Inca Empire, literally covered in gold. Looted by the first conquistadors, the temple was destroyed, though its foundation was used to buttress the uninspired seventeenth-century church. The church itself holds little of interest; more fascinating are the tales of the wealth of gold and precious jewels housed here to honor *Inti*, the Incan sun god. Hire a guide when visiting this building to gain a sense of its importance in the Incan world.

Avenida el Sol, at the base of the complex, is one of the most important commercial streets in central Cusco. Most of the major banks, larger grocery stores, airline offices, and tourist hotels are located here.

Southwest of the Plaza de Armas

One of the most peaceful plazas in the city sits just one block west of the Plaza de Armas. **Plaza Regocijo** is a small square surrounded by restaurants and hotels, and seems to attract more loungers than vendors. The **Municipalidad (City Hall)** looms over the plaza, flying the Incan and Peruvian flags; contemporary art exhibits are on display in the front rooms. The **Museo de Historia Regional (Regional History Museum)** facing the plaza on Calle Garcilazo is housed in the colonial home of Garcilaso de la Vega, a prominent author during the early colonial period. The museum houses a collection of religious art.

The church and monastery of **La Merced**, on Calle Mantas one block southwest of the Plaza Regocijo, is one of Cusco's more impressive buildings. The religious order of Merced was founded in Barcelona in 1218 by San Pedro Nolasco and there are paintings in the cloister depicting his life. Also in the cloister are tombs containing the remains of two of the most famous Spanish conquistadors, Gonzalo Pizarro and Diego de Almagro. The museum also has a lovely starry ceiling, a huge silver cross, and its most fabulous possession is an incredible, solid-gold monstrance, approximately one meter (just over three feet) in height and covered

with a dazzling array of jewels. Designed and built by Spanish jeweler Juan de Olmos, it contains over 600 pearls and more than 1,500 diamonds.

Near La Merced is the **Church and Convent of San Francisco**, dating from the sixteenth and seventeenth centuries. Although less ornate than some of the churches in this area, there is an interesting display of colonial religious paintings by local masters. Between San Francisco and the Estación San Pedro train station is the **Mercado Santa Ana** central market, a morass of stands offering everything from alpaca sweaters to purple potatoes. The market is fascinating, exciting, and a bit dangerous. Dump all extraneous belongings before wandering through the stalls. If you bring a camera (the photo opportunities are irresistible) keep a tight hold on it and have a companion carry your money in a hidden pouch.

Neighborhoods

Those with a bit of time to wander around Cusco should take the opportunity to visit **San Blas**, a small arty neighborhood northeast of the main plaza. The view of the city from atop a very steep hill is worth the climb, especially in the waning light of late afternoon. The **Chapel of San Blas** on Cuesta de San Blas houses an amazing pulpit ornately carved in cedar. The neighborhood is filled with artisan's workshops; though everything is shut tight as a drum in early afternoon, you may be able to visit in the morning or evening. **Plaza Nazarenas**, just a few blocks northeast of the cathedral on Calle Tucumán is fronted by the impressive colonial **Casa Cabrera** which now houses a bank.

Nearby Ruins

Visible from the Plaza de Armas and dominated by a large white cross are the hilltop ruins of **Sacsayhuamán**. The huge Incan fortress is located two kilometers (one mile) north of the city; steep streets and stairways lead up the hillside from the cathedral. You can trek to the site in about an hour, or hire a taxi or join a tour. The name of this ruin means "satisfied falcon." Today's visitor sees only about 20% of the original structures.

Bowl-shaped hats are part of traditional Quechua costumes.

The Spaniards tore down many walls and used the blocks to build houses in Cusco. The largest and most impressive of the original rocks remain, with one weighing 361 tons. Work on Sacsayhuamán began in the 1440s, initiated by Emperor Pachacutec. It took almost a century to finish it. It is hard to imagine the human toll exacted to move the massive stones to the site from the surrounding countryside.

The battle at Sacsayhuamán in 1536 was one of the most savage of the Spanish conquest. Thousands of dead Inca warriors scattered outside the fort attracted swarms of carrion-eating Andean condors, inspiring the inclusion of eight condors in Cusco's coat of arms. The site's main *esplanade* is the setting for the annual Inti Raymi festival of the sun on June 24, when thousands of visitors pack the site for the winter solstice. Admission to this site is included in the Cusco Tourist Ticket.

Qenko, located just twenty minutes by foot from Sacsayhuamán, is another significant Inca *huaca*, or sacred spot. This large limestone rock is carved with an intricate pattern of steps, seats, geometric designs in relief, and puma representations; it is thought to have been an important part of Inca worship. The name of the temple comes from the Quechua word for "zigzag." This design is carved in abundance into the stone. Large rocky outcroppings seemed to hold mystical relevance for the Inca people, as if they possessed a power from the spiritual dimension. At Qenko, there may have been sacrifices of *chicha* beer or llama blood, poured from the top of the structure, their patterns of descent interpreted by the priests for divine revelations. Admission is included in the Cusco Tourist Ticket.

Ask the guard at Qenko to point you toward **Salapunco**, a short walk uphill. A site less frequented than Sacsayhuamán or Qenko, it is nevertheless an interesting example of Inca workmanship in stone. Although historians are not sure of the rituals performed here or their significance, it was certainly an important and sacred center. There is also an impressive view of Cusco from this vantage point.

Six kilometers (nearly four miles) northeast of Cusco on the road to Pisac is **Puca Pucara**. If caught in the right light, the rocks here have a reddish hue, hence the name Puca Pucara, or "Red Fort." The exact nature of this site is not known, although some archaeologists believe it was a fort and others a lodge or inn for nobility. There is a semicircular protective wall under which are a number of stonewalled rooms. The ducts used to distribute water from a nearby spring are still visible.

Tambomachay, an Inca bath built in a sheltered gully near a spring, is less than fifteen minutes from Puca Pucara. The ruins here consist of three levels. The upper level has four niches, probably used as seats. Underground water emanates from a hole at the base of the stonework at the middle level and then tumbles down to the lower level, fashioning a natural shower. The baths were most likely reserved for the emperor and his cronies and used for ceremonial purposes.

Located about five kilometers (three miles) from Sacsayhuamán is the lesser-known site of **Chacan**. This ruin again demonstrates the importance of water to the Inca religion, with its underground water channels emerging from the rock. There is also terracing, rock carvings and several buildings. Nearby is **Quispe Huara**, a nearly overgrown ruin save for a large pyramid cut into the rock face and some stone walls which at one time may have been part of a religious bathing location.

SHOPPING

Cusco is a shopper's paradise, with an abundance of tempting items. Alpaca sweaters and capes may well be the most popular items, but you can also purchase llama rugs, brightly colored gloves and scarves, woven bags and backpacks, fine silver and gold jewelry, ceramics, and enough kitsch souvenirs to fill a newly-woven rucksack. Most of the expensive shops with high-quality goods are located around or near the Plaza de Armas, and the prices reflect the high demand. Smaller shops in outlying neighborhoods have lower prices.

Some shopkeepers offer to lower their prices, but bargaining is best accomplished with some finesse. Blatant dickering is ac-

ceptable and expected with the vendors who line the sidewalks around all Cusco's plazas and major tourist sites. The quality of their goods is often inferior. If you're interested in fine handicrafts, check the shops first and learn how to tell the difference between true alpaca or wool and synthetic fabrics.

One of the finest folk-art shops is **Pedazo** ((84) 242967 at Calle Plateros 334. Pottery, silver jewelry, weavings, and alpaca garments are all handcrafted by master artisans. High quality baby alpaca clothing is available at **Alpaca III** ((84) 226101 at Calle Ruinas 472 and **Alpaca Collection** ((84) 236581 at Plaza Santa Domingo 299. **H. Ormachea** ((84) 237061, at Calle Plateros 372, carries silver and gold jewelry in Inca designs. **Arte Peru** ((84) 225031, Calle Plateros 305, has a lovely

selection of silver earrings. **Josefina** on Santa Clara 501, which also has a smaller shop on Calle Plateros, specializes in antique ponchos and mantas. Most shops are open Monday through Saturday, 10 AM to 6 PM, though those around the plazas usually stay open later especially on Friday and Saturday nights. Most accept credit cards.

Several markets offer the opportunity for more interesting shopping, and should be explored. The largest market is the Mercado Santa Ana spreading for blocks by the Estación San Pedro. Smaller arcades with stalls displaying handicrafts are located in the **Feria Artesanal El Inka**, at the corner of San Andrés and Quera.

Mountain sunlight illuminates the wood balconies and stone façades of colonial-era buildings.

Photography supplies, including slide and black-and-white film and film processing, are available at **Foto Nishiyama (** (84) 227591 at Mantas 109.

WHERE TO STAY

Cusco would seem to have plenty of hotel rooms, though the most popular properties fill up quickly and advance reservations are advised especially during the high season from June through September and again around major holidays. Check to make sure the rate you are given includes the 18% tax and any service charges. The most expensive properties typically (but not always) have 24-hour hot and cold water, though this can only be guaranteed if the hotel has its own water tanks. Several of the more tourist-oriented places have interior windows facing the lobby and restaurant; noise from large tour groups can be infuriating in early morning. Nearly all will stash your luggage while you're off to the ruins or other tours. Most accept credit cards.

Very Expensive

For sheer cultural value, the **Hotel Monasterio de Cusco (** (84) 241777 FAX (84) 237111, Calle Palacio 136 Plaza Nazarenas, can't be beat. The building is by far the grandest hotel structure in Cusco, a former monastery dating from the seventeenth century. The architectural grandeur is reflected in its patios and handsome Chapel of San Antonio Abad, decorated with gold leaf and paintings from the Cusco school. The 122 rooms, on the other hand, are questionable; it's best to view a few before settling in. Some are quite cold and dark. All have private baths, cable television, direct-dial phones, minibars, and in-room safes.

The most elegantly modern accommodations are at the **Hotel Libertador (** (84) 231961 FAX (84) 233152, at Plazuela Santo Domingo 256. The palace built by Inca laborers under orders from Francisco Pizarro was refurbished in 1976 and now features 214 rooms, decorated in the Peruvian colonial style. The rooms are large by Cusco standards and come with climate control, bath, minibar, phone, television, and 24-hour room service. There is a restaurant which features Peruvian as well as international food and nightly traditional folklore performances.

Expensive

The **Posada del Inca (** (84) 227061 FAX (84) 233091 E-MAIL posada_cusco@el-olivar.com.pe, at Portal Espinar 142, is part of a chain of three wonderful hotels in the country where service and comfort are assured. The 40 rooms have golden-colored walls, firm mattresses, reading lamps, consistent hot water in the baths (with tubs), television by satellite, and direct-dial phones. The restaurant serves an excellent buffet breakfast, and the staff members do a fine job of making guests feel at home.

One of the newest properties in the city, the **Hotel Ruinas (** (84) 260644 FAX (84) 236391 E-MAIL ruinas@mail.nterplace.com.pe sits in a fairly quiet location at Calle Ruinas 472. The 34 rooms are small but thoroughly modern with satellite television, direct-dial phones, minibars, and tubs in every bathroom. A few have balconies over the street, and the third floor terrace is a pleasant, sunny spot with great views. The **El Dorado Inn (** (84) 233112 FAX (84) 232442 E-MAIL doratur@mail.cosapidata.com.pe, at Avenida el Sol 395, combines colonial and modern architecture. The remodeled lobby incorporates a freeform stucco pillar encasing an elevator; some of the 54 rooms have round beds. Interior balconies face fountains and gardens; exterior ones face a very busy street.

Said to be the oldest hotel in the city, the **Hotel Cusco (** (84) 224821 FAX (84) 222832, at Heladeros 150, is a worn-down grand dame. The lavish lobby, replete with murals and chandeliers, gives way to 105 rather plain rooms. Water service is a problem here, and the place could use remodeling. Still, it is one of the most popular places with tour groups and is often full. These same tour groups often fill the rooms at the **Don Carlos (** (84) 226207 on Avenida el Sol 602. The rooms are modern, with direct-dial phones, and televisions.

Moderate

Stone walls from the Inca era are but one of the charms at the **Hotel Royal Inka I (** (84) 231067 or (84) 263276 FAX (84)234221 E-MAIL royalinka@cosapifata.com.pe, at Plaza

Regocijo 299. You can't miss the bright blue doors at the entrance to this 300-year-old mansion, a historic monument. The hotel has 34 large rooms with safe deposit boxes, minibars, central heating; other facilities include an attractive restaurant and a sauna and Jacuzzi. Directly next door is the **Royal Inka II (** (84) 222284 FAX (84) 234221 at Calle Santa Teresa 335. It has 64 rooms and is a bit more expensive.

The **Picoaga Hotel (** (84) 252330 FAX (84) 221246 E-MAIL picoaga@correo.dnet.com.pe, at Santa Teresa 344, was the colonial-era mansion of the Spanish Marquis de Picoaga. The restored complex has 70 good-sized rooms with safe-deposit boxes, central heating, and minibars; some rooms have small wrought-iron balconies facing the street (where noise can be a problem). The architecture is lovely, with stone arches and pillars, and a fountain in the middle of a central courtyard. Highly recommended is the blue-and-white **Hostal Loreto (** (84) 226352, Calle Loreto 115. The most interesting rooms incorporate stones from the former Inca Temple of the Sun Virgins. All rooms have private bath and hot water.

Inexpensive

Rooms are a great bargain at the **Hotel Conquistador (** (84) 24461 FAX (84) 236314, Santa Catalina 149 by the main plaza. The 32 rooms all have private baths and are small but clean and comfortable; there is an extra charge for televisions and small refrigerators. **Andenes de Saphi (** (84) 227561 FAX (84) 235588, Calle Saphi 848, is a pleasantly quiet inn a ten-minute walk from the plaza. The 14 rooms are rustic in style with wood beams and bed frames; electric heaters cut the chill in the wood and stone building. **Hostal Imperial Palace (** (84) 223324, at Teccecocha 490, is a pleasant spot with 10 rooms (all with private baths) in a restored mansion. The rooms have carpeting, exterior windows and nice bathrooms, and the narrow street is very quiet.

In the low range the **Hostal Incawasi (** (84) 223992, at Portal de Panes 147 on the Plaza de Armas, has 23 basic rooms, some with private baths and firm mattresses. The proprietors are very helpful, and there is supposed to be a 24-hour supply of hot water.

The **Amaru Hostal (** (84) 225933, Cuesta San Blas 541, is a friendly spot with 24-hour hot water. Rock-bottom rates are the biggest reason for staying at the **Hostal Felix (** (84) 241848, Calle Carmen Alto 281, which is popular with young German tourists. Some rooms have private baths; all are a bit musty.

WHERE TO EAT

Every other building in Cusco seems to house a restaurant; it's hard to imagine how they all stay afloat. The menus are rather similar,

running the gamut from standard Peruvian dishes to pizzas to burgers and fries. Some places stand out for their better than average cooking; others for their decor or view of the plaza. Traditional dishes include stuffed chili peppers called *rocoto*, seared guinea pig, pork fritters, marinated meat, bean salad, roast suckling pig, corn-on-the-cob, and fresh cheese. As tourism rises, new places open and shut constantly, and cappuccino and espresso machines are all the rage these days. Prices are higher than in the smaller towns, and many restaurants accept credit cards.

Vibrant blue balconies decorate homes and hotels in downtown Cusco.

Moderate

Restaurant El Truco ((84) 235295, Plaza Regocijo 261, offers local specialties in an elegant setting. Good beef and fish dishes are served. Traditional Andean folk dancing is performed most evenings. **Mesón de los Espaderos** on Espaderos by the Plaza de Armas has a cozy upstairs dining room filled with colonial-style furnishings. Their specialty is *parrilladas*, platters of assorted grilled meats.

Inexpensive

Wonderful fresh salads and soups are the meal of choice at **Pucara** ((84) 222027 at Calle Plateros 309. The small dining room where soft Andean music plays in the background is crowded with travelers and locals at lunch and dinner. The soups alone are sufficient for moderate appetites, though the menu also offers large portions of beef, chicken, and fish main courses with crisp fresh vegetables.

There are numerous restaurants around the Plaza de Armas, most serving similar cuisine at competitive prices. One of the best is **Señoritas** ((84) 243422, Portal de Panes 147. The narrow counter in a second-floor balcony overlooking the plaza is a perfect spot for a breakfast of fruit, yogurt, and honey. The main dining room, painted a dusty orange and decorated with metal sculptures and original art, is a serene spot where diners feast on spinach salads, quiche, grilled sandwiches including a delicious one with cheese, egg, spinach, and bacon. The chef does a brilliant job with mountain trout — try the *ceviche*, chowder, or grilled varieties. Also worth repeat visits is **Café Roma** ((84) 245041 Portal de Panes 105. Original Inca stone walls, mirrors, and large windows facing the plaza provide a pleasurable ambience, and the spaghetti carbonara with bacon, egg and cheese is great. Beef, fish, and chicken dishes are served in huge portions.

Some of the best seats at the Plaza de Armas are on the second-floor balcony of the **Bagdad Café** ((84) 262405, Portal de Carnes 216. Meals are served all day, starting with a breakfast of muesli and ending with a warm *ponche* drink at night. Pastas, pizzas and sandwiches are the preferred items, and there is a set menu at lunch. **Café Allyu** ((84) 232357,

Portal de Carnes 208, serves one of the best breakfasts around, with hearty portions and mouth-watering pastries. Service is good, soft classical music plays in the background, and some tables have a view of the plaza. Also by the plaza is **La Yunta** ((84) 255103, Portal de Carnes 214, serving hearty omelets and pizzas. Healthy wholegrain breads and fresh juices are part of the attraction at **La Tertulia** ((84) 241422 at Calle Procuradores 50, part of the Amauta language school. The book exchange is another major plus. Run by Peruvian Hare Krishnas, **Govinda** is a pleasantly priced vegetarian restaurant with good, wholesome food. It is located on Espaderos between the Plaza de Armas and Regocijo. **Café Literario Varayoc**, Calle Espaderos 142, serves excellent espresso and cappuccino, sandwiches and pastries, and Swiss fondue. Japanese teriyaki and tempura delight homesick travelers at **Kin Taro** ((84) 226181 at Heladeros 149.

There are enough Italian restaurants in town to satisfying any pizza cravings. Among the best, and most popular, is **Tratorria Adriano** ((84) 233965, Mantas 105. A set menu including pasta is served at lunch, when the dining room is filled with office workers. Three pizza places face the pleasant Plaza Regocijo; all have outdoor café tables where groups gather for afternoon beers.

NIGHTLIFE

Outside Lima, Cusco probably has the most active nightlife scene in the country, offering pubs, bars, discos, *peñas,* and folkloric shows in some restaurants. These places are incredibly crowded on Friday and Saturday night. Carry your possessions in your pockets — leave purses and backpacks at your hotel. Carry a copy of your passport as well, in case you run into trouble. The **Cross Keys**, on the second floor of Portal Confiturías 233, has the feel of a traditional English pub with draft beer, malt whiskey, grilled sandwiches and soccer games on television. **Paddy Flaherty's**, on the second floor at Calle Triunfo 124, plays Irish music in the background as customers quaff imported beers. One of the longest-lasting and most popular dance spots is **Kamikase** ((84) 233865, tucked in a corner at Plaza Regocijo. The bar opens at 8:30 PM; dancing begins at 11:30 PM. English-language movies are screened on three large televisions, with the last showing at 9:30 PM at **Tumi's** at Saphi 478 by the plaza.

HOW TO GET THERE

Cusco's airport, **Aeropuerto Velasco Astete**, located three kilometers (two miles) south of the center of the city, is serviced by international flights with Lan Chile. Regional lines AeroPeru and AeroContinente have daily service from Lima and other major Peruvian cities. The most expensive taxis are located right outside the airport door; less expensive taxis and minibuses are located beyond the fence that separates the parking area from the road past the terminal.

If you are traveling by train from Puno (a rather miserable 14-hour journey), you will arrive at the **Huanchac train station** in the southeastern part of the city. Once again, a taxi is easy to acquire here to take you into the city proper. There are several different companies offering **bus** service to Cusco and where that bus discharges you will depend on the particular company.

CUSCO ENVIRONS

Northeast of Cusco, 162 km (100 miles) up into the Andes is the village of **Tres Cruces**. Overlooking the Amazon Basin from atop the mountain, the town is best known for its spectacular sunrises and vistas. Along the rough road from Cusco one passes through **Paucartambo**, where the annual Fiesta de la Virgen de Carmen in mid-July attracts hundreds of visitors. The town sits at the edge of Manú National Park in mountainous jungle, and has no tourist facilities.

The southeastern route from Cusco to Puno is dotted with interesting villages and ruins. Driving through this region without a guide is not advised, as there are few facilities and intermittent military checkpoints as well as rebel hideouts. The train ride from Cusco to Puno has potential, and passes by impressive scenery. The trains, however, are in wretched condition. If you do make it this way, stop off in **Sicuani** for the Sunday market and at **Raqchi**, site of the ruins of an Incan religious center. Travelers passing through in mid-July should check out the Fiesta de Raqchi for its traditional music and dance.

THE SACRED VALLEY

To the northwest of Cusco is the magnificent and fertile Sacred Valley of the Incas, also known as the Urubamba Valley (Valley of the Spiders). A patchwork of small towns, Inca ruins, rivers, and corn fields spread beneath the mountains, offering travelers the

opportunity to explore traditional Quechua communities outside the bustle of Cusco. In fact, the valley makes a perfect base for exploring the entire region. You can see Cusco's highlights in one or two day tours; catch the train to Machu Picchu, midway along its route; and sleep far from the city streets beneath starry skies.

My first glimpse of the Sacred Valley came from above when I flew via helicopter from Machu Picchu to Cusco. Snow-covered mountain peaks blended into fluffy white clouds in the background, while miles on miles of checkerboard brown and green fields spread below. It all looked vaguely barren and dry until a settlement appeared in a pocket between hills or along a riverbank.

On ground, the valley spreads through 60 km (36 miles) of incredibly beautiful scenery along the banks of the Río Urubamba and Río Vilcanota north of Cusco, running east to west to the base of Machu Picchu.

ABOVE: Quechua residents welcome visitors to the Sacred Valley. OVERLEAF: Rafters and hikers appreciate the beauty and power of the Río Urubamba.

March, April, and May are its best months, when the summer rains have turned the landscape into orchards and fields of every imaginable shade of green. The region along the Urubamba from **Pisac** to **Ollantaytambo**, was a favorite with the Inca nobles residing in Cusco, who escaped the city for their country homes and farms on holidays. They built terraces and temples between the river and mountains, carving out agricultural plots still in use today. Rich soil feeds fields and terraced hillsides planted with corn, coca and potatoes, irrigated by runoff from the glacier-capped mountains.

There is a decidedly mystical feel to the area, which captivated Inca sun and water worshipers. To those who feel its powers, the valley is the land of *Pachamama*, Mother Earth. Shamans and healers practice traditional ceremonies at *huanas* (sacred places). Travelers who believe in energy centers, vortexes, and spiritual sites are drawn to this area; many stay for a long while and some have made the valley their permanent home. Inns catering to spiritual questers are beginning to appear in small Quechua towns, and those who hang around a while can find guides interested in explaining the religious, medicinal, and meditative aspects of Inca culture.

The archaeological sites in the valley are evidence of the Inca architects' belief in combining human necessity with natural resources. There was a strong sense of ecology and a tremendous respect for the earth, sun, and water. The Sacred Valley and Machu

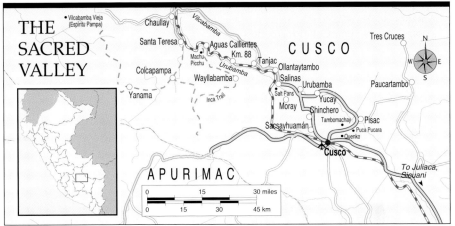

Picchu have become important destinations for those seeking to understand the connections between nature, the spirit, and orderly civilization. Most visitors speak of the strong spiritual stirrings aroused by simply being in the valley and connecting with the Andean peoples, who worshipped Pachamama and strove to live in harmony with her.

WHAT TO SEE AND DO

The geographical boundaries of the Sacred Valley are rather loosely defined. Traveling northwest from Cusco, the visual and archaeological signs of the valley begin just two kilometers (just over one mile) from the city at Sacsayhuamán (see WHAT TO SEE AND DO, page 133, under CUSCO), visible from the road to Urubamba. The drive, which takes about an hour without stops, travels past fields and pastures, small settlements of red clay homes, and young herders in traditional bright red shirts and trousers tending clusters of sheep, llama, alpaca, and cows. Massive pigs wander aimlessly across the road; schoolchildren gather at unmarked bus stops; and ladies in multiple skirts and felt hats walk to market bearing loads of potatoes and herbs wrapped in vivid *mantas*, the ubiquitous shawl, baby carrier, and native backpack. The largest settlement along this route is **Chinchero**, set against a backdrop of the Chicon and Wequey Wilca mountain peaks. The Sunday market in Chinchero is geared more toward locals than tourists, and residents from surrounding villages come to buy and sell vegetables, animals, and household goods.

Urubamba, located 78 km (47 miles) from Cusco, is a logical choice for a base in which to explore the Sacred Valley. Hotels, restaurants, and shops are scattered about the countryside on the banks of the Río Urubamba, which flows beneath the glaciers atop Chicon peak. Several Cusco-based adventure travel companies begin their river rafting and hiking trips here; it's best to set these up in Cusco. The town is the largest in the area, with bus stops for all major destinations in the valley. The large weekend market on Jirón Palacio is frequented by locals and tourists alike. Day trips from Urubamba include the **salt pans of Solinas** and **Moray**, ruins of an Inca agricultural center.

From Urubamba the main road travels east through several small settlements past remnants of Inca terraces and working farms. The town of **Yucay** is a peaceful spot with an excellent hotel. **Pisac**, the settlement closest to Cusco (30 km or 18 miles away) is accessible on a direct road from Cusco or from Urubamba. The town's market, held in the **Plaza Constitución** on Tuesday, Thursday and Sunday attracts villagers from around the area and enormous tour buses from Cusco. It's one of the best markets for purchasing alpaca and wool rugs, sweaters, pottery water jugs, and jewelry. The market is packed with tourists at midday, and is far more pleasant once the buses leave town.

There are two parts to Pisac, the colonial and modern village situated next to the river, and the Inca fortress located on the mountain above the river. A road winds its way up

A sense of serenity prevails in the Sacred Valley.

the mountain to the **citadel**; you can hire a taxi for a small fee, but the hour and a half walk up through the hillside is worth the effort. The view is spectacular. Scientists believe that these ruins were a fortress and refuge in times of war. The famous terraces that cover the mountainside and once supported Inca agriculture are still in use today. The citadel is an archaeological wonder, with terraces, water ducts, and steps cut from solid rock. In the upper portion of the ruins is the **Temple of the Sun**, built on an outcropping of volcanic rock. The position of the top of the temple

Ollantaytambo served as a fortress and a religious center between Cusco and Machu Picchu. The massive steps protecting the fortress are dramatic, and the bastion's walls, built with huge blocks of skillfully carved red granite, are an engineering feat. Seven monolithic stones at the top of the complex are etched with as yet undeciphered symbols, and may have been used for astronomical purposes and sun worship. The fortress was an important Incan stronghold during battles with the Spanish conquistadors. Rebel Inca Manco joined forces with nearby tribes

suggests that it may have been used for tracking significant stars. Also of interest at this site are ancient burial grounds, many of which have been plundered over the years.

At the far northwest end of the Sacred Valley is another important Inca site: the fortress of **Ollantaytambo**. Located 90 km (56 miles) from Cusco, the town beside the ruins is a major launching point for the Inca Trail and headquarters for travelers staying in the Sacred Valley. Local and tourist trains running between Cusco and Machu Picchu stop here; vendors selling tamales, breads, pottery, and rugs rush the train carriages during the short stop. The town is also accessible by road and is included in Sacred Valley tours from Cusco.

at this location and established an army so great in number that Pizarro, chasing him from Cusco, decided to abandon the pursuit and retreat. The Spaniards retreated so quickly they left much of their equipment behind.

The town of Ollantaytambo has retained much of its original Inca layout and is considered the most well-preserved example of Inca architecture still in use today. The town was divided into blocks or *canchas*, with each *cancha* having only one access. The entrance leads into a courtyard, from which individual houses were entered. The **Plaza Manyaraqui** is at the heart of the town and site of native folk dancing during fiestas.

WHERE TO STAY

Hotels and small inns are scattered throughout the valley, offering peaceful retreats amid Inca ruins and farms. Advance reservations are advised, as the hotels fill quickly with tour groups.

Expensive

The loveliest and most peaceful inn in the valley is the **Posada del Inca Yucay** ((84) 201346 FAX (84) 201345 E-MAIL posada_yucay

swimming pool, tennis courts, and a restaurant often crowded with tour groups.

Moderate

Though you must join a group to stay here, there is much to recommend the **Willka-T'ika Garden Guest Lodge** (no local phone) FAX (84) 201181 (or in the United States ((616) 977 0655 or (888) PERU070) E-MAIL info@ travelperu.com, on the road between Urubamba and Ollantaytambo. Owner Carol Cumes, author of *Journey to Machu Picchu* (see RECOMMENDED READING, page 281) chose

@el-olivar.com.pe, Plaza Manco II 123 in Yucay. Built in the style of a rambling hacienda, the hotel's golden-hued buildings sit against a mountain backdrop in a secluded compound. Fountains, gardens, and lawns provide peaceful areas for just sitting and enjoying the scenery. Some of the 65 rooms have balconies facing the gardens and mountains; all are spacious and comfortable. The bar with its blazing fireplace and traditional musicians playing Andean folk songs is an ideal place to while away the evening with friends or a good book.

In Urubamba **Hotel Valle Sagrado de los Inkas** ((84) 201126 FAX (84) 201071, at Km 69 on the highway to Cusco, is set close to the road and is more modern in style, with a

the property because of its 500-year-old *lukma* tree, sacred to the Inca, beside which she constructed a magical spiral garden of indigenous plants. Though she had intended to build a private garden and home, Cumes ended up creating the perfect retreat center for those interested in learning about Andean spirituality and the links to Pachamama (Mother Earth). The center's guest rooms were individually designed by Cumes to take in the garden views; all are filled with one-of-a-kind furnishings created by local artisans. When full, the property

LEFT: Ruins and rural restaurants attract wanderers to the Quechua village of Ollantaytambo.
ABOVE: Inca ruins form the base for colonial buildings in Chinchero.

holds only 24 guests, who are treated to an immersion course in the local lifestyle, with trips to Cusco, Machu Picchu, and private farms and homes in the area. Individual bookings are discouraged; instead, Cumes prefers that guests sign up with a like-minded group. Reservations must be arranged in advance; the exact address and phone number of the inn is kept private to prevent drop-in visitors. To arrange a stay for your yoga, meditation, healing, gardening, or other special interest group or to join and existing group contact Cumes through the fax number at the inn or the numbers in the United States.

Another spiritually oriented inn is the **Hotel Urpi Wasi (** (84) 201086 at Avenida Berriozabal 405 in Urubamba. The center, whose name means House of Peace, has a swimming pool, flower garden, sauna, and classes in massage, meditation, and healing. Bathrooms are shared but there is hot water. More mainstream is the **Royal Inka Pisac Hotel (**/FAX (84) 203064 or (84) 203065 TOLL-FREE IN THE UNITED STATES (800) 664 1819 on the road between Urubamba and Pisac. The hotel has 76 large rooms with views of the ruins of Pisac. There is also an indoor swimming pool with panoramic views, Jacuzzi, sauna, along with beauty and massage salons. Amenities include horse and bicycle rentals, a tennis court, and a mini basketball court. **El Albergue (** (84) 204014 FAX (84) 204025, in Ollantaytambo near the river and the train station at the far end of town, is popular with groups starting out on the Inca Trail hike. The rooms are spacious and nicely decorated and there is a sauna for relaxing after a hike up to the ruins.

Inexpensive

One of the nicest inns in the valley is the **Hotel Pisaq (** (84) 203058 or (84) 203062 (in Cusco) or (505) 758 0370 (in the United States) or 06301794653 (in Germany) WEBSITE www.aart .com/aart/HOTELPISAQ.html, at Plaza Constitución 333 in the center of Pisac. The decor blends Inca and American Southwest architecture and art; the dining room serves healthy fresh meals at inexpensive prices. The management offers tours of the valley. This is the perfect place to stay if you want to explore a typical town away from the crowds.

WHERE TO EAT

There are quite a few good places to eat in the Urubamba area. **Restaurant El Maizal** and the **Quinta Los Geranios**, both on the main road toward Cusco and open daily in the afternoons and early evenings, offer wholesome, typical regional food. A good less-expensive choice, is the **Restaurant Hirano**, Avenida Castilla 300, which serves lunch at a very reasonable price.

Pisac has several good restaurants. The most popular is **Restaurant Samana Wasi** on the corner of Plaza Constitución at Calle Mariscal Castilla. Bougainvillea vines shower the courtyard dining area with fuschia petals; caged birds chirp in the trees. There is an inexpensive set-menu lunch,

146

along with great breakfasts of scrambled eggs and omelets, and good salads and sandwiches. The **Café Restaurant Doña Clorinda** just off the plaza is a tiny place favored by the tour bus drivers and guides. The pies and cakes are terrific, as are the stews and soups.

In Ollantaytambo, **El Albergue** is probably your best bet. The breakfasts are particularly good. There are a couple of decent cafés around the main plaza. Try the **Restaurant La Nusta** or the **Bar Ollantay**.

HOW TO GET THERE

There are several ways to get to the Sacred Valley from Cusco. Companies offering bus service to the area include **Empressa Camino del Inca**, located in the northwest part of

the city near the train station at Calle Huáscar 128, and **Empressa de Transporte Turistico (** (84) 226157 or (84) 233009, at Calle Plateros 316. The latter has minibuses which go to all the main towns and sites in the Sacred Valley. Some days there are official guides on the buses and if you go on a Tuesday, Thursday, or Sunday you should get to experience the local craft market in **Pisac**. The tourist train from Cusco to Machu Picchu stops at **Ollantaytambo**, near the beginning of the **Inca Trail**. Sacred Valley tours are readily available in Cusco, and give visitors on tight schedules an opportunity to catch all the major sights in a day.

Wildflowers bloom in Cusco's countryside in April.

Machu Picchu and the Inca Trail

FEW TRAVELERS CAN VISIT SOUTH AMERICA AND RESIST the lure of the famed Inca city of Machu Picchu high in the Andes. Along with Ecuador's Galápagos Islands and Brazil's Amazon, Machu Picchu stands as a symbol for the entire continent. The ruined city rules as the most visible icon of the Inca Empire, the largest and most mysterious civilization of the New World.

The archeological site is readily accessible to all levels of travelers, provided they can wander up hills and granite stairways with relative comfort. True explorers prefer to approach the ruins via the Inca Trail, one of the most famous treks in the world. Hikers follow paths etched into mountainsides by Inca runners in the fifteenth century, albeit at a more comfortable speed than the messengers who raced between settlements. Whether you arrive via train, helicopter or ancient path, on a group tour or all alone, you're sure to be staggered by the beauty of this isolated, perfectly restored monument to nature and civilization.

MACHU PICCHU

Terraces etched in the Andean mountainside lead to ancient temples, palaces, towers, fountains, staircases, and the famous Hitching Post to the Sun, sprawling within a saddle between two mountains, backed by snowcapped glacial peaks. The Spanish conquistadors never discovered this mighty citadel, which sat relatively undisturbed until July 24, 1911, when Hiram Bingham,

by the studies of English historian John Hemmingway.

Still, Machu Picchu remains the most significant Inca site in South America, attracting international attention and speculation. Though Bingham is credited with bringing the site to international attention, he can hardly be called its discoverer. European and Peruvian explorers recorded the existence of the ruins earlier in the twentieth century. A local farmer, Augustine Lizárraga, inscribed his name on the Sacred Rock in 1901; his family led Bingham to the ruins a decade later.

Historians and archaeologists have determined that the site was built during the late fourteenth and early fifteenth centuries, during the reign of Pachacutec. It may have been a agricultural, religious or military center; debate over its purpose and manner of construction continues. The site was inhabited until the early seventeenth century, and then deserted for reasons not yet determined.

The ruins were declared a World Heritage Site by UNESCO in 1983, and archaeologists continue to discover more and more structures around the reconstructed site. Travelers with a mystical bent consider the ruins to be one of the most sacred spots in the world, and more than a few believers are convinced that Machu Picchu was created by extraterrestrial beings. No matter what you believe, you will never forget the beauty of this incredible Inca city.

a young North American expedition leader from Yale University, stumbled upon it by mistake. When local guides led Bingham up a steep cliff to a complex of terraces and mounds, he was sure he had discovered the fabled "lost city of the Incas," or Vilcabamba, the last stronghold of the Incas. Bingham's assertion held firm until the 1940s, when other explorers began to believe that Machu Picchu was actually an agricultural center for the inhabitants of Cusco. In 1964, archaeologist Gene Savoy from the United States led an expedition to Espíritu Pampa, deep in the jungle beyond the Urubamba Valley, a region explored by Bingham five decades earlier. Savoy's excavations uncovered an enormous city which he determined to be Vilcabamba, a theory further confirmed

GENERAL INFORMATION

Machu Picchu is located at a more comfortable elevation than Cusco at 2,350 m (7,708 ft) above sea level. The dry season is supposed to last from April or May until November, though in 1998 heavy rains began falling in late September. Mosquitoes and other irritating insects swarm about in August and September, when travelers caught unaware search frantically for repellent. Bring a rain poncho and bug repellent whatever the season. The climate is temperate year round, with warm days and chilly nights. The high season lasts from June through September and again from late December into February.

The Sacsayhuamán ruins dwarf tourists and serve as a backdrop for Cusco's Inti Raymi festival.

Advance reservations for the best hotels are necessary year round.

There are few tourist services at the ruins except for one hotel with an overpriced outdoor selfserve cafeteria, one souvenir and snack stand, a luggage storage area and bathrooms outside the site. You are not supposed to carry water bottles or food into the site; visible bottles are confiscated. I've always managed to hide water and snacks in my backpack.

Many travelers visit Machu Picchu on day trips from Cusco, which allows only about

is a good source for information on tours, hikes, and helicopter rides. **Qosqo Service** (/FAX (84) 212253, Avenida Pachacutec 103, is a full-service agency that changes traveler's checks and dollars, arranges train tickets and can provide guides to the ruins and hiking trails.

WHAT TO SEE AND DO

The whole reason for visiting this area is to explore the ruins of **Machu Picchu**, and those with a serious interest in Inca history and

three hours in the midday sun at the site. It is far better to spend at least one night in the area and arrive when the gates open as the sun is still rising and few tourists are about. The hordes descend between 10 AM and 11 AM. The site is open from 7 AM to 5 PM. Special sunrise and night tours of the ruins can be arranged through some agencies in Cusco. Admission costs $10; tickets for a second day at the ruins are half price if bought on the first day.

The area does not have a tourist information office. It's best to arrange tours and gather information in Cusco. **Rikuni Tours** ((84) 211151 FAX (84) 211036, Avenida Imperio de los Incas 123 in Aguas Calientes, or ((84) 241700, Calle Plateros 341 in Cusco,

archaeology should plan to spend at least two days here. I prefer staying in the town of Aguas Calientes (see WHERE TO STAY, page 156) and visiting the ruins when they open each morning. It's a sentimental thing. My first glimpse of the site came as I rode the bus up the Bingham Road one chilly morning at 6:30 AM, past wild orchids and streams. We passed campsites at the base of the road, where sleepy hikers warmed themselves by open fires. Distinct, regimented terraces etched the hillsides below thatched huts, part of the site's **Agricultural Sector**. Once inside the site I wandered about virtually undisturbed for two hours, petting soft brown alpacas on a plateau overlooking the ruins and climbing about structures in utter silence.

A group of people, their faces indistinguishable from the distance, stood in a circle atop the Temple of the Sun, their arms raised toward the sky. Never again have I experienced the sensations of that first morning, the feeling of absorbing the essence of a sacred place. I understand why friends pick Machu Picchu as a pilgrimage site when they're seeking spiritual solace or a special spot to mark life's passages.

The true wonder of Incan architecture becomes visible once you pass through the entrance and terraces to your first view of

must have felt after traveling the rigorous path from Cusco for many days.

Those who arrange to visit the site for sunrise begin at the **Temple of the Sun**, thought to be an astronomical observatory similar to the Mayan Caracol at Mexico's Chichén Itzá. Like the Maya, the Inca were superb astronomers, and this circular temple has trapezoidal windows facing the cardinal points. The niches throughout the structure are believed to have held offerings to the sun god, and a large natural stone slab altar is believed to have been used for reli-

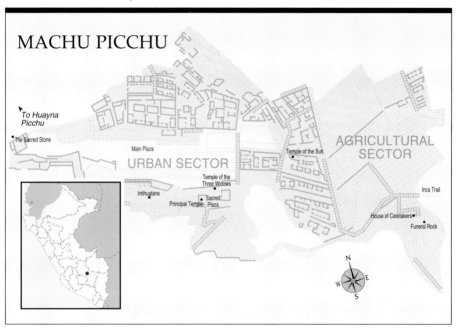

MACHU PICCHU

the entire city spread before the peak of **Machu Picchu** and **Huayna Picchu** towering behind the orderly granite buildings. Though the view is impressive year round, it's especially awesome just after the rainy season when the peaks are covered with lush green foliage. From here it's impossible to resist climbing the first level of steps to your left toward the original Inca entrance to the city. Stairs lead past the **House of the Caretakers**, the **Funeral Rock**, and the **Cemetery** to the **Inca Trail**, where backpackers who've been on the trail for days enter the site. A trio of alpaca who appear to have been here for an eternity graze in this area and pose for photos like proud peacocks. From here you can get an idea of how the original explorers

gious ceremonies. Closer to the entrance on a small rise is the famous **Intihuatana** or "Hitching Post to the Sun," thought to be an astronomical observatory. Atop the structure is a carved rock similar to a sundial, used to predict the winter and summer solstices and to help plan the planting and harvesting seasons. Every important Inca site had one of these carved columns, but most were destroyed by the conquistadors.

Within the main area, clustered around the **Main Plaza** and the **Sacred Plaza** are the **Principal Temple** and the **Temple of the Three Windows**, where one wall is constructed of a single rock with three large trap-

Precisely formed windows frame a view of the mountains around Machu Picchu.

ezoidal windows looking out toward the mountains. Nearby is the **Sacred Stone**, a huge slab of granite jutting out of the earth, facing east and west. Shamans and mystics consider the rock to be truly sacred and use this area for meditation and ceremonies. The peak of **Huayna Picchu** protrudes out behind the Sacred Rock over the Urubamba Valley at the northern edge of the Machu Picchu site. Climbers are allowed to follow a steep natural trail to the top after registering with a guard. It is a vigorous climb taking about 90 minutes and not advised for

those with vertigo or a fear of heights. The view from the pinnacle is breathtaking, encompassing the entire site and the surrounding mountains. On the way back down and to the right is the **Temple of the Moon**. The stonework here is some of the best, probably an indication that this was an important religious locale for the Inca people.

Many travelers visit Machu Picchu with a guide, and during the busy hours it's amazing to hear the echoes of Spanish, English, German, French, and Japanese descriptions of the various buildings. Guided visits are available through agencies in Cusco and Aguas Calientes and at the site. Though their explanations are helpful (if not always up-to-date), there is great value in wandering alone among the temples and terraces, absorbing the beauty of this magical place in solitude. The book *A Walking Tour of Machupicchu* by Pedro Sueldo Nava is available on the train and at shops in Aguas Calientes. Though far from complete, it offers a good overview of the structures and one of the few available maps of the site.

Hiking is superb in the region, and new trails are constantly being cleared. One of the most popular treks is a short version of the Inca Trail hike, from **Intipunku**, the original gateway to the site, to **Wiñay Wayna**. The name means "Forever Young," and the site is covered with ruins. The hike takes about two hours, and there is a simple Trekker Hotel with showers and a restaurant. If you hope to spend the night, hike in early and claim a bunk or floor space. You can also reach Wiñay Wayna by following the rail track from Aguas Calientes toward Cusco, past the hydroelectric plant. Within 15 minutes from the plant there is a marked trail and bridge over the Río Urubamba; from here the uphill hike takes about two hours. You can then spend the night at the trekkers' hotel or continue on the trail to Machu Picchu.

HOW TO GET THERE

Most travelers reach Machu Picchu via the **trains** from Cusco, which depart from the San Pedro Station. Local trains are extraordinarily inexpensive. But they are also dreadfully uncomfortable, slow (four hours or more) and crowded, and thefts are common. There are usually two morning trains and one in the afternoon. Far more desirable are the faster **autovagon** tourist trains, which cost about US$50 round trip. The comfort and safety afforded are worth the fare. The first train leaves Cusco at 6 AM and arrives at the ruins at 9:30 AM, then leaves for the return journey between 3 PM and 4 PM. A second train is supposed to leave Cusco daily at 9 AM and arrive in Machu Picchu at around noon. This train, however, is not always running. The train stops in Ollantaytambo; from here it's about two and a half hours to the ruins. The tourist trains used to run to the settlement at Puente Ruinas, past the town of Aguas Calientes. A new train station was built just east of Aguas Calientes in 1998, and includes a large waiting room, an information desk, and a snack shop. The station is a five-minute walk from Aguas Calientes, where buses depart to the ruins.

Always buy your train ticket at least one day in advance. Ticket windows at the San Pedro Station are open when trains are departing, or you can purchase a ticket throughout the day at the Huanchac train station. The easiest option is to buy your ticket from one of the reputable travel agencies in town.

An exciting, though costly way to get to Machu Picchu is by helicopter. **HeliCusco** offers a ride in a 24-passenger helicopter from the Cusco airport. The launch pad in Aguas Calientes is down the train tracks toward Cusco, about a 15-minute walk from town. Their office in Cusco (/FAX (84) 227283 or (84) 243555 is located at Calle Triunfo 379. In Aguas Calientes the office ((84) 211036 is on Avenida

miserable spot, with dirt trails leading past modest cement houses and souvenir stands. The town becomes more endearing once you settle in and visit with the workers and entrepreneurs who live in the shadows of the mountains. Conditions in town are improving steadily. Electricity and running water are available 24 hours a day (though the better hotels have their own generators and water tanks). Trash barrels would help the town's appearance considerably, as much litter is scattered about. The **thermal baths** are the town's biggest attraction, and are located a

Imperio de los Incas 123. You can also purchase tickets at the entrance to the ruins using credit cards, travelers' checks, or cash.

Buses depart from Aguas Calientes for the ruins starting at 6:30 AM; the last bus back leaves the ruins at 5:30 PM. The road to the ruins travels five miles up the mountainside with 14 steep curves. It was built in 1948 and is named for Dr. Hiram Bingham. Tickets are available in town.

AGUAS CALIENTES

The actual town by Machu Picchu is usually called **Aguas Calientes**, a name which refers to the thermal baths in the vicinity. The small settlement appears at first to be a rather

ten-minute uphill walk from the train tracks. They're open from 7 AM to 9 PM; there is an admission fee and towels are available.

There are no cars or taxis in the area, only a few trucks for hauling workers and supplies and the buses which travel the Bingham Road to the ruins. The train tracks, which run parallel to the Río Vilcanota, serve as the main road through town, called Avenida Imperio de los Incas. The tracks are lined with hotels, restaurants and shops. The main plaza is one block southeast of the tracks; a steep road winds south from here past more hotels and restaurants to the thermal baths.

LEFT: The precision of Inca stone-carving is evident at Pisac. ABOVE: Stones fit tightly without mortar in terraces and huts.

WHERE TO STAY

Most of the accommodations near the ruins are located in Aguas Calientes, and are more expensive than one might expect. Hot water is scarce in the cheapest places, and a poncho or sleeping bag comes in handy on cold nights. Advance reservations are strongly advised even in low season, as one never knows when large tour groups will be around. If you haven't secured reservations before arriving in Peru, do so with a travel agency in Lima or Cusco.

rocks. Red tiled roofs blend into a landscape of trees, their trunks laced with bromeliads. Hummingbirds hover about trumpet flowers, heliconias, and orchids flowering throughout the grounds. The rooms are decorated with eucalyptus wood beams, tiled floors, and cedar furnishings; some have balconies overlooking the forest, and each room has its own hot water heater. The restaurant is in a large main building with floor-to-ceiling windows facing the Río Vilcanota and town; fireplaces blaze on chilly evenings. The stone swimming pool in the central lawn

Rooms are usually less expensive when booked in advance; the rates posted for walk-in guests can be twice as much. You may be able to haggle for a lower rate if there are few tourists in town. Most hotels require guests to check out at 9 AM or 10 AM and will store your luggage until you depart.

Very Expensive

Despite the lure of the ruins, I had a hard time leaving the grounds of the **Machu Picchu Pueblo Hotel** ((84) 212032 FAX (84) 211124 E-MAIL reservas@inkaterra.com.pe. Set above the rail tracks on a slight hill, the 65-room inn consists of several white adobe cottages tucked amid gardens, with a stream running through the property, splashing over

offers a pleasant respite after hiking the ruins. Guided hikes of the orchid gardens and tea plantation are offered in the mornings, and bird watching is excellent. The hotel also has a campsite with hot-water showers, towels, and a comfortable setting. It's worth staying in the area an extra night just to enjoy this property. The only accommodations at the entrance to the ruins are in the very expensive **Hotel Machu Picchu Ruinas** ((84) 241777 FAX (84) 23-7111 E-MAIL reserlima@ peruhotel.com. The 32 rooms are uninspired, but have satellite television and phones (though the generator is shut off early in the night). A few rooms (numbers 39, 40, and 41) overlook the ruins (and the buses in the parking lot). If you're truly devoted to exploring the ruins no matter what the cost, this is the place to stay. You can explore in the early morning and late afternoon and rest while the crowds are swarming about. There is an indoor dining room serving a mediocre breakfast buffet and international cuisine. Unfortunately, there is no transportation to town in the evening and you're stuck at the hotel. Though the company can be congenial, the service and food are abysmal.

Moderate

Rooms overlooking the river are almost at the expensive level at the **Presidente Hostal** ((84) 212034 FAX (84) 211065, on Avenida Imperio de los Incas on the train tracks in Aguas Calientes. Those in the interior are less costly, but still expensive. The 25 rooms are immaculately clean and comfortable.

Inexpensive

The most popular rooms in town are at **Gringo Bill's Hostel** (/FAX (84) 211046 E-MAIL gringobill@yahoo.com, Calle Colla Raymi 104 near the plaza. The 18 rooms are located on several levels of a sprawling building; some have large private baths, some have balconies, and all have comfortable beds and mystical murals on the walls. Margarita and Bill Kaiser operate the hotel and are a valuable source of information and conversation. Their Margaritaville restaurant is one of the main hangouts for travelers sharing insights about local hikes and special spots throughout the country.

The **Machupicchu Hostal** ((84) 211034 FAX (84) 211065, Avenida Imperio de los Incas beside the Presidente, has 12 simple rooms, some with private baths. The price is a bit high for what you get, but the sound of the river below the property is a soothing accompaniment to sleep. Also recommended in this price range are **Hostal Ima Sumac** ((84) 212021 on Avenida Pachacutec, with private bathrooms and guide services, and the **Hostal Inca** ((84) 211034, Avenida Imperio de los Incas 135, which is clean and has private bathrooms.

WHERE TO EAT

The only dining facilities at the ruins are in the Hotel Machu Picchu Ruinas, where the cafeteria gets terribly crowded at lunch. Aguas Calientes is loaded with pizzerias, cafés and fullscale restaurants, most serving the same unremarkable meals. Reservations are essential at the nicest places when tourism is high. Many of the restaurants are closed on Sunday.

Moderate

The best restaurant in Aguas Calientes is **El Indio Feliz** ((84) 212090, Calle Lloque Yupanqui 4 above the plaza. Chef Patrick Vogin hails from France, while his wife, Cannie Pacheco, is from Cusco. Together, they have created an exquisite restaurant serving some of the finest cuisine in Peru. Though the menu features typical Peruvian dishes, none resemble ordinary fare. The *ceviche* is made from delicate pink mountain trout; the mixed vegetable salad is a delightful platter of shredded carrots, sliced tomatoes and cucumbers, diced apples and pineapple, and wedges of avocado all served with a mustard French dressing. Chicken and trout are served with delicate ginger or lemon sauces; don't miss the orange and apple pies with cappuccino. The best tables are on the second story beside windows overlooking town. I find it easy to spend several hours here listening to classical music over the sound system, lingering over several starters, and conversing with fellow diners. Reservations are essential in high season. It is closed on Sundays.

At the **Machu Picchu Pueblo Hotel** (see WHERE TO STAY, page 156), the cuisine rivals the best in Cusco. Three meals are served daily at set times in the dining room and on the balcony overlooking the river; reservations for lunch and dinner and suggested during high season. The soups alone are superb. If you're suffering from a cold (a quite common occurrence in rainy season), try the *aguadito norteño de pollo*, a dense broth seasoned with peppers and cilantro and loaded with vegetables, rice, and chicken. There are several excellent trout, beef and chicken preparations, along with fresh salads and pastas. The irresistible desserts include spice cake with rainforest nuts, caramelized apple pie, cream puffs, and lemon crêpes.

A Quechua woman displays her wares along the road of 12-sided stones.

Inexpensive

Gringo Bill's Hostel (see WHERE TO STAY, page 157) serves the best breakfast in town, starting at 5:30 AM; try the French toast and fresh fruit. Dinners include steaks, chicken, and pizza. Pizzas are the main draw at **Toto's House (** (84) 212013, on the tracks between the train station and town. The large restaurant is pleasantly decorated with folk art; pizzas are prepared in a wood-burning oven and the restaurant has a full bar with imported wines. The **Restaurant Allyu**, Avenida Imperio de los Incas 145, serves a wholesome breakfast and decent trout. Just down the road from here is the **Pizzeria La Chosa** serving Peruvian and Italian food. Also recommended is **Chez Maggy**, Avenida Pachacutec 156, with large tasty meals and a friendly atmosphere. Aside from the formal restaurants, there are food stalls in the market close to the police station which offer fruit juices and empanadas.

THE INCA TRAIL

Who hasn't heard of the Inca Trail? It is the classic adventurer's route to the outstanding site of Machu Picchu. The trail runs for 39.6 km (24.6 miles), peaking at 4,200 m (13,776 ft) above sea level, dipping and curving from riverbanks to mountain passes and back. The trail was the main route from Cusco and the Sacred Valley to the mountain citadel for the Inca, who traversed the route for both commerce and worship. These days it is thick with backpackers from June through September and sprinkled with hardier souls in rainy and colder months. Fortunately, the region is located within the boundaries of the Machupicchu Historical Sanctuary—one could only imagine the sorts of tourist facilities that would exist if developers were allowed to roam free.

Despite its popularity, the Inca Trail remains exciting, challenging, and both physically and spiritually uplifting. Some call the experience "sublime agony" and are happy to be done with it. Others repeat the trek again and again, finding side trails, solitary campsites and Quechua *campesinos* eager to mingle with curious gringos. The typical four-day route can easily double in time if you linger amid the scenery, examining rare birds and

cloud-forest plants. Sections of the route are accessible as day hikes from the ruins and the town of Aguas Calientes; hiking even a minor portion enhances your Machu Picchu experience.

GENERAL INFORMATION

It is possible to hike the trail in three days, but that's pushing it. A more realistic excursion is four days and three nights, with an extra night or two near Machu Picchu at the end of the trail. You can rent a tent, shop for supplies, get the latest information on trail conditions in Cusco, and do the trip on your own. But most people opt for a guided tour. International tour companies as well as their

counterparts in Lima and Cusco offer Inca Trail itineraries, as do countless vendors in Cusco's Plaza de Armas. Though you can hire a guide and do the trail in three nights for less than US$100, you may get even less than you paid for. You can expect meager food, inexperienced guides, and leaking tents. Qualified companies provide several types of tents for different seasons; check to be sure they are waterproof. Ask about the food in detail; many companies shave their costs in this area.

Make sure your voucher includes all pertinent details: the languages spoken by the guide, the type and quantity of food and fresh water, the quality of the equipment, and how many people will be in the group. Many of the tour companies supply porters to carry your stuff; tip them well. The tip is a major portion of their wage; ask the guide how much you should give them. See TOURS, page 129, under CUSCO, for tour companies.

The Inca Trail demands peak performance; the combination of altitude changes and serious trekking can overwhelm even experienced hikers. Try to acclimate yourself to Cusco's altitude for at least two days before starting the hike. Trail conditions are best in the dry months between June and September; the trail is also extraordinarily crowded at this time. The best time may well be in April and May, at the end of the rainy

Villagers rely on foot power to reach markets in the Sacred Valley.

season. The trails may be slippery and muddy at some points, but the vegetation is lush and green, birds and mammals abundant, and humans are scarce.

No matter when or how you go, essentials include a waterproof tent, backpack, a sleeping bag, comfortable hiking boots or shoes, and rain-repellent clothing. Other necessities include a hat, sunscreen, a flashlight, water purification tablets, and lots of strong insect repellent. Bring along some plastic bags; you will need to carry out all your garbage.

The second day tests the mettle of even hardy hikers. **Abra de Warmiwañusqa**, the first pass, is reached after about five hours of climbing. At 4,200 m (13,776 ft), it is the highest point on the trail and also the most challenging part of the trek. The view from this point is incredible, and the altitude rough on those suffering from *soroche* (altitude sickness). If the effects are intense, keep going down from the pass to the Río Pakaymayu valley campsites, at 3,290 m (10,791 ft). The second pass, **Abra de Runkuraqay**, contains one of the most interesting archaeological

THE INCA TRAIL

Huayna Picchu •   Aguas Calientes •

• Machu Picchu

| 0 | 2 | 4 miles |
| 0 | 2 | 4 | 6 km |

Trekkers' Hotel •

Urubamba

Wiñay Wayna •

• Puyupatamarka

Abra de Runkuraqay •

Sayacmarca •

Río Pakaymayu

Km. 88

Abra de Warmiwañusqa •

Llulluchayoc •

Wayllabamba ○   **Huayllabamba**

N

W   ✦   E

S

Río Cusichaca

WHAT TO SEE AND DO

There are two starting points for the Inca Trail. By road from Cusco to Ollantaytambo you will follow a dirt track to Km 82 of the Pan-American Highway. By train from Cusco to Ollantaytambo, you will begin at Km 88 of the Pan-American Highway. From here you hike over a suspension bridge spanning the Río Urubamba and up steep terrain until you reach **Wayllabamba**, the only inhabited village on the trail. This section of the trail takes four or five hours for most hikers, an adequate first-day's adaptation to backpacks, scenery, and the trail conditions. There are campsites here and in **Llulluchayoc**, one and a half kilometers (one mile) further along.

sites along the trail. The fortress-like complex sits above circular temples, about an hour's walk from a flight of stone steps leading up to the pre-Columbian complex of **Sayacmarca**, set up like a small town. There are campsites below Sayacmarca.

From Sayacmarca the trail leads gently downward through a tunnel carved in rock by the Inca and along a well-worn flagstone path to **Puyupatamarka**, the "Town Above the Clouds." Follow the trail down to five baths made of stone. There are places to camp here above the ruins, affording a spectacular view of Urubamba Valley.

Two or three more hours of rigorous descent will bring you to an impressive citadel known as **Wiñay Wayna**, also called Wiñay-huayna. The ruins in this area were excavated in the 1940s, and appear to be the largest complex on the route to Machu Picchu. There are six clusters of buildings in the complex, all similar in use to those at the nearby ruined city. Wiñay Wayna is a crossroads of sorts for travelers, just as it was for the Inca. It is accessible on a day hike from Machu Picchu, and has a small trekkers' hotel with beds and hot showers. The trail is well marked here, and leads down a steep descent for two more hours through dense jungle to Intipunku, the gateway to Machu Picchu.

Pampa uncovered an extensive complex buried in the dense jungle; future expeditions have unearthed hundreds of houses beyond a compound of plazas, temples, and palaces. Espíritu Pampa proved to have been a much larger settlement than Machu Picchu, and archaeologists now believe the famed Vilcabamba lost city is actually at Espíritu Pampa.

The region around Espíritu Pampa has a long revolutionary history, and was used by the Sendero Luminoso during the 1980s. There are still rumors of rebel camps in the

ESPÍRITU PAMPA

Hiram Bingham ventured beyond Machu Picchu during his famed 1911 expedition, but he overlooked significant ruins in his eagerness to proclaim his alleged discovery of the Lost City of the Incas. Bingham spent several weeks hiking west through the Cordillera Vilcabamba and river valleys before stumbling upon a few ruins at Espíritu Pampa, Plain of the Spirits. He decided the site was most likely an outpost for Incas fleeing from the Spanish during the conquest, and narrowed his sights on the far more impressive layout at Machu Picchu. Gene Savoy's 1964 expedition to find what he considered to be the real lost Incan city at Espíritu

remote area, and travelers should always employ a guide when venturing beyond Machu Picchu. The ruins of Espíritu Pampa are virtually inaccessible — no roads or rivers pass by and there are few settlements in the region. Those wishing to visit the ruins must hike and travel by mule and camp in the wilderness, which sounds enchanting until you're exhausted and bruised from the arduous trek. With advance notice a few of the adventure-travel companies in Cusco can arrange the Espíritu Pampa trek.

Rough-hewn houses mimic Inca stonework in the Espíritu Pampa region.

Puno and Lake Titicaca

TITICACA... LIKE TIMBUKTU AND KATMANDU, the name rolls off your tongue like an incantation, a word that seems to define *remote* and *exotic*. Author Arnold Toynbee called the lake a "vision of gods" when he ventured to this region in the 1950s. According to local Indian lore, it's also the abode of gods. One creation myth declares that the legendary Manco Capac and Mama Ocllo emerged from these sacred waters at the dawn of time to found the Inca civilization. But even before the advent of Inca power, the lake shores were home to numerous ancient cultures including the Pucara, Tiahuanaco, and Colla. Most of the modern-day Indians who live around the lake are Aymara, with a darker complexion and a different language than Inca descendants elsewhere in the Peruvian highlands.

The lake is a freak of nature, the only large body of water along the entire Andes spine and the world's largest high-altitude lake. Its deep-blue waters spill across 6,560 sq km (2,532 sq miles) of the *altiplano*, split about equally between Peru and Bolivia. That's comparable in size to Europe's Lake Geneva or Lake Ontario in North America. It sinks to 284 m (922 ft) below the surface at its deepest spot while its elevation is an incredible 3,820 m (12,500 ft) above sea level — which means that visitors coming directly from sea level will feel the negative effects of altitude (headaches, nausea, general malaise). And don't plan on a dip in Titicaca unless you brought your wetsuit: the average water temperature is a chilly 9°C (48°F).

Titicaca is also a natural wonder. Although the predominant hue is azure blue, you often see bands of intense color — the ochre of *totora* reeds growing along the lakeshore, the peagreen color of the algae that collects in certain bays, the reddish-brown of distant hillsides, and the puffy white clouds that hover in the superthin mountain air. All sorts of waterfowl take refuge here including the geese, ibis, coots, grebes, gulls, herons, teals, and flamingos, many of them protected within the confines of a new nature reserve that hugs much of the northern and eastern shore. The lake embraces 36 islands including Amantaní, Soto, and Taquile in Peruvian waters and Campanario, Luna, and Sol in Bolivian territory.

PUNO

With a population of 80,000, Puno is the largest city on the shores of Lake Titicaca and a thriving tourism center due to it being the only place on the Peruvian side where you can arrange transportation and tours to the lake islands.

Founded in 1668 by Spaniards eager to exploit the region's rich silver reserves, the city's official name is San Carlos de Puno. It was a fairly small provincial town until the late nineteenth century when the British-owned Peruvian Corp made the city its nexus for rail and steamship travel in the Titicaca region.

Puno's physical location is spectacular: set on a broad bay with mountains all around. It's especially attractive at night, the twinkle of golden lights around the edge of the water and crawling up the hillsides. However, the steep topography has severely limited the city's growth potential. As a result, nearby Juliaca has developed into a larger sister city of 100,000 people in recent years with an important rail junction and the region's only airport.

Because of its many traditional dances and festivals, Puno is often called the "Folklore Capital" of Peru. The most important annual event is the Virgin of the Candelaria fiesta in February. Other important celebrations include Puno Week at the start of November, the Alacitas handicraft fair in May, and Epiphany on January 6.

GENERAL INFORMATION

Puno's **Municipal Tourist Office** is situated at Jirón Lima 549, on the busy pedestrian street that runs off the Plaza de Armas. The staff are helpful if they happen to be there. The people manning the souvenir shop that shares space with the tourist office offer no assistance unless you want to buy.

Like many Peruvian cities, Puno now has its own e-mail café. **PunoNet (** (64) 369510 E-MAIL webmaster@punonet.com WEB SITE www.punonet.com, Jirón Lambayeque 145, is a pleasant retreat also offering fax services

Saint Francis dons an Indian hat for a sacred procession near Puno.

and general tourist information. It is open daily from 8 AM to 10 PM.

The **Bolivian Consulate** recently moved to Jirón Arequipa 120, one block from San Juan Plaza.

WHAT TO SEE AND DO

Puno has a rather modest **Plaza de Armas** compared to most Peruvian cities and there is always a heavy police presence given the number of banks and government buildings that surround the square. The plaza is domi-

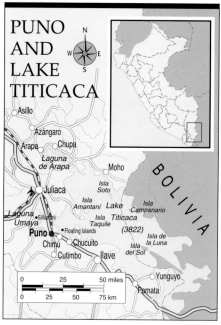

PUNO AND LAKE TITICACA

nated by the glass-fronted municipal building and the seventeenth-century **cathedral** that looks more like something from rural Mexico than the grander churches you find elsewhere in Peru. The interior is no more impressive: cold, dark, and humbly decorated, a rather cheerless place that betrays the poverty of the *altiplano*.

Right off the plaza is the **Museo Dreyer**, Conde de Lemos 289, with a modest collection of artifacts representing the various Indian cultures of the Titicaca region. It is closed on Sunday and charges admission.

If your legs and lungs have acclimated to the altitude, hike on up to **Huajsapata Park** which offers stunning views of the city and lake. The large white statue crowning the

bluff is legendary Inca leader Manco Capac. The reach the park from the Plaza de Armas, follow Jirón Deustua south, turn right onto Jirón Llave, left onto Jirón Bolognesi and left onto Pasaje Contique, a steep alley with many steps that leads to the summit.

It's difficult to view the lake from Puno's helter-skelter waterfront. But a short hike north of town is **Isla Esteves**, crowned by the modern Hotel Libertador but also part of the Titicaca National Preserve. A dirt path leads around the edge of the island, an excellent way to get a closeup view of the lakeshore and its reed vegetation. Birdwatchers should bring their binoculars because this is also a good place to scrutinize the local birdlife. You might also see fishermen in their wooden rowboats or Indian women cutting reeds along the banks.

Nearly everyone who comes to Puno visits the famous **Uros Floating Islands** in the Gulf of Chucuito. Most people organize their voyage through their hotel or local travel agent. You can also taxi to the foot of Avenida Titicaca and find your own boat. There will be plenty of people to help you choose, but ultimately everyone ends up in the next tourist boat departing for the Uros. Expect to pay S/12 to S/15 per person for a two-hour ride. It takes about half an hour for the slow-moving motorboat to reach the first of the floating settlements, a tourist village with souvenir stalls made from reed. The next two villages on the standard tour are much more interesting because Indians actually live and work in these places. The largest village features a lengthy waterfront and a wooden school (you have to wonder how it stays afloat on the reeds).

A few hard facts about the islands: most of the residents still live in reed dwellings, but they now have metal roofs to shield them from the elements. Reed canoes are nearly a thing of the past in this part of Titicaca, victims of a trend toward wooden rowboats and outboard motors. On the bright side, most of the island children now attend schools on the islands or the mainland and there are very few beggars compared to a few years ago.

Puno's latest attraction is a black and white steamship called the **MV** *Yavari* ((54) 622215 or (54) 369329. Built in Britain in 1862 by James Watt & Co. and Thames Iron Works and Shipbuilding, the vessel was commissioned for use on Lake Titicaca by the British-owned Peruvian Corporation. In order to transport her from Lima, the *Yavari* was broken down into 1,383 pieces and carted across the Andes on mule back. The job six years and the steamship was finally launched on Lake Titicaca in December of 1870. After numerous decades as a lake steamer, the vessel fell into disrepair and was eventually left to rot along the Puno waterfront. In the early 1990s, a London-based foundation

soon fade away as wooden boats with outboard motors become more popular with local fishermen. **Chucuito** (20 km or slightly over 12 miles) sports an ancient stone sundial in the Plaza de Armas, as well as a small ruin called the **Temple of Inca Uyo** and two old colonial churches.

Although the Titicaca region was part of the Inca's expansive empire, they never got around to building many stone monuments in this part of their realm. Many of the area's archaeological marvels predate the Incas. The most outstanding is **Sillustani** which sprawls

raised funds from all around the globe to refloat and repair the grand dame of Titicaca. It now takes pride of place on the Puno waterfront, one of the world's oldest surviving iron-hulled ships. Painted in the original colors of the Peruvian Corporation, many of the original fixtures have been lovingly restored including the Victorian-era steering gear and the Bolinder engine. The *Yavari* also contains a small museum dedicated to the maritime history of Lake Titicaca. Closed Monday and Tuesday, an admission fee is charged.

Along the south shore of Puno Bay are two interesting towns. **Chimú** (eight kilometers or five miles from Puno) is famous for its reed-boat industry, although it may

across a peninsula on Laguna Umayo about 30 km (20 miles) north of Puno. Developed by the Colla people before the rise of the Incas, the site contains giant stone towers called *chullpas*. The Colla buried their mummified rulers and priests in these circular and quadrilateral bastions, which are also found at other places around the shore of Titicaca. The tallest reach about 12 m (36 ft) in height and the stonework in many respects is even more complicated than what the Incas rendered at Cusco or Machu Picchu. Travel agencies in Puno arrange half-day tours to Sillustani, but you can also catch a taxi out to Laguna Umayo and explore the ruins on your own.

Medicinal herbs for sale at an *altiplano* market.

SHOPPING

The Titicaca region is known for its blankets, sweaters, hats, and other items woven from locally-grown wool and alpaca. Prices are generally much cheaper than for similar items sold in Cusco or Lima, but bargaining is still part of the game, especially on the islands and Puno's market.

Anyone who takes the short boat ride out to the Uros Floating Islands will find plenty of opportunity for shopping. You can get good sweaters for as little as US$7 if you know how to dicker. Bargains also await those who venture to Taquile and Amantaní islands.

Puno's Central Market is primarily a food and dry good's market for local residents. But around the fringe of the market at souvenir stalls and a few modest shops selling wool sweaters, Indian hats, Andean musical instruments, and toy llamas.

The city has very few arts and craft shops. **Qori Chasca Artesanía** at Jirón Lima 320 sells a wide variety of local pottery items, as well as other small souvenirs. **Artesanía Puno** at Alfonso Ugarte 150 (near the market) has a good general selection of local crafts. The tourist office on Jirón Lima (near the Plaza de Armas) shares space with a souvenir vendor. The **Hotel Libertador** has a small lobby boutique with high quality goods including alpaca sweaters and jewelry, but the prices are correspondingly high.

If you run out of film in Puno, try **Plus Color** at Jirón Moquegua 146, which offers both Kodak and Fuji, as well as print film processing.

WHERE TO STAY

Expensive

The only luxury abode in the Titicaca region is the **Hotel Libertador** ((54) 367780 FAX (54) 367879 WEB SITE www.libertador.com.pe, on Isla Esteves about five kilometers (three miles) north of the city center. About half of the 126 rooms overlook the lake, a spectacular view that takes in the Gulf of Chucuito and the nearby Uros Floating Islands. Amenities include the excellent Sillustani restaurant (more lake views) as well as piano bar, a games room, and sprawling lounge area

with free coffee and tea throughout the day. The only drawback is the front-desk staff who could be much more efficient and helpful given the amount of money they charge.

Moderate

My choice for the best place to stay in central Puno is the **Colón Inn** ((54) 351432 or (34) 357090, Calle Tacna 290. Situated in an old colonial-style mansion about halfway between the Plaza de Armas and the Central Market, the Colón exudes a certain antique charm that is sadly lacking in most of the city's hotels and hostels. All rooms include private bath with around-the-clock hot water, plus telephone and room service. There's a leafy courtyard in the center of the building, a panoramic terrace on the roof and a quite lounge downstairs where you can read or watch television. It's hard to go wrong with this place.

Another well-kept abode is the **Hotel Sillustani** ((54) 351881 FAX (54) 352641, Jirón Lambayeque 195. This four-story hotel near San Juan church feels a bit dated after several decades of business, but it's still one of the city's best bets. All rooms include private bath, hot water, and telephone. The room rate includes breakfast and you can negotiate a special weekly rate if you're spending some time in Puno.

Hotel El Búho ((54) 354214 or (54) 366122 FAX (54) 351409, Jirón Lambayeque 142, sports a sunny central courtyard and slightly funky decor. As with the other hotels in this category it features rooms with private bath and hot water, as well as its own restaurant and laundry service. El Búho also has its own travel agency, one of the best in Puno.

Inexpensive

Only a couple of minutes walk from the Plaza de Armas is the pleasant **Hotel Monterrey** ((54) 351691 FAX 351632, Jirón Lima 441. Rooms are set around a quiet courtyard away from the hustle and bustle of the nearby pedestrian precinct. The hotel has its own restaurant (open daily from 7 AM to 10 PM) plus laundry service. You can choose from rooms with or without private bath.

If you've just arrived by train from Cusco or Arequipa and don't feel like tramping around town in search of bed, try the **Hotel**

Ferrocarril ((54) 351752 or 352011 FAX (54) 351752, Avenida La Toree 185, across the street from the railroad station. Nothing fancy here, but the staff is friendly and the rooms come with private bath, hot water, and breakfast.

WHERE TO EAT

Puno is not the gourmet capital of the Andes (that would be Cusco), but there are a number of interesting restaurants from which to choose.

298. Pizzas come in three sizes (small, medium, and family) and about 15 different varieties including Hawaiian, chorizo, ham, sardine, mushroom, and vegetarian. The intimate setting includes red table clothes, flower-filled vases, and great views of the street outside (they throw open the windows during warm weather).

If you like freshwater fish make haste for **Don Gerolamo's Trout Palace (** (54) 356840, Jirón Lambayeque 141 where the house specialty is caught daily in Lake Titicaca. Situated in a restored eighteenth-century man-

Expensive
As with the hotel scene, the only things that qualifies as expensive in the Titicaca region is **Restaurant Sillustani** at the Hotel Libertador **(** (54) 367780 on Isla Esteves. The staff is friendly and efficient, the menu a mix of Peruvian and international dishes. And not everything is outrageously priced: ordering something like the Chinese rice, spaghetti bolognase, or tortilla lowers the cost to the inexpensive to moderate category. The best thing about the Libertador dining rooms is its wonderful views of the lake.

Moderate
I like both the pizza and the atmosphere at **Pizzeria Europa (** (54) 351432, Calle Tacna

sion, the restaurant also offers folklore shows and *peña* music from 8 PM each evening.

Inexpensive
The ideal place in Puno to sample local "game" is **Apu Salkantay Café** at Jirón Lima 341, where such Andean delights as guinea pig and alpaca steak feature on the menu. There is a wide array of other dishes including trout, kingfish, chicken, pork and sandwiches. They also do one of Puno's best breakfast selections including yogurt, muesli, and pancakes.

New on the Puno scene is a pleasant little restaurant called **Así es mi Peru**, at Calle

Aymara Indians mix old and new fashion in Puno.

Libertad 172. The solarium-style dining area is pleasant both day and night while the menu features a number of tasty dishes including *ceviche*, *corvina* (sea bass), *chicharrón de pollo* (deep-fried chicken), *lechón al horno* (roast suckling pig), *lomo a lo pobre* (beef steak), *palta a la reyna* (avocado salad), and *trucha frita* (fried trout).

An old favorite among travelers is **Restaurant Don Piero** ((54) 351766, Jirón Lima 364. The wide-ranging menu includes many chicken, beef, and pasta dishes, as well as fresh trout from Lake Titicaca. Right up

washed out in the El Niño storms of 1998 and is still in rough repair. Expect delays and a journey of at least 14 hours despite the shorter distance. The road journey between Puno and Juliaca takes about 45 minutes by taxi.

AeroPeru and AeroContinente provide daily air service from Juliaca's Manco Capac Airport to Lima (two hours) and Arequipa (20 minutes). Strangely there is no direct service from Juliaca to Cusco at the present time; you must detour through Arequipa or Lima.

A more romantic (and much longer) way to reach Arequipa and Cusco from Puno is

the street is another standby, the **Bar Delta Café** at Jirón Lima 284. The fare is a bit lighter here including sandwiches, desserts, fresh fruit juices, and cold beer. Delta also serves breakfast. The only drawback is the cramped, dark dining room.

HOW TO GET THERE

Puno is 389 km (241 miles) southeast of Cusco and 323 km (200 miles) northeast of Arequipa via road. There is daily bus and *colectivo* service to and from both cities, as well as bus, *colectivo*, and taxi service to and from Juliaca. The highway to Cusco is paved and in good repair, a journey that takes about 12 hours. The road across the *altiplano* to Arequipa was

the Southern Railroad via Juliaca. Rail service to Cusco departs three times per week for a journey of 11 hours across the *altiplano* reaching a high point of 4,313 m (14,146 ft) at La Raya. Fares are S/25 for *económico* class (no reclining seats, very crowded), US$19 for *turismo* class (reclining seats but often crowded), and US$24 for "Inka" first class (declining seats, no crowds, secure compartments). Trains to Arequipa depart Puno twice a week for an overnight journey of about nine hours that arrives in Arequipa the following morning. Fares are S/18.50 for *económico* class and S/30 for "Pullman" first class. The train schedules are erratic; check at the station for current departure information.

TAQUILE AND AMANTANÍ

Floating islands aside, Titicaca's most visited islands are Taquile and Amantaní, about three hours sail to the east of Puno. These are not reed islands but solid chunks of earth and stone that rise precipitously from the lake.

Archeological finds show that **Taquile** had been a fulcrum of civilization in this region for at least 10,000 years. It was an Aymara stronghold until the thirteenth cen-

ichu grass. In fact, this is probably the closest anywhere in Peru to a genuine ancient Inca lifestyle. The primary crops (as elsewhere in the *altiplano*) are potatoes, corn, and beans. Alpaca wool provides the basic raw material for local looms which spin out fine sweaters, shawls, and blankets at a fraction of the price of what you would pay in Lima. The main village perches on a rocky slope high above the shoreline and much of the landscape is covered by Inca agricultural terraces. Elsewhere on the island are ancient hilltop ruins including **Uray K'ari** and **Hanan K'ari**,

tury when it was seized by an armada of Inca reed boats. After the Spanish conquest, the island was purchased by an Iberian nobleman Pedro Gonzalez de Taquile who transformed it into his private hacienda with local Indians as his slaves. By the early twentieth century it had become a Peruvian version of Alcatraz, a place of exile for high-profile criminals and political prisoners. Sixty years ago the local Indians regained ownership of their own land by buying it back from the government.

These days the island is populated by farmers, fishermen, and weavers. There are only about 1,200 inhabitants and many of them still wear traditional Andean clothing. They dwell in stone houses roofed with local

developed by the Tiahuanaco people about 1,200 years ago.

Taquile sports few manifestations of twentieth-century life — solar panels provide the only electricity, toilets are primitive at best, blankets and wood fires provide warmth from the Andean chill, and the only form of locomotion is your own two feet. Taquile has no hotels or hostels. All visitors stay in private homes, either pre-booked in Puno through a local travel agent or arranged at the dock upon arrival in Taquile.

Amantaní boasts a similar ambience with stone terraces that creep up the hillsides,

LEFT: Outboards compete with reed boats on Lake Titicaca. ABOVE: The Aymara inhabit both the lakeshore and islands.

inhabitants who cling to ancient ways despite the onslaught of "progress" elsewhere in Peru, and very little in the way of modern conveniences. The major handicraft here is basket weaving. With around 5,000 people it has a much larger population than Taquile, but it receives fewer tourists and has fewer visitor services. Once again, room and board are in private homes.

Daily boats connect Puno with both Taquile and Amantaní. It's best to leave early in the morning so that you reach the islands by noon. At least one overnight stay is recommended because of the amount of time (at least three hours) it takes to reach either island. If your Spanish (and Quechua) are good enough, you can make all the arrangements yourself and save a few dollars. Or you can simply have a Puno travel agency do the legwork. I find that standard prices for overnight packages are actually quite reasonable. **American Tours (** (54) 351409 or (54) 366122, Jirón Lambayeque 142, offers several options. Their one-day tour includes stops at the Inca temple in Chucuito, at one of the floating islands, and in Taquile. It departs Puno at 7 AM, returning at 6 PM that evening. The S/30 price includes boats, ground transfers, lunch, entrance fees, and English speaking guides. Their two-day tour includes a visit to the MV *Yavari* in Puno Bay, an overnight stay in Amantaní, and a one-hour visit to Taquile the following morning. The S/40 price includes transportation, meals, accommodation, and an English-speaking guide.

An alternative way to explore Lake Titicaca is a **trout fishing tour** offered by Cualquier Tours (54) 356840 FAX (54) 351400, Jirón Lambayeque 141 in Puno. Five hours of fishing on a private boat called *Los Andes* costs US$25. The price includes ground transport from your hotel to Charcas village south of Puno, all sportsfishing equipment, personal advice and assistance from a local fisherman, a visit to the Inca temple at Chucuito, and transportation back to Puno at the end of the day. The tour departs daily at 9 AM.

Aymara women cooking on the Uros Floating Islands near Puno.

The Southern Desert

THE SOUTHERN COAST OF PERU IS ONE OF THE world's most desolate places, an empty and starkly beautiful desert landscape that stretches all the way into northern Chile, where it merges with the even harsher Atacama Desert. This is desert in the most extreme sense — shifting sand dunes, dry river beds, rocky plains, and chestnut-colored mountains that announce the western frontier of the Andes. Sandstorms and dust devils are far more common than rain showers. In fact years can pass between downpours, rendering this region one of the earth's driest places. Temperatures can drop to near freezing at night and easily soar above 40°C (104°F) by day. And there are vast tracts where *nothing* grows — not even cactus or scrub.

Despite these ruthless conditions, the southern desert gave birth to some of Peru's most fabulous ancient civilizations. The Paracas and Nazca cultures both thrived here, churning out a wealth of textiles and pottery, plus the famous Nazca Lines. In later years, this area was an integral part of the Inca Empire. The Spanish conquistadors founded some of their first settlements along this desolate stretch of coast. There were two reasons why human life could flourish amid this desert bleakness — amazingly rich fishing waters off the coast which provided a ready and easy food source, and the presence of oasis valleys fed by snowmelt from the Andes.

These lush valleys provide the sustenance of life even today, a chain of emerald gems strung along the Pan-American Highway —

Pisco, Ica, Palpa, Nazca, Yauca, Camaná, Chili, and Tambo. Each one of them like a tiny Nile Delta, a nucleus of life for several thousand years and now a bulwark of civilization against the constantly encroaching desert. Like the ancient societies that prospered here, various crops find the climate and soil most appealing: grapes, rice, asparagus, olives, avocados, and cotton provide a good living for local farmers, complementing fishing activities and slowly increasing tourism.

The Pan-American Highway is in excellent condition in this part of Peru, little affected by the El Niño storms that washed away so much of the roadway in the north. It provides a wonderful means to explore the varied attractions of the south — the wild-

life around Paracas, the wine and pisco produced in Ica, the mysterious desert lines and haunting cemetery of Nazca, and the Spanish colonial heritage of Arequipa. It's truly amazing how so much life can thrive in such an inhospitable place.

PISCO AND PARACAS

Lying about half a day's drive south of Lima, the small city of Pisco and nearby Paracas Peninsula offer a welcome diversion from the archeological sights that dominate so much of the tourist trail along Peru's coast. The attractions here are profuse wildlife and unfettered coastal scenery, especially in the giant Paracas National Reserve which could be described as Peru's version of the Galápagos Islands.

But the area has history too. The Paracas civilization flourished here between 1300 BC and AD 200, living off the rich offshore waters and producing a wealth of textiles that are considered the most sophisticated of pre-Columbian times. Fast-forwarding more than a millennium, Paracas Bay is where José de San Martín landed in 1821 at the start of his liberation of Peru, an event marked by a stark, modern monument on a desert hill overlooking the village.

GENERAL INFORMATION

Pisco is a rather sleepy town centered around a dusty Plaza de Armas. There is no official tourist office, but nearly every hotel and travel agent can fill you in on the area's attractions. **Ballestas Full Tours (** (34) 533491, Avenida San Francisco 113, next to the Hostal Pisco, offers trips to both the offshore islands and the mainland part of Paracas Reserve with English-speaking guides.

WHAT TO SEE AND DO

Most people who travel to Pisco have one thing in mind: the wild and rugged **Paracas National Reserve**. Established in 1975, this is Peru's premier coastal park, a massive park that embraces over 280,000 hectares (700,000 acres) of shoreline, mountains, and desert.

The sprawling high desert near Arequipa.

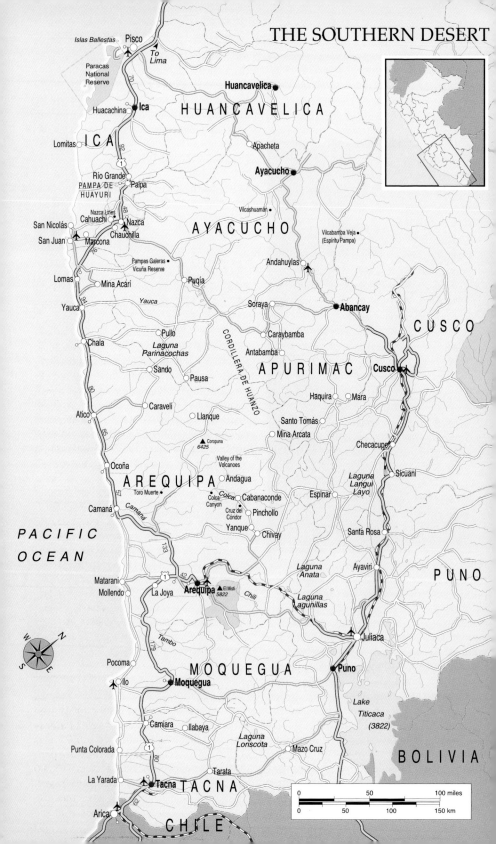

THE SOUTHERN DESERT

PACIFIC OCEAN

Islas Ballestas
Pisco
To Lima
Paracas National Reserve
Huancachina
Ica
Lomitas
ICA
Apacheta
Río Grande
Palpa
PAMPA DE HUAYURI
Nazca Lines
Cahuachi
Nazca
Chauchilla
San Nicolás
Marcona
San Juan
Pampas Galeras Vicuña Reserve
Lomas
Mina Acarí
Yauca
Yauca
Pullo
Chala
Laguna Parinacochas
Sando
Pausa
Atico
Caravelí
Llanque
Coropuna 6425
Ocoña
Valley of the Volcanoes
AREQUIPA
Andagua
Toro Muerte
Camaná
Colca Canyon
Colca
Cabanaconde
Cruz del Cóndor
Pinchollo
Yanque
Chivay
Matarani
Mollendo
La Joya
Arequipa
El Misti 5822
Chili
Pocoma
Tambo
Illo
Moquegua
MOQUEGUA
Camiara
Ilabaya
Laguna Loriscota
Mazo Cruz
Punta Colorada
Tarata
La Yarada
Tacna
TACNA
Arica
CHILE

HUANCAVELICA
Huancavelica
Ayacucho
AYACUCHO
Vilcashuamán
Vilcabamba Veja (Espíritu Pampa)
Andahuylas
Puqia
Soraya
Abancay
Caraybamba
Antabamba
APURIMAC
Haquira
Mara
Santo Tomás
Mina Arcata
Espinar
Cusco
CUSCO
Checacupe
Sicuani
Laguna Langui Layo
Ayaviri
Santa Rosa
PUNO
Laguna Anata
Laguna Lagunillas
Juliaca
Puno
Lake Titicaca (3822)
BOLIVIA

0 50 100 miles
0 50 100 150 km

Numerous sea creatures take refuge in its deep blue waters including dolphins, whales, sea lions, penguins, leatherneck turtles, hammerhead sharks, manta rays, condors, pelicans, and flamingos.

The famous **Islas Ballestas** with their sea lions and myriad bird life are technically part of the reserve, but you don't actually have to go into the park to reach them. Tour boats leave at frequent intervals from the main pier in Paracas village. Most hotels in the Pisco–Paracas area will gladly arrange your boat trip. Expect to pay about S/20 for a three-hour trip. Do not settle for a boat that doesn't provide lifejackets.

But there's much more to the reserve than the offshore islands. The park's main road runs around the edge of Paracas Bay to the fascinating Tello Museum (with its exhibits on the area's pre-Columbian civilization) and the famous **Candelabra** image carved into a steep hillside above Paracas Bay. Like the Nazca Lines, no one is sure who created the cactus-like image, but it was probably some sort of pre-Inca religious icon. Unpaved roads (four-wheel drive recommended) lead to several ruggedly handsome beaches like **Playa Mendieta** and **Playa Carhaus**, and the sea lion gallery at **Mirador de Lobos**. One of the most efficient ways to tour the park if you don't have much time is by guided minibus tour. They can be arranged through local hotels and travel agencies and usually run about S/15 for five hours.

Pisco's newest tourist attraction is **Acorema** at Avenida San Martín 1471, a private research institute devoted to the research and public awareness of the marine environment in the Pisco–Paracas region. It's quite modest compared to Western marine parks and aquariums, but provides good insight into what local people are doing to protect wildlife and marine resources. It is closed on Sunday. Admission is free, but they ask a small donation to fund the institute.

WHERE TO STAY

Expensive
The best resort along this stretch of coast is the **Hotel Paracas** ((34) 221736 FAX (34) 4225379, which is located right on the beach in Paracas village. It's been around since the late 1940s when it started attracting the rich and famous of Lima. Today it caters mostly to upmarket tourists with a wide range if amenities including three pools, tennis courts, miniature golf, and waterskiing, as well as a fine restaurant. The front desk will gladly arrange sport fishing or an excursion to the islands.

Inexpensive
Pisco offers two types of budget accommodation: an "upper level" favored by Peruvians that runs US$20 to US$30 per night and a "lower level" favored by young backpackers that runs less than US$10 per night.

Perhaps the best of the upper-level abodes is **El Candelabro Hostal** ((34) 532620, at the corner of Jirón Callao and Pedemonte, which features a friendly staff, clean and comfortable rooms, and a very nice continental breakfast. Rooms have televisions, minibars and private baths. Drawbacks include lukewarm shower water, paper-thin walls, and street noise from the nearby bus and *colectivo* stops. Closer to the nature reserve is **Hotel El Mirador** — call their booking office in Lima at ((1) 4325757 FAX (1) 4320109 — on the outskirts of Paracas village, with rooms that feature private bath and hot water at a cost of US$25.

Hotel Embassy ((34) 532809, Jirón Comercio 180, is a friendly place that perches above Pisco's pedestrian street. It's immaculate and run by a friendly lady who goes out of her way to help guests. Rooms include private bath and hot water for US$10 to US$15. Across the way is the brand new **Suite San Jorge Hostal** ((34) 534200, Jirón Comercio 187, which offers a choice of rooms with hot or cold water for US$13.

An old favorite with overland travelers is the **Hostal Pisco** ((34) 532018, San Francisco 115 on the Plaza de Armas. Situated in a funky old colonial mansion with white-washed walls set around a pleasant courtyard, it offers rooms with and without private bath for around US$10.

WHERE TO EAT

One of Pisco's few upscale restaurants is the **As de Oro** ((34) 532010, Avenida San Martín 472, which is popular with locals and visiting businessmen. It doesn't offer much in the way of atmosphere (although you can eat by candlelight during blackouts), but the food is probably the best in town including *ceviche*, soups and salads, various seafood, and chicken and meat dishes. Top off the meal with an Irish coffee.

Closer to the town center is **Restaurant Don Manuel** ((34) 532035, Jirón Comercio 179, on the pedestrian street that runs off the Plaza de Armas. The specialty here is seafood including *ceviche*, octopus, shellfish, squid, and sea bass.

Pisco features a number of modest restaurants favored by locals and backpack travelers including **La Fontana** at Jirón Callao 132, **Snack Bar Catamaran** at Jirón Comercio 166, and **El Tridente** inside the Hostal Pisco on the north side of the Plaza de Armas. The latter has an especially good breakfast menu including egg dishes and banana milk. Backpackers also flock to the **Panadería Pastelería** next door to the Hostal Pisco, open from 6 AM to 10 PM daily. The menu includes sandwiches, hot dogs, hamburgers, fresh fruit juices, chorizo, and oven-fresh baked goods.

HOW TO GET THERE

Pisco is 235 km (145 miles) south of Lima and 80 km (50 miles) north of Ica via the Pan-American Highway. There are frequent buses and *colectivos* from Lima and Ica, plus several daily services to Nazca and Arequipa. The journey from Lima takes about four hours; the journey from Ica about 90 minutes.

Paracas village and the entrance to the national reserve are about 15 km (10 miles) south of Pisco along a coast road that runs through San Andreas fishing village and past numerous smelly fishmeal factories. The best ways to reach the area from Pisco are via taxi or *colectivo*.

ICA

Like an *Arabian Nights* fantasy in the middle of the desert, Ica is a lush oasis town set amid sifting dunes and hard-baked desert barrens. Founded in 1563 and one of the oldest towns along the southern coast, the Ica Valley is fed by runoff from the Andes, water that nourishes the area's many vineyards. Grapes are

the area's life blood. Wine and pisco brandy are produced at about 60 different bodegas ranging from family affairs to major industrial concerns. Unfortunately the same river that makes the valley so fertile overflowed during the El Niño storms in 1997 and 1998, devastating both downtown Ica and many of the lower-income homes that surround the city.

GENERAL INFORMATION

Ica's tiny **tourist office** is located near the intersection of Avenida Grau and Jirón Ayacucho, one block east of the Plaza de Armas. It's generally open Monday to Friday 9 AM to 6 PM, although it sometimes opens later and closes earlier than the posted hours.

WHAT TO SEE AND DO

One of the finest archeological collections in southern Peru is the **Museo Regional de Ica** on Avenida Ayabaca in the southwest part of the city. Exhibits run the gamut from mummies and trophy heads to textiles and ceramics. The emphasis falls squarely on various peoples that thrived along this coast including the Paracas and Nazca cultures. It is open daily and admission is charged.

The city's other pride is the **Museo de Piedra**, Bolívar 170 on the Plaza de Armas, which contains an intriguing collection of engraved stones that no one has been able to attribute to a specific culture or epoch. It is open daily and admission is charged. The church overlooking the Plaza de Armas is the petit **La Merced** dating from 1874. One block west of the plaza, along Avenida Municipalidad, is the much grander **San Francisco** church.

The luxuriant **Huacachina Oasis** lies six kilometers (four miles) southwest of downtown Ica, a reddish-blue lagoon surrounded by fine white dunes that tower more than a 100 m (325 ft). Developed as a posh resort during the 1940s, Huacachina maintains a bygone air with a palm-shaded promenade that stretches around most of the lake, several outdoor cafés, and a stylish old hotel that wouldn't look out of place in *Casablanca*. You can swim in the lagoon (reputed to have healing powers) or rent a paddle boat for a

Lichen thrives at some of the higher elevations in Arequipa province.

casual cruise. Those with a bit more energy can rent sandboards (similar to snowboards) and surf the dunes.

A number of wineries in the Ica Valley welcome visitors. One of the smaller establishments is family run **El Catador Bodega** ((34) 403263, about five minutes north of the Pan-American Highway at Km 296. As well as a fine selection of their own wines and pisco, El Catador can whip up a pretty mean pisco sour too. There is a restaurant and a small museum on site. Free tours of the vineyard and processing area are available upon

request. At the other end of the spectrum is the huge **Vista Alegre** winery ((34) 232919, largest in the valley and maker of fine wines, sangria, and pisco for more than 140 years. Tours and tasting every day, but you may have to fight off the bus tourists.

WHERE TO STAY

Moderate

For a taste of old Peru nothing beats the **Hotel Mossone** ((34) 213630 FAX (34) 236137 E-MAIL mossone@invertur.com.pe. Situated in the heart of Huacachina Oasis, the place has a real 1940s ambience with rooms set around a Spanish colonial courtyard shaded by huge *ficus* trees. The pool area is small but secluded

and includes playground equipment. Both the bar and restaurant feature terraces that overlook the lake. It offers good value for your money at around US$44.

On the outskirts of Ica is the excellent **Las Dunas Resort** ((34) 256224 FAX 256231 E-MAIL invertur@protelsa.com.pe, Panamericana Sur Km 300, a rather large hotel (110 rooms) by local standards and popular with weekenders from Lima. Many of the rooms feature terraces that overlook the nearby sand dunes and there is a golf course and a great pool.

Another good bet in the moderate range is **Hotel Ocucaje** ((34) 220215 E-MAIL ocucaje @amauta.rcp.net.pe, Panamericana Sur Km 336, which bills itself as a "sun and wine resort" with features such as a swimming pool and sauna.

Inexpensive

Perhaps the best budget hotel is **Hostal Sol de Ica** ((34) 236168 or (34) 227189, Jirón Lima 265, which offers 70 rooms with private bath, hot water and television. Other amenities include a swimming pool, Turkish baths, a travel agency, and a disco. **Posada Hispana Hostal** ((34) 536363, Avenida Bolognesi 236, is one block off the Plaza de Armas. Rooms feature private bath with hot water; the owners speak English, French, and Italian.

WHERE TO EAT

Many of Ica's restaurants were wiped out during the El Niño storms and have not returned. However, a new crop of eateries is taking root. **Zambos Sandwiches** on the south side of the Plaza de Armas offers light meals such as sandwiches, desserts, and fruit juices. For a more substantial meal try **Nueva Castilla Restaurant**, on Avenida Libertad between the Plaza de Armas and Jirón San Martín. **La Taberna Restaurant** ((34) 403263 at El Catador Winery features a good menu of local dishes and a fine selection of wines and pisco.

HOW TO GET THERE

Ica is roughly 300 km (200 miles) south of Lima and 140 km (86 miles) north of Nazca via the Pan-American Highway. There are frequent buses and *colectivos* to and from those other cities. The Lima drive takes about four hours and the Nazca drive about three hours, mostly through open desert. There are also services to Pisco and Arequipa.

NAZCA

The town of Nazca, tucked amid the shifting dunes and desert mountains, was never especially important in Spanish colonial times. It would have no doubt remained a hot and dusty crossroads if not for the discovery of the Nazca Lines about 70 years ago.

Although no one knows for sure, the Lines were probably created by the ancient people who populated this region in pre-Columbian times. An offshoot of the coastal Paracas culture, the Nazca civilization prospered from about 300 BC to AD 700, at the same time that Moche culture was flourishing in northern Peru. Like the Moche, the Nazca people were diehard potters, generating a wealth of ceramics that show daily life in ancient times.

Nazca is now one of country's foremost travel destinations, a "must stop" on the tourist trail that winds across southern Peru. Despite all this attention, it remains a small town at heart with friendly inhabitants and a bygone ambience that centers around the Plaza de Armas.

Much of Nazca, which sits atop a geological rift equivalent in size and power to California's San Andreas fault, was leveled by an earthquake in the early 1990s. Giant heaps of brick and adobe — the refuse of quake destruction — cover huge areas on the outskirts of town.

GENERAL INFORMATION

There is no tourist office, but both the Nazca Lines Hotel and the Hostal Alegría can provide general tourist information or hook you up with local guides and travel agents. **Nazca Trails Travel**, Jirón Morsequi 122 (on the east side of the triangular plaza outside the Nazca Lines Hotel), can also arrange scenic flights over the Lines, visits to the Chauchilla Cemetery, or journeys to the Pampas Galeras vicuña reserve. English-speaking drivers and guides are available.

WHAT TO SEE AND DO

Discovered by Paul Kosok in 1929 and investigated by Maria Reiche for nearly five decades between 1940 and her death in 1998, the **Nazca Lines** are one of South America's enduring mysteries. Researchers believe they were made by the ancient Nazca culture, although we may never be sure of their precise origin. There are all kinds of wacky theories about aliens drawing the lines — could they be "space maps" or UFO runways? But

most likely they are some kind of astrological or religious rendering related to the constellations or heavens. In addition to huge trapezoids and triangles, there are 11 major figures drawn on the Pampas de San José north of Nazca city including a condor, a hummingbird, a monkey, a pelican, a whale, a spider, and the famous hillside astronaut that gave birth to the *X-Files* suppositions.

Scenic flights over the Nazca Lines run anywhere from US$45 to US$60 dollars per person depending on the operator and season. **AeroCondor** ℂ (34) 522402 is one of the most reputable operators and the first air-

LEFT: Polychrome bottle with geometric designs made by the ancient Nazca people. ABOVE: The Paracas culture was famed for its fabulous textiles.

line that offered scenic flights, charging US$55 per person for a 40-minute journey that takes in most of the major figures. Flights are best in the early morning when the air is less hazy and turbulent. You can book through your hotel front desk or the AeroCondor office at Nazca Airport.

If you want to see the Lines from closer range, hop in a taxi to the **Mirador**, an observation tower on the Pan-American Highway about 20 km (12 miles) north of Nazca. The drawback is that you can really only see three of the figures — Lizard, Hands, and Tree —

but the drive gives you a good sense of the solitude of this sacred plain. The man who collects admission to the Mirador runs a side business painting Nazca Line images on small stones.

Continuing north, the highway descends from the plateau to a tiny village called San Pedro where you find **Maria Reiche's House**. Since her death in early 1998, the house has been transformed into a little museum of her life and work including her hand-drawn blueprints and calculations of the various Lines, many personal photographs, her surveying equipment and box cameras, and her flower-covered grave in the garden. It is closed on Sunday, and admission is charged.

Nazca's other archeological marvel is **Chauchilla Cemetery**, a necropolis of the ancient Nazca culture that lies 30 km (20 miles) southwest of Nazca via the Pan-American Highway and a rough desert road. Thousands of graves are scattered across dunes on the edge of the verdant Nazca Valley. You literally step on human bones, braided hair fragments, and funeral shrouds as you ex-

plore the graveyard. In 1998, local authorities upgraded the site by excavating 13 tombs. Mummies squat inside these mudbrick graves, wrapped in thick layers of funeral cloth and cotton, their skeletal faces facing the rising sun. It's enough to send a shiver up your spine. There is an admission fee.

A much less-visited site is **Cahuachi**, the remains of an ancient city in the desert west of modern-day Nazca. The Nazca culture construction an adobe *huaca* and other buildings here, but it's difficult to find without a local guide. **Pampas Galeras** vicuña reserve is about 90 km (60 miles) east of Nazca in the high mountains that mark that western flank of the Andes. It's best to explore the reserve with a guide from Nazca.

WHERE TO STAY

Moderate

For more than 50 years the **Nazca Lines Hotel** ((34) 522293 FAX (34) 522112 E-MAIL invertur @protelsa.com.pe, on Jirón Bolognesi, has been a favorite with travelers and visiting archaeologists. It has a wonderful hacienda-style design with rooms set around a leafy central courtyard with swimming pool. Maria Reiche lived here for much of the last decade of her life and often gave lectures in the hotel lounge. The front desk can arrange flights over the Nazca Lines and transportation to other nearby archeological sites.

Inexpensive

Hostal Alegría ((34) 522702 FAX (34) 522444, Jirón Lima 168, is a magnet for backpack travelers offering rooms with private baths and hot water, as well as a swimming pool, laundry service, a book exchange, and a computer room with Internet service. Nearby are the bus stops for Arequipa, Ica and Lima.

Closer to the center of town is **Hotel Mirador** ((34) 523121, Jirón Tacna 436, a brand-new establishment overlooking the Plaza de Armas. With a narrow oval courtyard that opens to the stars, rooms are clean and comfortable with private baths, hot water, and television upon request. The rate includes breakfast.

Hostal Las Líneas ((34) 522488, Jirón Arica 299A, offers rooms with private bath, hot water, and televisions, at rates ranging from US$15 to US$22. At the bottom end of the budget category but still pleasant is the family run **Hosteria El Sol** ((34) 522064, Jirón Tacna 476. Rooms are simple but clean and some feature private bath with hot water. Rates run from US$5 to US$7.

WHERE TO EAT

The popular **La Taberna** at Jirón Lima 321 offers delicious food and an eclectic menu featuring all sorts of dishes including chicken, steak, fish, and pasta. The pisco the hotel is the new **El Portón** with its pleasant courtyard dining area. The food is standard tourist fare — sandwiches, pizza, pasta, and seafood dishes — but this is probably the most romantic place to dine in Nazca.

One of Nazca's best-value restaurants is **Pizzeria Trattoria La Púa** next to the Hostal Alegría, which serves a good selection of pizza, pasta, chicken, and fish dishes as well as salads, sandwiches, fresh fruit juices, and breakfast. **El Griego Restaurant** at Bolognesi 287, popular with the young backpacker

sours are delectable, the beer served ice cold. There's live music every night, Andean flute tunes or soulful gypsy melodies. And the café's walls are smothered in graffiti penned by travelers from all around the world. Feel free to add your own name and words of wisdom.

Pin Point Café next to La Taberna is a small coffee bar which features cappuccino, fresh fruit juices, breakfast, and sandwiches. During the late afternoon happy hour everything is 15% cheaper.

The restaurant at the **Nazca Lines Hotel** offers a good selection of Peruvian and international dishes at reasonable prices. The bar next door has a happy hour from 7 PM to 9 PM each evening. Across the plaza from

crowd, has a typical Peruvian menu with lots of meat, chicken, and fish dishes.

HOW TO GET THERE

Nazca lies about 440 km (272 miles) south of Lima and 570 km (353 miles) north of Arequipa on the Pan-American Highway. There is frequent bus service to and from both cities, as well as bus and *colectivo* service to Ica. The drive from Lima takes about eight hours, the journey to Arequipa about ten.

Another alternative is hopping a two-hour flight from Lima. AeroCondor and

OPPOSITE: The high desert close to Arequipa. ABOVE: A truck rumbles along the Pan-American Highway.

other small airlines offer service upon request, but there is no regular schedule.

AREQUIPA

As the largest city between Santiago and Lima, Arequipa is a bastion of European civilization in the midst of a vast desert wilderness. In many respects it has never cast off its colonial mantle, a city that remains staunchly conservative and deeply proud of its Spanish colonial traditions. During the terror years, the Shining Path and Túpac Amaru never gained a foothold here. And it's said that Peru's economic renaissance in recent years is largely fueled by Arequipa's enterprising entrepreneurs.

Pizarro established the city in 1540 on the banks of the Río Chili, a lush area already occupied by Inca farmers. He christened his new outpost Villa Hermosa, but the old Quechua name refused to fade — *ari quipay*, which is supposed to mean "let's stay here." Which is probably what the Inca's said when they first stumbled upon this green space amid the barrens. Since the late nineteenth century, Arequipa has been a center of right-wing political power that supported numerous coup d'états and launched the careers of several prominent military dictators (including Belaúnde). Family ties are still important here, the sort of place that values blood lines.

Since 1540 the city has endured 12 major earthquakes. But with so many buildings constructed of white volcanic stone, much of the bygone architecture remains, especially around the Plaza de Armas and a wealthy suburb called Yanahuara. In fact, Arequipa is often called the "White City" because of its favorite building stone. Despite increased urbanization you can still find alfalfa and onion fields along the Río Chili, which splits the city into eastern and western halves.

Arequipa has grown into Peru's second largest city, with more than one and a half million people. In recent years vast shanty-towns have taken shape on the outskirts, populated mostly by displaced Indian farmers from the highlands. Needless to say, this has created friction with the old-time residents, most of them European in origin, who view residents of the *pueblos jovenes* as parasites and freeloaders.

GENERAL INFORMATION

The **tourist office** ((54) 211021, extension 30, is situated on the south side of the Plaza de Armas at Portal de la Municipalidad 112. Open Monday to Friday 8 AM to 4 PM.

The **Bolivian Consulate** is on the fourth floor of Galerías Gamesa commercial center at Jirón Mercaderes 212. Open Monday to Friday 9 AM to 2 PM. The staff is not especially helpful.

Anyone wishing to ship things home from Arequipa will find the **DHL/Western Union** office ((54) 234288 at Santa Catalina 115.

WHAT TO SEE AND DO

Arequipa's **Plaza de Armas** is one of the cleanest and safest central squares in all of Peru. And also one of the most picturesque, especially when the air is crystal clear and you can see El Misti volcano towering above the plaza's white-stone cathedral. Every Sunday morning at 11 AM, thousands of residents gather in the square for a flag-raising ceremony, military band concert, and parade of local school, church, and union groups, a colorful ceremony that spills over into the surrounding streets.

The massive **cathedral** takes up the entire eastern flank of the plaza, essentially a nineteenth-century design that replaced the original seventeenth-century cathedral that was destroyed by an earthquake. Despite the imposing façade, the interior is something of a disappointment, much less ornate than most Peruvian churches and reflective of the austere times when the church was rebuilt. Several of the statues at the rear of the cathedral are noteworthy including the Virgin of the Sighs in her white wedding dress and Beata Ana de Los Angeles, a nun from Santa Catalina Monastery who was beatified by Pope John Paul II when he visited Arequipa in 1990.

But that's not to say that Arequipa doesn't have its baroque churches. **La Compañía**, perched on the southeast corner of the plaza, was the city's original Jesuit church (1698), fashioned from white volcanic stone with an ornate façade. Jesuit-founder Saint Ignatius of Loyola features in a statue above the main altar while the niche to the left of the altar harbors the church's most impressive artwork, the massive *Retablo de los Fundadores*. The adjacent Chapel of Saint Ignatius boasts original oil paintings by Bernardo Bitti and other masters of the Cusco School as well as a baptismal font hewn from a single piece of *piedra de Huamanga* (a hard white stone found around Ayacucho). The chapel is closed on Sunday. Before leaving the main church, take note of the Virgin of the Macarena shrine near the rear of the church and the fully clothed Jesús Cautivo behind glass.

market. On the west side of the plaza is the **City History Museum**, housed in the old Sala Naval dating from 1804. It contains various exhibits on local history, archeology, architecture, and natural history including many photos of bygone Arequipa. It is closed Saturday and Sunday and there is an admission fee.

Farther north, on the outskirts of the downtown area, lies **Plaza San Lazaro**, a nice little Belle Époque square at the top of Avenida Santa Catalina. Its green wrought-iron benches offer superb views of the snow-

Another ornate construction is **Santo Domingo Church**, two blocks east of the plaza via Calle Moran, which boasts wonderful brick arches and stone domes like the famous Mesquita mosque in Córdoba, Spain. Notice the hundreds of silver *milagros* (small votive offerings) on the wall to the left of main alter. The cloisters around the back are still part of an active Dominican monastery.

Yet another impressive structure is the sixteenth-century **San Francisco Church** on Calle Melgar with its solid silver altar. Around the right side of the church are the cloisters and a small chapel. **Plazuela de San Francisco** is one of the city's more pleasant squares, a leafy quad with jacaranda trees, a statue of Saint Francis, and a hippie flea

capped volcanoes towering over Arequipa. **Barrio San Lazaro** beyond the plaza features narrow lanes and whitewashed houses reminiscent of southern Spain.

Across Puente Grau, on the western banks of the Río Chili, is **Yanahuara** district, renowned for both its architecture and its leafy plazas. The main square in front of the town hall features towering palm trees, fountains, lawns, and benches to snooze away the afternoon. The adjacent **mirador** affords wonderful views of the volcanoes and central Arequipa. **Yanahuara Church** (1783) has amazing goldleaf sanctuaries on either side of the nave, impressive wrought-iron chandeliers,

Arequipa's Plaza de Armas is one of the most picturesque squares in all of Peru.

and a glass coffin with a Christ figure that is paraded outside on holy days. Also on the west side of the river is **La Recoleta Monastery**, a Franciscan enclave constructed in 1648 that contains one of Peru's most important libraries (many historical books and maps) and a collection of Amazon artifacts assembled by Catholic missionaries. It is closed on Sunday and charges admission.

Santa Catalina Monastery

Arequipa's premier tourist attraction and most astounding cultural treasure is Santa

Catalina Monastery, a veritable "city within a city," located three blocks north of the Plaza de Armas (via Calle Santa Catalina). It's actually a convent rather than a monastery, opened in 1580 as an exclusive retreat for nuns from wealthy colonial families. It was completely shut off from the world until 1970 when local authorities insisted that the monastery comply with local building codes including running water and electricity. In order to pay for the improvements, the nuns threw open their doors to tourism. But don't expect to see the two dozen that remain — they are still secluded behind closed doors in an off-limits area.

Prior to the late nineteenth century, almost medieval conditions persisted in Santa

Catalina. In order for a young woman to enter the convent her family had pay a dowry of a thousand silver coins. She was allowed to bring in 25 household and personal items that would be used during her stay. But lest you think they lived a tough life, consider the fact that the items often included expensive furnishings, artwork, and china sets. Nuns were also allowed to have personal servants, as many as two or three, paid for by their families.

The one-hour guided tour takes in most of the important sights inside the walls including the Courtyard of Silence where teenage novices lived for the first year, the Cloister of the Orange Trees with its vivid murals representing the exorcism of Saint Ignatius, Zubaran Sala with its collection of antique dowry items, the Bañera where the nuns took their holy baths, and various "cells" where they lived in secluded luxury.

Santa Catalina is open daily from 9 AM to 5 PM with last entry at 4 PM. Admission is S/12 including the obligatory guided tour. Once the tour is complete you are free to wander around the grounds on your own. Tours are available in Spanish, English, French, German, and Italian. The guides are superb and a small tip is common. The monastery has a small café with snacks and drinks.

SHOPPING

With good prices, pleasant shops, and a wide variety of merchandise Arequipa is one of the better cities in Peru for souvenir shopping.

The Cloisters (Claustros de la Compañía), at General Moran 118 in central Arequipa, is an old Jesuit compound converted into an upmarket arts and crafts center with about two dozen shops selling alpaca, silver, T-shirts, and other locally made items. **Anselmo's Baby Alpaca** and **El Dorado Baby Alpaca** both carry a wide variety of alpaca fashion including scarves, sweaters, vests, shawls, and wall hangings. Anselmo's Baby Alpaca has another outlet at Pasaje Catedral 117 behind the cathedral. The merchandise is slightly different including one of the best T-shirt selections you will find anywhere in Peru, and good postcards too. **Arte Peru** specializes in antique items including jewelry, religious icons, and ceramics. **Paulet Joyas Peruanas (** (54) 287786, carries a wide variety of silver picture frames and jewelry including interesting broaches and earrings patterned after the Nazca Lines.

The city's largest collection of arts and crafts stalls is the **Fundo el Fierro** in the cobblestone courtyard opposite San Francisco church. About 40 vendors carry a wide variety of items including sweaters, wall hangings, T-shirts, jewelry, ceramics, and small silver trinkets. Outside, on the church steps, a small **flea market** takes shape every day with mostly jewelry for sale.

Several interesting antique shops are found in close proximity to San Francisco church. **Curiosidades (** (54) 232703, Zela 207, is a tiny shop crammed full of all kinds of precious and semiprecious items such as *retablos, milagros* (small silver offerings), old postcards and photos, watches, religious icons, vases and lamps, furniture, and weapons. Nearby is **Galería de Arte Jerico (** (54) 228893 or (54) 215093 at Santa Catalina 400. The selection here runs the gamut from ceramics, silver, and gramophones to furniture, paintings, and even a complete suit of armor.

Arequipa's most convenient supermarket is **El Super** on the south side of Plaza de Armas near the municipal tourist office.

WHERE TO STAY

Expensive

On the outskirts of downtown Arequipa is the superb **Hotel Libertador (** (54) 215110 FAX (54) 241933 E-MAIL www.libertador .com.pe, Plaza Bolívar opposite Selva Alegra Park. Built in 1940, the place is like a sprawling Spanish colonial villa with a profusion of arches, wrought-iron windows, and a large garden area in the back with a swimming pool and lawn. The food at Restaurant Los Robles is among the best in the city and the hotel bar offers a happy hour from 7 PM to 9 PM each evening (two pisco sours for the price of one!). Best of all were the front-desk staff, who went out of their way to meet my most eccentric needs.

Closer to the center of town is the **Portman Hotel (** (54) 215530 FAX (54) 234374, Portal de Flores 116 on the Plaza de Armas. The Portman is well-run establishment, but also fairly dull, with little of the Spanish colonial atmosphere that permeates the rest of Arequipa. Some rooms overlook the square.

Moderate

Anyone who enjoys the monastic atmosphere of Santa Catalina should stay at **La Hosteria (** (54) 289269 FAX (54) 281779, Bolívar 405. Situated in a wonderful old Spanish-colonial mansion, the hotel features marvelous touches like skylights in the bathrooms,

suites with stone fireplaces, an upstairs lounge with big overstuffed sofas, and a central courtyard smothered in bougainvillea. Many rooms boast reproduction antique furnishings and white volcanic stone walls.

A slight monastic air also pervades the **Hotel Maison Plaza (** (54) 218929 FAX 218931, Portal de San Agustín 143 on the Plaza de Armas. The lobby sports a vaulted ceiling of white volcanic stone and religious paintings, while the guest rooms are comfortable and much quieter than in other hotels that overlook the plaza. They come equipped with cable television, telephone, and minibar.

OPPOSITE: Santa Catalina was once a retreat for nuns from wealthy colonial families. ABOVE: La Compañía is built from white volcanic stone.

Inexpensive

My favorite budget hotel in Arequipa and one of the best-value hotels in all of Peru is **La Casa de mi Abuela** ((54) 241206 FAX (54) 242761, Calle Jerusalén 606. I can't say enough good things about this place. It has nearly everything you need in a small hotel including expansive gardens, a swimming pool, a playground, laundry service, secure parking, a games room, a library with Internet connection, and proximity to most of the city's major tourist attractions. Rooms come with private bath, hot water, minibars, and television; there are also bungalows with kitchenettes. And you've got to love that old Fiat van that now serves as a garden ornament.

Arequipa's best backpacker abode is **Hostal Regis**, Ugarte 202. Situated on the second floor of a lovely old mansion, for about US$5 the Regis features a sunny roof garden, laundry service, and safe deposit boxes. Rooms are basic but clean. Shared baths occasionally have hot water. However it can get a bit noisy at times with all the traffic outside.

Also offering great value for money is **Santa Catalina Hostal**, Santa Catalina 500. The place is clean and friendly; rooms come with private bath and hot water. There's a pleasant central courtyard where you can read or relax and a roof terrace where you can hang your laundry. Another favorite with shoestring travelers is **Tambo Viejo Hostal** ((54) 288195 FAX (54) 284747, Malecón Socabaya 107 near the train station. The people behind the front desk speak English. There is a coffee shop on the ground floor, room service is available, as is laundry service, and hot water in the bathrooms.

Down on the Plaza de Armas is the clean and comfortable **La Portada del Mirador Hostal** ((54) 211539, Portal de Flores 102, which offers rooms with private bath and hot water for US$5.

WHERE TO EAT

Moderate

The atmosphere isn't much to write home about, but **Restaurant Los Robles** ((54) 215110, in the Hotel Libertador, Plaza Bolívar in Selva Alegre, offers perhaps the best mix of local and international cuisine in all of Arequipa.

There a several good "Creole" restaurants in suburban districts including **Tradición Arequipena** ((54) 426467 or (54) 242385, Avenida Dolores 111 in Paucarpata; and **La Cantarilla** ((54) 251515, Tahuaycani 106 in Sachaca. My personal favorite is **Sol de Mayo** ((54) 254148, Calle Jerusalén 207 in Yanahuara, a series of adobe pavilions set around a leafy central courtyard with cactus plants and eucalyptus trees. All three offer a wide range of local dishes including *rocoto relleno* (stuffed bell peppers), *ocopa arequipena* (boiled potato slices in a slightly spicy cheese sauce), and *cuy chactado* (roast guinea pig). These restaurants tend to attract more of a lunch crowd and usually close in the early evening.

Seafood is also popular in Arequipa. **Mixto's Cebichería**, at Pasaje Catedral 115 offers myriad seafood dishes as well as chicken, meat, and pasta selections. You might try the fried sea bass in shrimp sauce or the delicious shellfish *empanadas*. Dine indoors or the terrace overlooking a whitestone cathedral passage.

Continuing the seafood theme is **Aji Limón Cebichería**, Plaza San Francisco 300, a tiny place with only five tables that allegedly serves the best marinated raw fish south of Lima. The cozy little **La Casita de José Antonio Cebichería** ((54) 289327, Plaza San Francisco 401, offers *ceviche* and other fascinating seafood dishes like *machitas a la criola* (pink clams in a Peruvian sauce), *corvina de la macho* (sea bass in a hearty seafood sauce), *tortilla de erizo* (sea urchin omelet), and *parihuela* (seafood casserole).

Inexpensive

Arequipa is one of Peru's best cities for bargain restaurants with good food. There are a number in the downtown area including **Le Bistrot** ((54) 215579 or (54) 281770, Santa Catalina 208 in the Alliance Française compound, offers a wide variety of mouth-watering dinner and dessert crêpes including asparagus and ham, mozzarella and spinach, strawberry, and chocolate, as well as baguette sandwiches, chocolate *gâteaux*, and myriad coffee drinks. The owners also offer magazines and board games for the pleasure of patrons, making it the kind of place where you can lounge all day if your heart desires.

Anyone browsing the ancient San Lazaro neighborhood should duck into **El Conquistador Picantería** ((54) 286009, Bayoneta 106, for a quick snack or a jug of their savory homemade sangria. This place is *very* local with a menu that includes pork's head salad, pork pies, stuffed green peppers, and *caldo blanco* soup.

Another good bet is **Petit Restaurant** at San Fernando 129, a cozy café with lots of wood paneling and a menu that includes both coffees and snacks. If you're in the mood for Mexican, duck into **Snack Tenampa**, Pasaje

remaining after the ceremony and parade in the plaza.

NIGHTLIFE

In keeping with its staid image, Arequipa is not a wild and crazy town after dark. But there are a couple of places where you can let your hair down. My top choice for traditional Peruvian music is **Las Quenas** ((54) 281115 or (54) 215468, Santa Catalina 302, opposite the monastery entrance. This is the city's best *peña* with music that ranges from

Catedral 108. The menu includes burritos, enchiladas, and tacos. Just around the corner is **Restaurant Central Garden** ((54) 284318, Plaza San Francisco 127, with a good local menu and a flashy decor that features mirrors and plastic flowers. **Restaurant Govinda**, at Calle Jerusalén 500-A, serves up the same tasty vegetarian fare as its sister restaurant in Lima.

Half a dozen cheap eateries fill the balcony above the Portal San Agustín on the west side of the Plaza de Armas including **Tuturutu** and **Qosqo**. All offer roughly the same fare: Peruvian specialties and barely recognizable versions of European and American food. There is usually a rowdy Sunday afternoon lunch crowd of Peruvians

Andean flute bands to Creole guitar masters. The bartender blends up some pretty mean drinks including pisco sours, cuba libres, and caiparinas. There is music from 8 PM Monday to Saturday.

Another hot spot for local tunes is **La Troica** ((54) 225690, Calle Jerusalén 522-A, which showcases both Afro-Peruvian and Latin American music. It is open Monday to Saturday from 7 PM. The **Sumptuous Disco Pub**, in the rear courtyard of The Cloisters at General Moran 118, swings on Friday and Saturday nights to the house DJ. If you're in the mood for a cold beer and conversation try **Pub Tenzaro**, at Melgar 119,

A Spanish church in the Colca Valley.

which offers darts, backgammon, and rock music.

How to Get There

Arequipa is 1,020 km (632 miles) south of Lima and 400 km (248 miles) north of Tacna via the Pan-American Highway. There is frequent bus and *colectivo* service from both cities, as well as from Moquegua and Nazca. There is also bus service to and from Cusco, Juliaca, and Puno across the *altiplano*, but the roads are unpaved and the journey long and

bumpy. El Niño storms wiped out the main road between Arequipa and Puno in 1998. The city-to-city journey usually takes six hours, but with the washouts I had to endure a 14-hour marathon along various detours.

As the air travel hub of southern Peru, the city can also be reached by plane. Several daily services on AeroContinente and AeroPeru connect Arequipa with Lima, Cusco, Juliaca (Puno), and Tacna. The flight from Lima is about one hour; the flight from Cusco about 30 minutes, the flights from Tacna and Juliaca about 20 minutes.

Yet another way to reach the city is via the Southern Railroad, which stretches from Juliaca and Puno across the *altiplano* to

Arequipa. It runs twice a week (Sunday and Wednesday) departing Puno at 10 PM with 6:30 AM arrival in Arequipa. The return service departs Arequipa at 9 PM and arrives in Puno at around 8 AM the following morning. The schedule is erratic; check at the train station in Lima, or the stations in Arequipa, Puno or Juliaca, to confirm the current timetable. First-class, "Pullman" fare is S/30 per person, second-class *económico* fare is S/18.50 per person.

At Juliaca you can transfer to the Cusco train, a journey that takes another 10 hours. The train from Arequipa arrives in Juliaca around 6 AM. Disembark and wait for the northbound Cusco train which should arrive from Puno around 9 AM.

COLCA CANYON

As one of Peru's most outstanding natural attractions, Colca Canyon has gained its fair share of tourism over the past decade. Peruvians claim this is the world's deepest canyon, a vertical drop of roughly one kilometer (slightly over half a mile) from rim to river. Truth be told, it's far less impressive at first sight than the Grand Canyon or Mexico's Copper Canyon because Colca is basically monotone — a giant brown slash in the ground. With Colca you have to catch the right views at the right time. The canyon is best seen in the early morning when it's often filled with low clouds or fog, or at sunset, when auburn light filters up from the west. The name derives from the *colcas* or stone warehouses used by prehistoric Indians to store grain for the villages along the canyon walls.

Most tourist services are along the south rim, especially in **Chivay**, which sports several hotels and restaurants. A fairly good road links Chivay with other villages along the south rim including Yanque, Achoma, Maca, and Pinchollo. Many of these towns have ancient colonial churches made from white volcanic stone and most of the residents are Collagua Indians whose ancestors have dwelt along the canyon rim for more than 2,000 years.

There are plenty of ways to enjoy the canyon. One of the most popular is an excursion to **Cruz del Condor**, a windy viewpoint between Pinchollo and Cabanaconde villages

where condors like to congregate, apparently preferring dusk and dawn; but they can appear at any time of day and are sometimes absent during the alleged peak periods. Even with no giant bird sighting, the view from here—1,200 m (nearly 4,000 ft) straight down into the canyon — is simply breathtaking.

Other ways to explore the canyon include whitewater rafting and hiking. Rafting on the **Río Colca** is only possible between December and March; trips can be arranged through travel agencies in Arequipa. As many of the paths are poorly marked, hikers should only venture into this vast, arid wilderness with a local escort. One experienced guide is Carlos Zarate who lives in Arequipa ((54) 263107. He charges roughly US$30 per day plus expenses.

Most people explore Colca Canyon on one- and two-day package tours out of Arequipa. These tours, which include overnight accommodation and meals, run between US$21 and US$35 per person. Among the Arequipa-based operators are Santa Catalina Tours ((54) 216994 or (54) 215705 and Colonial Tours. Santa Catalina charges US$21 for a two-day trip that includes one night of simple accommodation in Chivay, all meals, a folklore show, and a stop at the condor cross. Colonial charges US$25 for a two-day tour with better food and rooms that includes a stop at a hot springs.

OPPOSITE: An Indian woman from the oasis farmlands around Arequipa. ABOVE: Achoma explodes with color each year during the Festival of the Three Wise Men.

Several other natural wonders lie directly west of Colca Canyon, although they are difficult to reach without your own four-wheel-drive transportation.

The **Valley of the Volcanoes** is a 65-km (40-mile) trench scarred with 80 extinct cinder cones and craters, more like the surface of Mars than something you'd expect to find on planet Earth. Overlooking the valley is the still active **Coropuna Volcano**, highest in Peru and tenth tallest in the Andes. **Andagua** village sits amid all this geologic upheaval. Simple lodging and meals are available. It can be reached by daily bus from Arequipa, a journey that takes roughly half a day. Make sure you've got a good map if you explore the volcanic zone on your own.

Much closer to Arequipa are the **Toro Muerto** ("Dead Bull") petroglyphs in the Río Majes valley near Corire village. Prehistoric people scrawled pictures of animals, dancers, and geometric patterns on hundreds of volcanic rocks scattered across the desert. There is a daily bus from Arequipa to Corire and then a two-hour walk into the wilderness before you reach the first petroglyphs.

Travel agencies in Arequipa can organize transportation and guides to both the Valley of the Volcanoes and Toro Muerto.

WHERE TO STAY

Relax in a hot springs while viewing the canyon at **Fundo Puye Lodge** ((54) 245199

FAX (54) 242088 E-MAIL colcalodge@grupoinca .com, in Llanque, is a brand new wilderness resort tucked into the upper reaches of Colca Canyon, not far from Chivay. The thatched-roof bungalows are clean and comfortable, with terraces that overlook the river and springs. Horseback riding through the nearby canyon-lands can be arranged through the front desk.

Nearby is another good small hotel, **El Parador del Colca** ((54) 288440 FAX (54) 218608, Fundo Curina in Llanque. It features seven suites and one of the better restaurants in the canyon region.

Chivay's best accommodation is the **Rumi Llaqta** (/FAX (54) 521098 E-MAIL rumillaktacolca@lared, Calle Huayna Capac.

Rooms feature private baths with hot water, and room service is available from the hotel's restaurant.

Hostal Anita ((54) 210231, extension 14 (in Chivay), or (54) 213114 (in Arequipa), on the Plaza de Armas in the heart of Chivay, is a modest *hostal* offering rooms with shared bath and hot water. Other budget inns in Chivay including the **Hostal Plaza** on the Plaza de Armas, the **Hostal Colca** at Calle Salaverry 307, and the **Pousada del Inca** at Calle Salaverry 323. Most do not have private baths or hot water, but the prices are hard to beat.

Stone farm terraces in the Colca Valley.

SOUTH FROM AREQUIPA

The Pan-American Highway continues south from Arequipa toward the Peru–Chile frontier, a journey of nearly 400 km (250 miles). Along the way are two major cities, Tacna and Moquegua, both of them nearly overwhelmed by the surrounding desert. Neither have much in the way of tourist appeal, but if you're on your way to Chile you could find yourself with an overnight stay or a few hours to kill in either city.

suyo, and a small ridge called Cerro Baúl at the north end of Jirón Lima which provides an excellent panorama of the mud-brick skyline.

Where to Stay

Without a doubt the best place to overnight is the **Hotel El Mirador** ((54) 761765 FAX (54) 761895, Alto de la Villa, on the outskirts of town. It offers 16 rooms and 12 bungalows, plus a restaurant with a local and international menu. Other features include a swimming pool and a handball court.

MOQUEGUA

There probably wouldn't even be a city here — and certainly not one with more than 10,000 souls — were it not for the nearby copper mines and the presence of the Río Moquegua which dribbles through on its intermittent journey to the coast. Farming and highway-related activities (gas stations, garages, and such) maintain the rest of the population.

Despite a glaring lack of visitors, Moquegua maintains a small **tourist office** ((54) 762236 at Jirón Callao 435. They've got information in local sights including the Church of Santo Domingo, a new archeological collection called the Museo Conti-

There are more than a dozen small budget hotels including **Hostal Comercio** on Calle Moquegua (one block north of the Plaza de Armas) and **Hostal Los Limoneros** on Jirón Lima (two blocks west of the plaza).

How to Get There

Moquegua is roughly 220 km (136 miles) southeast of Arequipa and 150 km (100 miles) northwest of Tacna. There are daily bus and *colectivo* services to both cities.

TACNA

Spreading its wings across the desert, Tacna is a much larger city than Moquegua. As the primary gateway to Chile, in many respects it has more in common with Peru's southern neighbor than with the jungles of Iquitos or the Inca heritage of Cusco. In fact, Tacna was part of Chile from 1880 (when Peru lost the War of the Pacific) until 1929 when the local populous decided to vote their way back into Peruvian hands.

For travelers, Tacna is mostly a way station on the road to Chile, but there are a few worthwhile sights. Foremost is the **cathedral**, designed by the French architect and engineer Gustave Eiffel in the 1870s but not completed until 1929. Eiffel also designed the

bronze fountain in the plaza outside. Train buffs should make a beeline for the **Museo Ferroviario** in the Train Station which features antique engines and rolling stock, while anyone with an interest in the War of the Pacific should duck into the **Casa de Cultura** on Jirón Bolívar, two blocks south of the Plaza de Armas.

Where to Stay

Top of the heap is the **Gran Hotel Tacna** ((54) 724193 FAX (54) 722015, Avenida Bolognesi 300, which offers 85 rooms and several suites. It features a fine restaurant with local and international dishes, as well as a bar with ice-cold beer, a swimming pool, tennis courts, and a leafy garden.

Another good bet in the moderate category is the **Camino Real Hotel** ((54) 713451 or (54) 721891 FAX (54) 726433 or (54) 711588, San Martín 855, on the eastern outskirts of downtown Tacna. The clean and quiet rooms come equipped with minibar and television. If you're on a tight budget try **Las Lidos Hotel**, at San Martín 876, which is comfortable, clean, and cheap. Rooms have private bath and hot water.

How to Get There

Tacna is about 370 km (230 miles) south of Arequipa and 150 km (100 miles) from Moquegua along the Pan-American Highway. There are daily bus and *colectivo* services from both cities.

You can also fly from Arequipa on Aero-Peru or AeroContinente, daily services that take about 20 minutes from runway to runway. Cheap airfares (US$40) can be purchased from travel agents around the Plaza de Armas in Arequipa.

GOING TO CHILE

About 40 km (25 miles) south of Tacna, the international border is open daily from 9 AM to 10 PM, with no crossing in the middle of the night.

A very slow and ancient train rumbles three times daily between Tacna and Arica, the northernmost Chilean town, about 25 km (15 miles) south of the border. While this is the cheapest way to travel across the frontier, it's definitely the slowest and often the most frustrating.

Most people take a bus or *colectivo* from Tacna's Terminal Terrestre to the border, a journey of about one hour. Expect to pay S/10 (including the terminal tax) for a *colectivo* seat and slightly less for the bus journey. Coming up from Chile, the bus ride from Arica to Tacna will cost you about 900 Chilean pesos.

OPPOSITE: Desert copper mine near Arequipa. ABOVE: The Colca Valley offers a respite from the relentless desert.

The North Coast

COMPARED TO THE WELL-BEATEN SOUTH COAST and the southern Andes, Peru's northern reaches are almost virgin territory when it comes to tourism. It's not uncommon to go for days without seeing another overseas traveler save the occasional backpacker. You might feel a bit lonely at times, but there are distinct advantages: you rarely need hotel or restaurant reservations, public transportation is not crowded, and you might find that you have a famous ruin or an intriguing museum all to yourself.

Almost a mirror image of the south coast, the north is dominated by unrelenting desert, vast stretches of arid wilderness — stony plains, sand dunes, stark mountains — divided by fertile river valleys. These valleys, fed by snow in the Cordillera Blanca and other lofty outriders of the Andes, are oases for both agriculture and civilization, the location of huge plantations and most of the north's largest cities — Trujillo, Piura, and Chiclayo.

From an archaeological standpoint, the north is Peru's richest region, far more important in the overall scheme of things than the Cusco area, which reached its apex near the end of the pre-Columbian era. Agriculture took root in the north nearly seven thousand years ago, around the same time as similar cultures were developing in the Nile Valley and Mesopotamia. The region's early urban societies — Chavín and Sechín — began to evolve around 1200 BC, before the advent of the Greek city states or the Roman Empire. Ancient Peruvian artistic expression

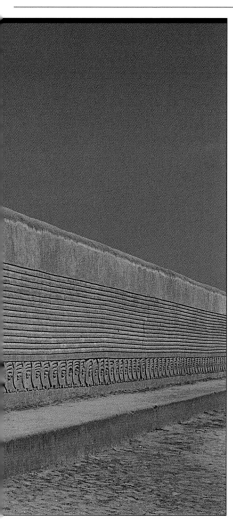

of the capital. Along this stretch is a fascinating coastal ecosystem protected within the confines of **Lomas de Lachay National Reserve**. Often shrouded in thick coastal fog, the *lomas* are gently rounded hills that tower around 600 m (1,800 ft) above sea level, covered in dune grass and wild flowers at lower elevations, bushes and small trees on the upper reaches. The fog nourishes their growth, and in turn this lush vegetation supports rich bird and mammal life including parrots, hummingbirds, and deer. You can explore the park on your own along various hiking trails or join a guided tour offered by adventure travel outfits in Lima.

Continuing north, the highway passes through the **Supe Valley**, which was of little interest until the discovery of **Caral** in early 1998. Perched on an alluvial terrace above the Río Supe 22 km (15 miles) east of Barranca, Caral is believed to date from at least 2500 BC, which would make it the oldest urban civilization in South America and parallel to the development of early Mesopotamian cultures. Among the structures that have been uncovered are temples, pyramids, an eternal flame pit and adobe homes, leading archaeologists to surmise that Caral was a sacred city ruled by priests.

Just north of Barranca — and easily seen from the Pan-American Highway — is the giant **Fortress of Paramonga**. Captured by the Incas in the late fifteenth century, this huge adobe bastion with seven defensive walls was constructed by the Chimú people to mark the southern boundary of their empire. It probably doubled as a place of worship, perhaps dedicated to sun worship given the fact that it overlooks the sea. The fortress is open daily and admission includes a visit to the small site museum.

reached its apex with the Moche culture that prevailed along the north coast during the first millennium AD and the Chan Chan culture that just predated the Incas.

The north is for travelers who enjoy solitude: vast desert spaces, empty beaches, remote ruins, and a style of life that seems far removed from the twentieth century — not everyone's cup of tea. But then again, those of us who cherish the north would rather have it that way.

NORTH FROM LIMA

The Pan-American Highway provides a quick and convenient exit from Lima, a wonderful four-lane divided highway as far north as Huacho, 150 km (100 miles) north

CASMA

There are a lot of worthwhile sights on the long stretch of desert coast between Lima and Trujillo, but the only place with a nucleus of tourist facilities is the town of Casma, 370 km (230 miles) north of Lima on the Pan-American Highway. Founded in 1751 by Spanish priest Bach Fernando de Castro, Casma is

Chan Chan was the paramount achievement of the Chimu culture.

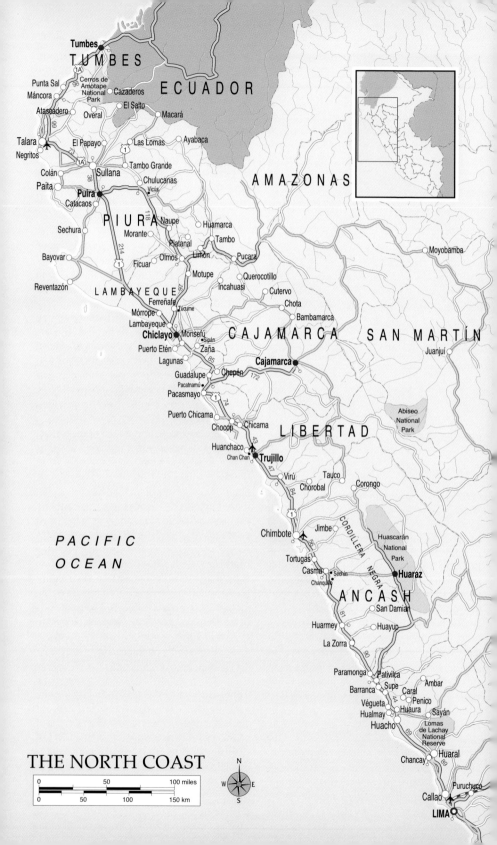

Tumbes

TUMBES

ECUADOR

Punta Sal
Máncora
Cerros de
Amotape
National
Park
Cazaderos
Atascadero
Overal
El Salto
Macará

Talara
El Papayo
Las Lomas
Ayabaca
Negritos

Colán
Sullana
Tambo Grande
Paita
Chulucanas
Vicús

Piura
Catacaos

PIURA
Naupe
Huamarca

Sechura
Morante
Tambo

Bayovar
Ficuar
Olmos
Limón
Pucara

Reventazón
Motupe
Incahuasi
Querocotillo

LAMBAYEQUE
Cutervo
Chota

Ferreñafe
Bambamarca

Mórrope
Túcume
Lambayeque

Chiclayo
Monsefú
Sipán
CAJAMARCA
SAN MARTÍN

Puerto Etén
Zaña
Juanjuí

Lagunas
Chepén
Cajamarca

Guadalupe
Pacatnamú
172

Pacasmayo

Abiseo
National
Park

Puerto Chicama

Chocop
Chicama
LIBERTAD

Huanchaco
Chan Chan
Trujillo

Virú
Tauco

Chorobal
Corongo

**PACIFIC
OCEAN**

Chimbote
Jimbe

Huascarán
National
Park

Tortugas

Casma
Sechin
Huaraz

Chanquillo

ANCASH

San Damian

Huarmey
Huayup

La Zorra

Paramonga
Pativilca
Ambar
Barranca
Supe
Caral
Véqueta
Penico
Hualmay
Huaura
Sayán

Huacho

Lomas
de Lachay
National
Reserve

Chancay
Huaral

Puruchuco

Callao

LIMA

THE NORTH COAST

| 0 | 50 | 100 miles |
| 0 | 50 | 100 | 150 km |

N
W E
S

AMAZONAS

called the "city of eternal sun" because of its pleasant weather and fine beaches.

Casma's municipal **tourist office** ((44) 711062 is situated on the Plaza de Armas. Local travel agencies that can help you explore the nearby ruins include **Sechín Tours** ((44) 711421, in the Centro Comercial Montecarlo on Avenida Nepeña, and **Tur-Juv Adventures** ((44) 711064. For a private guide contact the **Asociación de Guías de Turismo** ((44) 711116 or (44) 333344.

WHAT TO SEE AND DO

More than a dozen archeological sites dot the fertile river valley south of Casma including the temple complex of **Sechín**, one of the most important ruins on the north coast. Constructed around 750 BC, the outer walls are decorated with granite slabs bearing images of ancient warriors. There are several theories about what these portraits represent: most researchers feel they are prisoners of war, a concept boosted by the fact that many of them seem to be tortured and mutilated. But another theory suggests they may be celebrating a religious or victory rite — dancing around like dervishes in some sort of drug-induced trance.

On the mesa behind the temple is an even older sight called **Sechín Alto**, an immense U-shaped construction dating from around 1400 BC, possibly the genesis of the religious rituals and artistic styles that came to dominate this coast in subsequent centuries. A fine little **site museum** describes the various ruins found in this valley. Sechín, and other sites like Moxeke, were first excavated by Dr. Julia Tello in 1937. The site is open daily and there is an entrance fee.

Perched on a mighty hilltop above the Sechín Valley is the massive granite fortress of **Chanquillo**, with three concentric walls enclosing a central platform with two round towers. Little is known about the people who constructed it, but the bastion was probably built around 350 BC. It's considered the largest fortress of its kind along the entire South American coast, although it has never been clear if it was used for real warfare or just ritual battles. Chanquillo isn't easy to reach or find. Follow the Pan-American Highway 15 km (10 miles) south from Casma to a dirt

road on the left marked by three small red flags. Follow this road about two kilometers (one mile) due east into the desert until you see the rugged outline of the granite fort. There are no hours or admission fees.

Looking down from Chanquillo you can make out several other ruins in the desert including a palace complex and an unusual structure called the **Thirteen Towers** that may have been used for lunar worship or astronomy. Another unique archaeological site seen by few tourists is **Pampa de las Llamas-Moxeke**, which dates from around 1500 BC and is considered one of the earliest examples of urban planning in the Americas. The ruins consist of two large adobe pyramids and several mudbrick plazas, plus the remains of warehouses, offices and houses.

Ruins aside, Casma is also known for its beaches, long empty strands, and isolated coves. **La Gramita**, about 45 minutes south of Casma along the Pan-American Highway, offers pristine sand and fine surf, as well as a small fishing fleet. About one kilometer (half a mile) north of the beach is **Las Aldas**, a small ruin crowning a bluff above the sea. Dating from roughly 2000 BC, the site embraces four large plazas and a number of stone mounds that may have once been a temple.

WHERE TO STAY

The inexpensive **El Farol Inn** ((44) 711064 FAX (44) 712183, Avenida Túpac Amaru 450 in central Casma, has just about everything you need for an overnight stay on the road between Lima and Trujillo including rooms with private bath and hot water, a restaurant and bar, a playground and a swimming pool. There's also an expansive lawn shaded by huge mango trees. The entire compound is surrounded by a stout wall that gives it the feel of a Foreign Legion fort in the Sahara Desert. An even cheaper option is **Hostal Ernesto's** ((44) 711475, Avenida Garcilaso de la Vega 340.

WHERE TO EAT

Despite the snail-paced service, the outdoor restaurant at **El Farol** offers fairly good Peruvian fare including many fresh seafood dishes, as well as cold beer.

Restaurant Libertad ((44) 711309, Avenida Magdalena 519, offers regional specialties including duck *ceviche* and *picante de cuy* (guinea pig) as well as seafood and meat dishes. You can find a similar regional menu at **Los Pacaes** ((44) 711505 on Avenida Bolívar.

HOW TO GET THERE

Casma is 370 km (230 miles) north of Lima and 190 km (118 miles) south of Trujillo on the Pan-American Highway. Many buses and *colectivos* pass through Casma on their way to larger cities, but few have scheduled stops. If you want to disembark here, inform the driver ahead of time. As an alternative you can hop a *colectivo* to Chimbote, which offers much better connections to Lima and Trujillo. It's also possible to catch a bus from Huaraz to Casma via high mountain passes and a dirt road that winds down to the coast.

NORTH TO TRUJILLO

The desert picks up again north of Casma but it's not long before you come to **Tortugas**, a fine little beach resort that's just off the Pan-American Highway. Tortugas is set on a deep blue bay tucked between desert hills and shifting dunes. You can fish and snorkel along the shore, or hire one of the local boats for a sports fishing expedition into deeper waters. Even if you don't spend the night, you should detour into Tortugas for a taste of the local *ceviche*, which is my pick for the best along the entire north coast.

If you like the look of Tortugas and decide to linger there are several options. **Hotel El Farol** ((44) 711064, perched on rocks on the south side of the bay, is probably the best place to bed down for the night. Besides splendid sea views, the place features a playground, a restaurant, a bar, and ample parking. The hotel can help arrange boat and fishing trips. Two other small hotels you might consider are **Las Terrazas** ((1) 9649573 with private terraces and bay views, and **Hostal Gabriela** ((44) 711761 which offers discounts to anyone who wants to stay for a week or a month.

The local seafood is excellent, especially the *ceviche* at **La Cabaña Marina** restaurant, the first place on the right when you come

down from the Pan-American Highway. Other dining choices include **Restaurant Tortugas** next door and **Tono Restaurant de Playa** farther up the beach.

The next outpost of civilization is **Chimbote**, one of the largest cities in the north coast and probably the most repulsive city in all of Peru. You can literally smell Chimbote before you reach it, an overwhelming stench generated by the fishmeal and seafood processing plants that dominate this hardworking port. More than three-quarters of Peru's fishing industry is based here, and the population has grown by leaps and bounds in recent years. Chimbote is also graced by a steel mill, numerous dive bars and a thriving prostitution trade. In other words: avoid it at all cost. Unfortunately the Pan-American Highway runs right through the middle of town.

In the desert about 20 km (14 miles) north of Chimbote is a seldom-visited archaeological wonder called the **Great Wall of Peru**. Made from stone and adobe, the rampart was probably built around AD 900, although nobody knows for sure who built it.

The last stop before reaching Trujillo is the verdant Virú Valley where the sugar cane industry remains king. Giant irrigation schemes are taking shape in the desert both north and south of Virú, huge agricultural projects that are among the largest of their kind in the world.

TRUJILLO

With nearly a million inhabitants and a history that stretches back to early colonial times, Trujillo is the queen of the north. Founded in 1536 as a foil to Chan Chan, Pizarro named the new settlement after his birthplace in Spain. The Incas soon destroyed it, butchering most of the Spanish inhabitants. But Trujillo was rebuilt and became a thriving port-of-call for ships lugging the treasure of the Incas from Lima to Panama and thence onward to Spain.

More than any other major Peruvian city, Trujillo retains its colonial ambience and attitudes. The old Spanish families that still constitute the ruling class are a proud people who revel in bullfights and the spectacle of *caballos de paso* — high-stepping horses originally bred to traverse sandy wastelands but now used in ornate dressage competitions. For the traveler, Trujillo offers many riches including the fabulous ruins of Chan Chan, the funky beach resort of Huanchaco, and a wealth of Spanish colonial architecture.

Trujillo's most renowned festival is **Primavera**, which takes place a the start of spring each year, usually the last week of September and the first week of October. Festivities includes youth parades and religious processions, the coronation of the Primavera Queen at the Municipal Theatre, various concerts (including *peña*, classical, and rock), and plenty of *marinera* dancing, which is another local specialty. Activities reach a crescendo on the final weekend with a gala ball, a paso horse competition, and an outdoor extravaganza at Mansiche Stadium.

GENERAL INFORMATION

Trujillo's **tourist office** (run by the Tourist Police) is located at Jirón Independencia 630. You can also ask for information at the Tourist Police desk in the Municipalidad on the Plaza de Armas. The latter is open daily 9 AM to 5 PM.

Several local travel agencies offer city tours, visits to outlying archeological sights and private guide service. One of the best is **Guía Tours ₵** (44) 245170 FAX (44) 246353, Jirón Independencia 527. Open Monday to Friday from 9 AM to 1 PM and 4 PM to 8 PM, Saturday from 9 AM to 1 PM. Among the tours offered are Chan Chan, the Pyramids of the Sun and Moon, El Brujo, and the Chicama Valley.

AeroPeru ₵ (44) 242727 or (44) 234241 can be found at Jirón Pizarro 470 on the Plaza de Armas. **DHL/Western Union ₵** (44) 203689 is at Jirón Pizarro 356.

WHAT TO SEE AND DO

Like so many Peruvian cities, Trujillo's social, political and religious life swirls around the **Plaza de Armas**. With its glazed concrete, the plaza seems waxed and shined, and in fact this is one of the most tidy squares in Peru. The Soviet-style statue in the middle of the square depicts various battles of the Wars of Independence. The plaza is the haunt for shoeshine boys (don't pay more than one

sol for a shine), smooching students, and elderly photographers with box cameras. The plaza is packed on Sunday mornings for a flag raising ceremony at 10 AM that includes military marching bands, political speeches, and a community parade.

A number of impressive colonial structures are arrayed around the plaza, including the **Basilica Menor**, a seventeenth-century cathedral with a rather dour façade by Peruvian standards. The interior of the church is simple but effective with massive marble columns, crystal chandeliers, and

modest stained glass. The cathedral museum with religious keepsakes and old paintings is closed Sunday and there is an entrance fee. The plaza's north side is dominated by the **Hotel Libertador Trujillo** with its rusty colored façade and the attractive **Casa Bracamonte**, home of a charitable organization that looks after local cemeteries. Across the street is **La Compañía**, a small Jesuit church with an ochre façade, which is now used by Trujillo University for nonreligious functions. On the plaza's southern flank is the **Municipalidad** (City Hall) and the **Casa Urquiaga** — where Simón Bolívar stayed during his sojourn in Trujillo.

Trujillo's daily life still centers on the Plaza de Armas.

The downtown area boasts a number of colonial mansions that have been restored and/or converted to twentieth-century functions. **Casa Orbegoso**, at the corner of Jirón Orbegoso and Bolívar, is probably the most engaging, a sprawling villa filled with Spanish colonial furniture, paintings and decorative arts. The bathroom is especially noteworthy with its huge marble tubs and sylvan murals. Casa Orbegoso is owned by a local bank which pays for its upkeep and occasionally organizes private functions or public art exhibits. Evening concerts are sometimes staged in the courtyard. The house is closed Sunday and entrance is free.

Another splendid structure is **La Casa de Emancipación** at the corner of Jirón Pizarro and Gamarra, which doubles as a modern bank and a fascinating little museum. The library contains a scale model of sixteenth-century Trujillo complete with city walls and many of the churches that are standing today. There is also an exhibit on Bishop Baltazar Jaime Martinez Companon who commissioned an exhaustive tome on daily life in northern Peru in the seventeenth century including illustrations of farming, fiestas, and town life. And there is a small tribute to Trujillo-born poet Cesar Vallejo. The rear courtyard is a real haven of peace with its Moorish-style fountain. The house is closed Sunday and entrance is free.

At the other end of the same block is the **Palacio Iturregui** at Jirón Pizarro 688, an opulent nineteenth-century Republican-style mansion that now houses the exclusive Central Club. Besides being a retreat of the local ruling class, the club is involved in various philanthropic activities like sponsoring the 1998 Peruvian South Pole expedition. The house is open to the general public Monday to Friday from 8 AM to 11 AM only, admission is free.

On the northern outskirts of Trujillo, sequestered beneath a Mobil service station, is one of Peru's most unusual collections, the **Cassinelli Archeological Museum (** (44) 231801, Avenida Nicolás de Piérola 607. José Cassinelli started the collection 40 years ago and it now contains nearly 5,000 pieces, 2,000 of which are on display in this basement museum. The core of the collection is Moche ceramics, but there are also examples of pottery from various other ancient cultures including Inca, Nazca, Virú, Wari, Chimú, and Cajamarca. Some of the more intriguing pieces include Moche pots that seem to represent Negro and Chinese figures, and a large clay figure that's the spitting image of Jimmy Carter. There's also an assortment of ancient musical instruments, a small collection of Chimú silver, and a mummified newborn baby girl beneath a glass cover. Señor Cassinelli plans a five-story museum that would house his entire collection but he has yet to raise the funding for such an ambitious project. The museum is closed Sunday and there is an entrance fee.

Just up the Pan-American Highway from the gas station museum is **Huaca Arco Iris** in suburban Esperanza. This mudbrick pyramid — also called the Rainbow Temple because of its distinctive motif — was built around AD 1200 by the Chimú people and was probably once part of the Chan Chan metropolis. Since its excavation in 1963 it has been largely reconstructed, a good example of what a Chimú ceremonial complex must have looked like a thousand years ago.

On the western outskirts of Trujillo are the fabulous ruins of **Chan Chan**, one of the country's most important archeological sites. This was the capital of the Chimú Empire that thrived along the north coast from around AD 1100 to 1470, when the Inca armies swept down from the highlands and destroyed what was essentially a more advanced but less aggressive civilization. At its apex, Chan Chan supported more than 50,000 people spread across nine royal precincts, the largest and perhaps the richest metropolis in the Americas. Chimú artisans churned out pottery and gold work in great abundance. The surrounding valley was well irrigated: a bounty of food production. However by the time the conquistadors arrived in the 1530s, the city had been completely abandoned, and virtually ignored by the Incas.

Only one of the nine precincts has been restored — the **Tschudi Complex** — which offers a small but fascinating insight into ancient Chimú art, architecture, and religion. The central courtyard is surrounded by mudbrick friezes with geometric designs and zoomorphic figures including fish and rodents. Elsewhere in the complex are a royal necropolis, huge cistern, military barracks, and a highly unusual assembly room with 24 niche-like seats. A modern steel tower provides a panoramic view of the entire compound including the nearby Pacific Ocean. The ruins are open daily and there is an entrance fee. Note: your Chan Chan ticket is also valid for entrance to Huaca Esmeralda and Huaca Arco Iris on the same or following day.

The eight other Chan Chan compounds are open to the public, but they are unguarded and tourist muggings have been reported in

walk away across the desert. It's much smaller in size but has generated far more artifacts than its larger cousin. The frescoes here are especially noteworthy, retaining much of their original color. The ruins are open daily. There is an entrance fee to Huaca de la Luna.

WHERE TO STAY

Expensive

Trujillo's finest abode is the charming **Hotel Libertador** ((44) 232741 or (44) 244999

recent years. It's not recommended that you visit these areas without a local guide.

If you're not tired of visiting ruins after a day at Chan Chan, there are other important archaeological sights in the surrounding desert. **Huaca del Sol (Pyramid of the Sun)** and **Huaca de la Luna (Pyramid of the Moon)** sit almost side-by-side on the southern fringe of the city, remnants of the Moche culture that thrived along the north coast during the first millennium AD. The Huaca del Sol pyramid is the largest pre-Columbian structure in Peru, a massive adobe temple that rivals the Pyramids of Giza. Reaching a maximum height of 45 m (135 ft), an estimated 140 million bricks were used in its construction. The Huaca de la Luna is a short

FAX (44) 235641, Jirón Independencia 485. It's hard to beat the location — overlooking the Plaza de Armas in the town center — but the atmosphere is also captivating, a Spanish-style building that summons up the ambience of colonial mansions that once graced the square. A swimming pool with a small waterfall graces the courtyard. The 78 rooms include air conditioning, color television, minibar and safe-deposit box. Besides a fine restaurant downstairs (El Chalán) there is also 24-hour room service. If you happen to show up without a reservation, the front desk is not averse to negotiating a lower rate that puts your room in the moderate category.

Geometric designs in abode at Chan Chan, one of Peru's top archeological sites.

Moderate

The city has quite a few good moderate hotels but my favorite is **Los Conquistadores (** (44) 244505 or (44) 235917 FAX (44) 235917, Diego de Almagro 586, because of its central location and friendly staff. There's nothing especially fancy about most of the rooms, but they are clean and comfortable, equipped with television and minibar. The second floor restaurant serves a very good breakfast which is included in the price and the hotel has its own secure parking lot. You can negotiate a 10% discount of you're staying more than one night.

Inexpensive

The best of Trujillo's budget abodes is the brand new **Pullman Hotel (** (44) 203624 FAX (44) 205448, Jirón Pizarro 879. Situated on a pedestrian street near the Plazuela el Recreo, the Pullman features a sunny terrace and valet parking, and charges lower rates if you pay in cash.

The rucksack brigade flocks to the **Hotel Americano (** (44) 241361, Jirón Pizarro 764. Once the grandest hotel in Trujillo, the Americano has fallen upon bad times. But it still exudes a certain faded charm: elaborate wooden balconies, a huge lobby dripping in marble, and a vintage Royal typewriter perched on the front desk. You can get rooms with and without private bath.

WHERE TO EAT

Moderate

I have two favorite restaurants in Trujillo and I can never decide which is better because the food at both establishments is tasty and well priced. One is **Romano (** (44)

252251, Jirón Pizarro 747, which offers pasta with a dozen different tasty sauces including carbonara, alfredo, pescado and mushroom, plus a dozen different soups like garlic, vegetable, asparagus and borscht. The other is **El Mochica (** (44) 231944, Jirón Bolívar 462, which offers a wide selection of tasty Peruvian dishes at very reasonable prices. On weekend nights they have traditional Trujillo music and dancing in the back room.

Two other fine restaurants sit side-by-side in downtown Trujillo. **Austrias (** (44) 258100, Jirón Pizarro 741, attracts the older crowd on Friday and Saturday night, usually dressed to the nines, reflecting the fact that this is where Trujillo high society like to spend their cash. **De Marco (** (44) 234251, Jirón Pizarro 725, offers good Peruvian food and an expansive menu. But the real treat here is the dessert table — it's hard to resist the Black Forest cake.

Inexpensive

Plaza Pollería ((44) 262589 is a popular roast chicken restaurant on the corner of Plaza de Armas and Jirón Pizarro. **Amareto (** (44) 228845, Jirón Gamarra 368, is a nice little café with a pink façade and pleasant wooden tables which offers sandwiches, fruit juices, coffee, and other simple treats.

Also new is **Pizarrito**, at Jirón Pizarro 543 (opposite La Merced church), a nice little café set inside a gallery. The menu features sandwiches, yogurts, deserts, fresh juices, and breakfast. For a taste of the Orient try **Chifu El Rey**, Jirón Pizarro 890 on pedestrian street near the Plazuela el Recreo. There are several modest cafés and bars with outdoor tables on the plazuela including **El Rincón del Recreo** and **Las Tradiciones** for barbecued meat dishes.

HOW TO GET THERE

Trujillo is 560 km (347 miles) north of Lima and 200 km (124 miles) south of Chiclayo via the Pan-American Highway. There is frequent bus and *colectivo* service to and from the capital as well as to other cities in the north like Chiclayo, Chimbote, Cajamarca, and Piura. Driving time from Lima is about nine hours; from Chiclayo about three.

There is also daily airline service from Lima and other major cities including Piura, Chiclayo, and Iquitos. The primary carriers are AeroPeru and AeroContinente.

HUANCHACO

Huanchaco is Trujillo's spirited beach suburb, 15 km (10 miles) west of the city center and adjacent to the airport. It's like a whole different world out here, the realm of die-hard surfers and solitary fishermen who still set out to sea each morning astride their

abandon. Not exactly the lost world of the Chimú. But then again, the ancients probably never had this much fun.

WHERE TO STAY

My favorite seaside retreat is **Caballito de Totora Hostal** ((44) 461004, Avenida La Rivera 219 near the pier. Most rooms have terraces overlooking the beach, and there's a swimming pool and outdoor café. At the south end of the beach is **Hostal Bracamonte** ((44) 461162 FAX (44) 461266, Los Olivos 503,

sturdy *caballitos* (little horses): tiny boats made from locally grown totora reeds. This is perhaps the last place along the Peruvian coast where you can see traditional reed boats used on an almost daily basis.

Weekdays are best for surfing and beach-combing because there isn't much of a crowd. But weekends are best for people watching when there are thousands of people wandering up and down the seafront promenade and the little **wooden pier**. A small arts and crafts market sets up beneath tarps near the head of the pier, and vendors ply their wares along the strand — tropical fruits, ice cream, tacky key chains, you name it. The local **seafood restaurants** overflow with hungry customers and cold beer flows with reckless

with a swimming pool, restaurant, and bar. Next door is **Hostal El Ancla** ((44) 461030 or (44) 461327, Avenida La Rivera 101, which offers oceans views and hot water. However it can get a little noisy with traffic from the busy street outside.

Farther up the shore is the **Huanchaco International Hostal** ((44) 461272, Jirón Victor Larco 287, a huge yellow building that overlooks a wide, sandy beach. The biggest drawback is the fact that it's quite a walk to cafés or bars in town. It's also near the end of the airport runway. But this is the place to bunk down if you want nothing but endless sand.

OPPOSITE: Making a house from *caña brava* in the northern desert. ABOVE: Cabo Blanco near Talara is famed for both its sports and commercial fishing.

WHERE TO EAT

Cafés up and down the waterfront offer similar seafood fare. Among the standbys are the **Huanchaco Beach Restaurant**, Larco 602, which offers a breezy terrace on the second floor; and **Big Ben** ((44) 461378, Larco 832. There are several modest cafés around the Plaza de Armas, including the **Club Colonial**, at San Martín 801 and **Pizzas Tere** ((44) 461197, on Larco 280.

NORTH TO CHICLAYO

The lush **Chicama Valley** north of Trujillo is the realm of sugar cane plantations and haciendas where fighting bulls and *paso* horses are bred. **Puerto Chicama**, a fishing village and surfer haven, is 16 km (12 miles) off the Pan-American Highway. It's supposed to have the world's longest left-hand break, but surf conditions depend on the tides, the winds, and El Niño. The best beach for sunbathing is south of town, below the tall sandstone cliffs.

Another surfer hangout is **Pacasmayo**, about 100 km (62 miles) north of Trujillo along the Pan-American Highway. Unless you've brought your baggies and board, the only reason to linger in this area is a visit to the ancient city of **Pacatnamú** at the mouth of the Río Jecetepeque. Often called the City of Sanctuaries, the site was first developed around AD 350 by the Gallinazo people. It was later occupied by the Mochica and Chimú before falling into ruin.

If you find yourself in need of a bed in Pacasmayo try the **Hotel Pakatnamú** ((44) 522368 FAX (44) 523255, Malecón Grau 103, on the waterfront. This three-star abode is cheap but comfortable.

There are several interesting archaeological sites off the Pan-American Highway just south of Chiclayo. **San José de Moro** is an unassuming village where the tomb of a Moche high priestess was uncovered in the early 1990s, including artifacts that confirmed the existence of a human blood-drinking cult among the Moche hierarchy. **Zaña** presents the eerie ruins remains of a sixteenth-century Spanish colonial city called Santiago de Miraflores de Zaña, destroyed in 1720 by an El Niño flood and now nothing but a ghost town that is partially submerged in the shifting sands.

CHICLAYO

Barely overshadowed by Trujillo as the north's most important metropolis, Chiclayo is a wealthy modern city that lies at the crossroads of the Pan-American Highway and a major land route from the Peruvian Amazon. It flourishes on trade and transportation (and probably money laundering from drug-related activities). Chiclayo was hard-hit by the El Niño floods of 1997 and 1998. The big highway bridge across the Río Reque was wiped out and may not be replaced for some years.

GENERAL INFORMATION

As Chiclayo does not have a tourist office at the present time, the best source of local information is probably your hotel front desk. You can find the **tourist police** ((74) 236700, at Avenida Saenz Peña 820.

AeroPeru ((74) 233503 is at Avenida Balta 815; **AeroContinente** ((74) 209916 or (74) 209917 at Avenida San José 604. Vehicle rental is available from **Chiclayo Rent-A-Car** ((74) 229390 FAX (74) 237512, Avenida Grau 520 in the Santa Victoria district. The local **DHL/Western Union** agent is Tumi Tours at ((74) 225371, Avenida Elias Aguirre 576.

WHAT TO SEE AND DO

Chiclayo is much older than it looks at first glance, founded by Spanish colonial settlers in the mid-sixteenth century but overshadowed by nearby Lambayeque until fairly recently. Much of the city's old colonial heart has faded away in favor of modern steel-and-glass buildings. The Plaza de Armas is dominated by a baroque **cathedral**, somewhat modest by Peruvian standards. A much more attractive church is the **Basilica San Antonio** with its ochre-and-rust façade and double bell towers.

One of Chiclayo's strangest sights is the **Paseo Las Musas**, a leafy promenade decorated with mock Greek temples and statuary.

Popular with lovers and children, it's a good place to see how Chiclayo residents let their hair down. Also popular with locals is the **Parque de Diversiones** across the street from the Gran Hotel, a fun fair with rides, games, and Peruvian-style carnival food that's open until midnight on weekends and holiday eves.

The sprawling **Mercado Modelo** is north of the Plaza de Armas, a typical Peruvian municipal market dominated by fresh food and household goods. But over in the market's southeast corner (close to the intersection of Balta and Anca) is the fascinating **Shaman's Market**, several dozen stalls selling the various accoutrements of the shaman's trade in the Chiclayo region. There's a wide variety of weird merchandize including deer legs, snake skins and toucan beaks, crucifixes and voodoo dolls, bells and scented candles, statues of St. Anthony and Buddha, sulfur powder and fool's gold, aphrodisiacs and perfumes, and various hallucinogenic plants like the San Pedro cactus.

WHERE TO STAY

Moderate

The local version of the Hilton or Sheraton is the **Gran Hotel Chiclayo** ((74) 234911 FAX (74) 223961 or (74) 224031 E-MAIL granhotel@lima.business.com.pe WEB SITE www.business.com.pe/granhotel, Avenida Federico Villareal 115. Situated near the heart of downtown Chiclayo, the Gran is popular with visiting businessmen and archaeologists. The second-floor restaurant is expensive by local standards but does present a pretty good breakfast buffet. Other facilities include swimming pool, car rental, travel agency, bar, and casino in case you want to gamble your cash away. The rooms are a little austere, but the staff is friendly and eager to please.

The **Garza Hotel** ((74) 228172 or (74) 226098 FAX (74) 228171, Avenida Bolognesi 756, is another moderate choice, but nearly as grand as the Gran. The Garza does have a swimming pool, cable television, restaurant and bar, but its location in the bus station/colectivo area makes many of the rooms quite noisy.

Inexpensive

One of the better budget places is the **Hotel el Sol** ((74) 232120 FAX (74) 231070, Avenida Elias Aguirre 119, which features a swimming pool, as well as televisions in every room and private baths with hot water.

Other good bets in this category include the **Hotel America** ((74) 229305 FAX (74) 241627 at Avenida Luis Gonzales 943; the **Inca Hotel** ((74) 235931 FAX (74) 227651, Avenida Luis Gonzales 622; and **Sipán Hotel** ((74) 242564 FAX (74) 242408, Calle Virgilio Dall'Orso 150. Most rooms at these establishments feature private bath with hot water plus television.

There's a whole row of super-cheap hotels along Avenida Balta between the Mercado Modelo and the Plaza de Armas including the **Adriatico**, the **Cruz de Chalpon**, the **Chimú**, and the **Balta**. These places run towards the seedy. Most come without private bath, hot water or air conditioning (which is essential during Chiclayo's sweltering summer). But the rates are hard to beat.

WHERE TO EAT

Moderate

Chiclayo isn't known for its fine dining, but one of the better eateries is **El Mirador** restaurant at the Gran Hotel ((74) 234911, Avenida Frederico Villareal. The menu includes many northern specialties like *cabrito al horno* (roast goat), *arroz con pato* (duck rice), *pato la naranja en almíbar* (honey-glazed duck in an orange sauce), plus a pretty mean *pollo a la suiza* (breaded chicken breast baked in a cheese sauce).

Two other restaurants that offer a good choice of local meat and seafood dishes are **Las Tinajas**, Avenida Libertad 155, and **Fiestas** ((74) 201970 or (74) 228441, Avenida Salaverry 1820.

Inexpensive

My favorite restaurant in Chiclayo — and the best pizza place in northern Peru — is **Caffe Pizzeria Cappuccino** on the ground floor of the Gran Hotel ((74) 234911. The pasta dishes (lasagna, spaghetti, tagliatelle) are only average, but the pizzas are great. Choose from 21 different varieties including ham and pineapple, vegetarian, sausage, spinach, and capricciosa (which I can't resist).

Another outstanding eatery is **Romana** ((74) 223598, Avenida Balta 512, which offers a wide range of Peruvian and Italian dishes. I highly recommend the *pollo a la Milanesa*. They serve great salads too, including the *ensalada Romana* which contains asparagus, chicken, ham, and celery.

El Huaralino ((74) 2700330, La Libertad 155 in Santa Victoria district, also offers a fine local menu including roast goat, duck rice, ray fish omelets, mashed potatoes with shrimp, and duck *ceviche*.

HOW TO GET THERE

Chiclayo lies 770 km (477 miles) north of Lima and 210 km (130 miles) north of Trujillo via the Pan-American Highway. There is frequent bus and *colectivo* service from Lima, Trujillo, Piura, Tumbes and Cajamarca. In addition, AeroPeru and AeroContinente offer daily flights from a number of Peruvian destinations including Lima, Trujillo, Piura, Cajamarca, Tumbes, and Iquitos.

SIPÁN

Thirty kilometers (20 miles) east of Chiclayo is a village called **Sipán** which burst into world headlines in 1987 with the discovery of the most amazing tomb ever unearthed in the Americas. This extraordinary site was first located by grave robbers who tried to sell pilfered gold pieces in Chiclayo. Alerted to the possibility of a major archaeological treasure, Dr. Walter Alva and Luis Chero of the Brüning Museum in Lambayeque made haste to Sipán, where they excavated the first of 11 Moche tombs — the grave of a high-ranking noble who was later dubbed the Lord of Sipán. Since then Sipán has yielded more gold and silver treasure that any other archeological sight in Peru.

The ancient city of Sipán flourished between AD 200 and 600 as one of the fulcrums of the Moche Empire. Today the site consists of two large adobe pyramids with a platform between them, a burial mound, and the remains of a city that once held an estimated 12,000 people. You should scale the largest pyramid for a panoramic view of the entire sight. The *huaca* you're standing on was the religious heart of ancient Sipán; the smaller *huaca* was the probably the palace of the local rulers and their courtiers.

Beyond the ticket office, an earthen ramp leads to the Lord of Sipán's tomb, which is filled with replicas of the fabulous treasure that was uncovered here. To the right of the tomb is a small enclosure full of funeral pots that once contained food for the deceased to eat in the afterlife. To the left of the tomb are about a dozen adobe bricks that contain family or clan brands or marks — possibly mandatory donations to the lord's tomb from various upstanding members of the community.

Other significant tombs discovered during the past decade include the Old Lord of Sipán and the High Priest. The latest excavations, still in process at the time of publication, are the tombs of a shaman's assistant (number 12) and a high-ranking warrior (number 11).

The site museum is small but interesting. It houses some original items from the tombs and many fine reproductions, but more interesting are drawings showing how Sipán (and its residents) must have looked during the city's heyday. The site is open daily and there is an entrance fee.

LAMBAYEQUE

Founded in the sixteenth century as the primary Spanish settlement in this region, Lambayeque was a flourishing city until the early twentieth century when it was overtaken by Chiclayo in both wealth and political importance. Slow-paced and quiet, Lambayeque is a pleasant contrast to the hustle-bustle of larger Peruvian cities.

The town's Plaza de Armas and surrounding streets harbor a treasure of colonial architecture. Dominating the square is the well-kept **Iglesia San Pedro** (1557) with its soft yellow façade. Behind is a chapel dedicated to San Francisco de Assisi. The **Municipalidad** (1874) opposite the church is a fine example of the French-inspired style that predominated in late nineteenth-century Peru. **Colegio Nacional** occupies the beautiful ochre building on the western flank of the square, while lovely **Casa Leguía** (Calle Atahualpa 431) with its blue façade dominates the plaza's south side.

The whitewashed house **Casa de la Logia**, Sol de Mayo 108, is where Lambayeque declared its independence from Spanish rule in 1820 and now contains the longest wooden balcony in South America. Historian Augusto Alejandro Castillo was born and raised in the blue house at Sol de Mayo 514.

Lambayeque's primary tourist attraction is the excellent **Brüning Museum (** (74) 282110 or (74) 283440, two blocks east of the Plaza de Armas. This squat modern building contains many of the Sipán treasures, as well as locally excavated artifacts of the Chimú, Chavín, and Inca cultures. It's especially strong on ceramics with an excellent collection of Moche pottery including erotic pieces and depictions of human freaks (Siamese twins and elephantiasis victims). The displays are well-conceived and modern, making this one of Peru's best regional museums. The museum is open daily and there is an entrance fee.

One of the few places to stay overnight in Lambayeque is **Hostal Karla**, a modest three-star establishment across the street from the Brüning Museum. It features a small restaurant and shop on the ground floor (they sell film). The town's best restaurant is **El Cántaro (** (74) 282196, Dos de Mayo 180, with many regional specialties including *arroz con pato* (duck rice), *mollejitas* (chicken innards), and *humitas* (corn tamales). It offers good food at reasonable prices. Many of the museum people eat here.

TÚCUME

One of Peru's most impressive and least visited archaeological wonders is the ruined city of Túcume about 30 km (20 miles) north of Lambayeque. Developed by the Sican culture between AD 800 and 1200, this vast mudbrick metropolis contains no less than 26 pyramids and many other lesser buildings.

Huaca El Mirador is the first you approach after visiting the site museum. Thirty meters (just under 100 ft) tall, it was probably built around 1200 and has the longest access ramp at Túcume. The upper parts of the pyramid includes rooms set aside for food preparation, garbage disposal, storage, and residences for the nobility. Mirador has

yielded many ceremonial instruments and food offerings including petrified maize, avocado seeds, *zapalo* (a type of pumpkin), *lucuma* (a small nutty-tasting fruit), and *guanábana* (soursop) — a fascinating insight into what the ancients ate.

Nearby is **Huaca Larga**, the largest adobe structure in Peru, a massive construction that measures 700 m (765 yards) by 280 m (306 yards) by 30 m (33 yards). It's basically a huge platform with large interior spaces including ceremonial yards and squares, residential and managerial areas, temples and

markets. Excavations have shown that three successive cultures — Sican, Chimú, and Inca — occupied the sacred site. Over the last decade this huaca has yielded a wealth of artifacts including silver jewelry, pottery, wooden tools, wall paintings and mummies, as well as the remains of an Inca stone temple built atop the adobe superstructure.

Looming over the ruined city is a cactus-studded hill called **Cerro Purgatorio**. This rocky mount is supposed to be a very magical place, revered by the area's shamans. It's also called Cerro La Raya after a legend about a magical ray that flew out of the sea and now inhabits the place. Purgatorio was the

Among the treasures of the Brüning Museum is this Lambayeque vase.

central focus of the ancient religious complex at Túcume and the object of a special cult. It was once surrounded by an adobe wall barring entrance to anyone without high religious or political standing in the community. The Inca built stone platforms and terraces on the side of the hill, probably for ceremonies. You can climb to the top of its 197 m (600 ft) for a vast panorama of Túcume and the surrounding countryside. It's especially moving at sunset when you can almost feel the magical aura of the mountain stir beneath you.

Alfred Kroeber of the University of California was the first archeologist to study Túcume (1925–1926). Wendall Bennett of the American Museum of Natural History undertook the first excavations in 1930s, discovering several tombs from the Inca epoch. Wooden objects recovered by Herman Trimborn in the 1970s have been carbon dated to between 1010 to 1290. Thor Heyerdahl sponsored the 1989 dig, and a fullscale replica of his *Kon Tiki* sits rotting beneath a shed between Huaca Mirador and Huaca Larga. The site is open daily and there is an entrance fee.

PIURA

Beyond the lush Lambayeque Valley there is nothing but stark desert for several hundred kilometers until you reach Piura, gateway to the country's northern extremes. The oldest colonial outpost in Peru, Piura was founded in 1532 by Francisco Pizarro and quickly prospered into a trade transhipment and cotton growing center. The verdant fields of the Piura Valley still produce more than 30% of the country's cotton crop.

Most overseas visitors pass right through Piura without bothering to explore the city or its environs. But the area has always been popular with Peruvians, who find the sleepy, sultry north a rather exotic place compared to the hustle bustle of Lima.

Piura was hard-hit by the El Niño storms of 1997 and 1998, which caused numerous casualties and millions of dollars in damage. The main highway bridge across the Río Piura was washed away and the city was cut off from the south for many months. However, communication and transportation

links were restored and the residents were back on their feet by the end of 1998.

GENERAL INFORMATION

There is no longer a tourist office in Piura. Your best sources of information are probably hotel staff and local travel agencies.

WHAT TO SEE AND DO

Piura really doesn't have much in the way of sights compared to other large Peruvian cities. You can probably hit all of the top spots in a single morning. The town's ancient **cathedral** towers over the Plaza de Armas. It was originally constructed in the 1580s but largely rebuilt after numerous earthquakes.

Two blocks south of the plaza via Avenida Tacna is **Casa Grau**, former home of Admiral Miguel Grau, hero of the War of the Pacific (1879-1883) against Chile. It contains ship models and other nineteenth-century military mementos. The house is closed Sunday and entrance is free. The city's other historical collection is the **Museo de la Cultura** at the corner of Avenida Huánuco and Sullana, about a fifteen-minute walk from the main plaza. The emphasis here is on pre-Columbian artifacts with items from various ruins and digs in the Piura region. The museum is closed Sunday and there is an entrance fee.

Just outside Piura is a village called **Catacaos**, renowned for its artisans. Among the crafts sold in the local market and shops are handwoven hammocks, filigree silver and gold items, Panama hats and wood carvings. Catacaos is 12 km (eight miles) from downtown Piura on the road to Sechura. The only major archaeological site within easy reach of Piura is **Cerro Vicús**, developed by the Vicús culture around two thousand years ago. All that remains today of this once-great city are adobe ruins and a few tombs.

The closest beaches to Piura are situated near **Sechura** (54 km or about 33 miles to the southwest) and **Paita** (50 km or about 32 miles due west). The strands are packed with Piurans during school holidays but the rest of the time they are serenely empty.

Máncora and **Punta Sal**, about 150 km (100 miles) north of Piura via the Pan-American Highway, have become increasingly popular with middle-class Peruvians over the past few years and now sport a number of beach resort hotels. Máncora and Punta Sal offer some of Peru's most beautiful beaches, as well as warm sea water and pretty fair waves for surfers. There's also a bit of literary history: Ernest Hemingway went deep-sea fishing in this area in the 1930s, an experience that allegedly inspired him to write *The Old Man and the Sea*.

WHERE TO STAY

Despite its size, Piura doesn't have a great selection of overnight accommodation. Top of the line is **Hotel Vicús** ((74) 343201 FAX (74) 343249, Avenida Guardia Civil B-3 in suburban Miraflores district, which tenders clean and comfortable rooms as well as a swimming pool. Not far behind is the **Río Verde Hotel** ((74) 328486 FAX (74) 303098, Avenida Ramón Mujica, in suburban San Eduardo district. Amenities include swimming pool, air conditioning, room service, cable television, and a restaurant.

Closer to the city center is **Hostal Los Portales** ((74) 321161 FAX (74) 325920, Calle Libertad 875, situated in a lovely old colonial building off the Plaza de Armas. Slightly cheaper is the **Hotel Piura** ((74) 321161 FAX (74) 325920, Jirón Libertad 875.

Máncora offers the best accommodation along the far north coast. My favorite is the **Máncora Beach Bungalows** ((1) 2416116 FAX (1) 2416115 (in Lima), owned and operated by the same crew that runs the excellent Hotel Antigua Miraflores. Besides kitchenettes and private bath, the eight units feature balconies or terraces overlooking the strand, all of them equipped with hammocks. Turn off at Panamericana Norte Km 1164, just south of Máncora village.

Next door is another fine beach abode called **Las Arenas de Máncora** ((1) 4411542 or (1) 4214226 (in Lima). Other choices include **Punta Bellenas Inn** ((74) 858104, **Hostal Sausalito** ((74) 858058, and **Las Pocitas** ((74) 858010.

Another 30 km (20 miles) north along the coast is the excellent **Punta Sal Beach Club** ((74) 608373 FAX (74) 521386. Features include swimming pool, sports facilities, room service, cable television, and a restaurant—but

unfortunately no air conditioning for those steamy north-coast nights. Turn off at Panamericana Norte Km 1192.

WHERE TO EAT

The **Río Verde Hotel** ((74) 328486 on Avenida Ramón Mujica has a pretty good restaurant, a menu that includes typical local dishes and pseudo-international food. Another good choice for local food is **Las Tres Estrellas** ((74) 328472, Avenida Arequipa 702. For Peruvian-style Chinese try **Chifa Tay Loy** at Avenida

Callao 828. Backpackers flock to the **Heladería Chalán** on the Plaza de Armas, a funky little place that doles out sandwiches, fresh fruit juices, ice cream, and other snacks.

HOW TO GET THERE

Piura is 1,033 km (640 miles) north of Lima and 282 km (175 miles) south of Tumbes via the Pan-American Highway. There is frequent bus and *colectivo* service from both cities, as well as long-distance coach service from Lima and Trujillo. In addition, there are daily flights from Chiclayo, Trujillo, and Lima.

Residents beat the heat at one of Piura's public parks.

The Northern Andes

WITH JAGGED, SNOWCAPPED PEAKS AND DEEP jungle valleys, the Northern Andes is one of Peru's most spectacular regions. But it's also one of the least-visited areas because of poor transportation links, lack of tourist facilities, and personal-safety issues. The ragtag remnants of the Sendero Luminoso terrorist group that plagued the country during the 1980s still hide among these misty northern ridges, and the region is a prime drug-smuggling route. Many of the more remote areas remain beyond police or military control.

Tourism in the Northern Andes centers on three distinct areas: the Callejón de Huaylas valley with its dramatic mountain landscapes; the city of Cajamarca with its notorious history and relaxing thermal baths; and isolated Tarapoto on the cusp between the Andes and the Amazon. Those who take the time to explore this region will be rewarded with unmatched scenery, profound adventures, and encounters with amiable residents who haven't been spoiled by the onslaught of mass tourism.

CALLEJÓN DE HUAYLAS

The astonishing Callejón de Huaylas is Peru's most spectacular highland region, a long valley carved by the Río Santa and flanked by two towering mountain chains: the Cordillera Negra (Black Mountains) in the west and the Cordillera Blanca (White Mountains) in the east. Not even the High Andes around Machu Picchu can match the majesty of this place, which looks more like the Swiss Alps or the Canadian Rockies than something you would expect to find in Peru.

With a wealth of snowcapped peaks, flower-filled meadows, and glaciers and aquamarine lakes, the scenery is nothing short of stunning, much of it protected within the boundaries of Huascarán National Park which runs nearly the entire length of the Cordillera Blanca. Most of the area perches above 3,000 m (9,840 ft) and nearly 50 peaks soar beyond 6,000 m (19,680 ft) including mighty Huascarán and Alpamayo—shaped like a shark's dorsal fin and considered among the world's most perfectly proportioned mountains.

In many respects the Callejón de Huaylas is Peru's premier adventure-sports area.

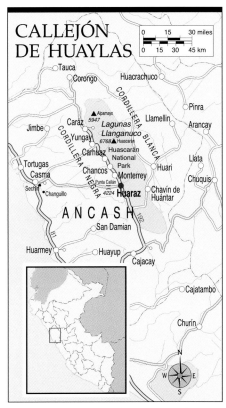

There are hundreds of kilometers of hiking and mountain-bike trails, many of them following the routes of pre-Columbian trails through the woods and mountains. This is a mountaineering wonderland that offers some of the easiest and toughest technical ascents in the Peruvian Andes. Experienced climbers can choose from any number of vertical rock faces — some dropping more than 1,000 m (3,280 ft) — and virgin routes that have never been conquered. Another local sport is whitewater rafting along the rough and tumble waters of the Río Santa.

Going beyond the great outdoors, Callejón de Huaylas also has its human history. Just beyond the valley are the ruins of ancient Chavín, one of the countries most important archaeological sites. Lastly, there is the high-mountain ambience of Huaraz, the valley's largest town and staging point for adventures into the surrounding mountains. A paved road runs the entire length of

LEFT: Wide-open spaces in Ancash province.
OVERLEAF: The famed Cordillera Blanca hovers above Callejón de Huaylas.

the valley from north to south, linking Huaraz to other communities and providing quick access to various parts of the national park.

GENERAL INFORMATION

Like many Peruvian cities, the Huaraz **tourist office** — which can provide information on attractions throughout the region — is located on the Plaza de Armas in the middle of town. It is open weekdays from around 9 AM to around 6 PM (although frequently closed for lunch). Information on Huascarán

Armas, which houses mummies and trepanned skulls as well as a good collection of Chavín, Chimú, Wari, Moche, and Recuay ceramics. In the garden are stone monoliths typical of this region. The museum is open daily and there is an entrance fee.

Another worthwhile collection is the **Museo de Miniaturas**, Jirón Lúcar y Torre 460, a collection of local folk art and crafts including about a hundred dolls dressed in traditional costumes. There's also prehistoric art and a scale model of the town of Yungay before it was obliterated in the 1970 earth-

National Park can be obtained from the **national park office** on Avenida Raimondi (inside the Ministry of Agriculture Building), which is open Monday to Friday.

WHAT TO SEE AND DO

The busy little town of **Huaraz** (the name means "Dawn Star" in Quechua) nestles near the southern end of the Callejón de Huaylas and is where most people base their visit to the region. Besides its abundance of budget hotels, restaurants, and adventure-travel outfits, the town boasts several interesting sights. Chief among them is the small but eclectic **Ancash Archaeological Museum**, on Avenida Luzuriaga facing the Plaza de

quake. On the eastern outskirts of town, on Avenida Confraternidad Internacional Oeste, is the **Piscigranja de Truchas** (trout farm). Privately owned, it's open to visitors daily for a small admission. For the best view of Huaraz and the surrounding mountains, be sure to climb **Mirador de Retaquenua**, southeast of the city.

The people of the Callejón de Huaylas are very talented in craft production, including hats, scarves, blankets, and leather goods. A good place to shop for these items is the **municipal market** on Avenida Luzuriaga, which takes place daily in the afternoons and evenings.

Monterrey, a small town about seven kilometers (four miles) north of Huaraz, is famed for its *baños termales* (thermal baths). The vast, natural hot-spring complex comprises two pools plus a number of smaller pools for individual or family use. About the same distance west of Huaraz, **Punta Callán** offers breathtaking views of the Cordillera Blanca and, on clear days, the ice-capped Huascarán. The Huascarán also looks magnificent from **Lagunas Llanganuco**, the most accessible of the area's several hundred glacial lakes. Situated some 3,850 m (12,628 ft) above sea level, the lakes seem to change color depending on the time of day and the season.

tall as 12 m (36 ft). Named after local explorer and botanist Antonio Raimondi — often called the "Darwin of Peru" — the plant is a member of the pineapple family that only grows at high altitudes. Wildlife that you can expect to come across in the park includes foxes, gray deer, hummingbirds, and viscacha (rabbit-like creatures). May to August is the primary climbing season, but other activities are possible throughout the year. Anyone entering the park is required to register at one of the ranger stations and pay a small entrance fee.

Dominating the eastern flank of the valley is **Huascarán National Park**, established in 1975 and one of the country's most important nature preserves and recreation areas. With a total area of 3,400 sq km (1,312 sq miles), the park comprises the whole of the Cordillera Blanca above 4,000 m (13,120 ft). The area is a paradise for outdoor enthusiasts with hundreds of kilometers of hiking trails (many of them also ideal for mountain bikes), several dozen snowcapped peaks that are just begging to be climbed, and vertical rock walls to match anything you might find in Yosemite or the Eiger.

The park is also rich in native flora and fauna. Among the indigenous plants is the giant *Puya raimondi* plant which grows as

About 30 km (18 miles) north of Huaraz are the hot springs of **Chancos**. Comprising a collection of natural saunas within caves, these thermal waters are rather rustic and tend to get really crowded on weekends when locals visit. Private cubicles are available. Nearby is **Carhuaz**, the valley's second major town, famous for its Sunday market when the streets off the Plaza de Armas are chock-full of food and craft stalls staffed by vendors in traditional local dress.

In 1970, during the middle of a grand fiesta, an earthquake (measuring 7.7 on the Richter scale) and avalanche destroyed the

OPPOSITE: Huascarán National Park shelters some of Peru's best mountain scenery. ABOVE: A reconstructed wall at Chavín de Huántar.

town of **Yungay** near the north end of the valley. Although an accurate tally of the casualties was impossible to calculate, it's estimated that some 70,000 people may have lost their lives on that fateful afternoon. Today you can visit the site of the devastation. The top of the cathedral and a few petrified palm trees protrude from the rubble of what used to be the town's Plaza de Armas. Perhaps the cemetery gives you the best vantage point, spread beneath a statue of Christ holding his hands up towards the mountains as if to ask them

doesn't look very impressive because many of the important artifacts are underground and the area was covered by a landslide in 1945 which buried much of the aboveground structures. Even though he never visited the site, artist Pablo Picasso was quite taken by drawings of the Chavín motifs. "Of all the ancient cultures that I admire," Picasso once said, "that of Chavín amazes me the most. Actually, it has been the inspiration behind most of my art." What better recommendation do you need to visit Chavín de Huántar?

"Why?" Yungay has been rebuilt a little farther north but has no real appeal, comprising modern buildings and prefabricated structures which were sent as part of the relief effort from the former Soviet Union.

A good five-hour drive from Huaraz is the ancient temple complex of **Chavín de Huántar**. The Chavín culture, which flourished between 1300 and 400 BC, is the oldest advanced civilization known to have existed in Peru, predating the Incas by about 2,000 years. Theories about the origin of its religious inspiration run the gamut from extraterrestrial influences to ideas that it infiltrated down from the various cultures of Central America. Don't be put off by your first impressions. The site

ADVENTURE SPORTS

Copa Tours ((44) 722619, Jirón Simón Bolívar 611615, can help you arrange various outdoor activities in the Callejón de Huaylas region including trekking, whitewater rafting and horseback riding, as well as high-altitude mountain services including guides, porters, cooks, donkeys, and climbing equipment. Other source for guides and equipment include **Casa de Guías** ((44) 721811 on Plaza Ginebra; and **Pyramid Adventures** ((44) 721864, Avenida Luzuriaga 530.

The local cycling specialist is **Julio's Mountain Bike Adventures** ((44) 724259 FAX (44) 724888 E-MAIL olaza@mail.cosapidata .com.pe. Owner Julia Olaza rents bikes and helmets, can help plan your route through the surrounding mountains, and provides mechanical service for anyone who brings their own bike. They have two locations: Jirón Lúcar y Torre 538 (one block from Avenida Luzuriaga) and Jirón Julio Arguedas 1246.

WHERE TO STAY

Moderate

Probably the best accommodation in Huaraz is the **Andino Club** ((44) 721662 FAX (44) 723028, Avenida Pedro Cochachín 387, a

with private baths and hot water. Situated near the bus terminals, it also offers luggage storage.

Churup Albergue ((44) 722584, Jirón Pedro Campos 735 in La Soledad, is a friendly hostel that features rooms with shared bathrooms (hot water) as well as laundry service and luggage deposit. Owners Nelly and Juan Quiros are a fountain of information on trekking and climbing in the Huaraz region. Another good bet in the budget bracket is **Copa Hostal** ((44) 722619, Jirón Simón Bolívar 611-615. Rooms have private bath,

three-star establishment with 40 rooms that include private bath, hot water, and central heating. There's a restaurant on the premises, plus room service. The **Gran Hotel Huascarán** ((44) 721640 or (44) 721709 FAX (44) 722821, in Block 10 of Avenida Centenario, offers clean and spacious rooms with private baths.

Inexpensive

With so many trekkers and climbers gathering here, Huaraz was developed a surplus of budget accommodation, the best selection in all of northern Peru. One of my favorites is **Hostal Residential Los Portales** ((44) 721402 FAX (44) 721247, Avenida Raimondi 903, which offers modern, clean rooms

hot water and color TV; there's also a restaurant, laundry, and fax service, and the front desk can help you organize adventure trips. **Hostal Gyula** ((44) 721567, Parque Ginebra 632, is another of the better budget places. Rooms have private bath and hot water.

One of the town's newer hotels is the **Santa Victoria** ((44) 722422 FAX (44) 724870, Avenida Gamarra 690, which offers spacious rooms with televisions, phones and private baths. **Hostal El Pacifico** ((44) 721662 or (44) 721683, Avenida Luzuriaga 630, tenders rooms with private bath, but the hot water flows only in the mornings and evenings. **Hostal El Tumi** ((44) 721913 Jirón José de

Among items for sale in the Carhuaz market are felt hats LEFT and locally grown peppers ABOVE.

San Martín 1121, has comfortable and quiet rooms with private baths and televisions.

Other choices include the multilingual **Edward's Inn (** (44) 722692, Avenida Bolognesi 121 (private baths, hot water, laundry); and **NG Residencial (** (44) 721831, Pasaje Carlos Valenzuela 837, in the Belén district (private bath, hot water, restaurant).

WHERE TO EAT

Huaraz has plenty of small restaurants that offer typical local dishes and simple international fare at modest prices. **Chez Pepe (** (44) 726482, Avenida Luzuriaga 570, bakes a pretty mean pizza, as well as offering pasta dishes, garlic bread, and wine. **Bistro de los Andes** on Jirón Morales cooks up a great breakfast every morning including pancakes, omelets, fresh fruit juices, and fine coffee. Right down the street is the city's best coffee house, a cozy little place called **Café Andino**, open from 6 AM to midnight, with great espresso. Another good choice is the **Restaurant Chalet Suisse (** (44) 722830, Avenida Pedro Cochachín 357 in the Club Andino hotel.

For local Chinese try **Chifa MinHua**, Avenida Luzuriaga 418. **Crêperie Patrick**, Avenida Luzuriaga 422, offers continental dishes including a variety of crêpes. For large portions at rock-bottom prices it's hard to beat **Las Puyas**, Jirón Morales 535, popular with the backpacker crowd. **Restaurant Monte Rosa**, Avenida Luzuriaga 496, offers Italian dishes and light snacks.

HOW TO GET THERE

The only way to reach the Callejón de Huaylas region is by road. There are three routes up from the coast. The most reliable, and the only paved route, runs between Huaraz to Pativilca and then onwards to Lima, a total distance of 406 km (152 miles). Normal driving time is about eight hours. A scenic alternative is the Casma–Huaraz road, an unpaved route that starts at Km 370 of the Pan-American Highway that climbs up and over the cordillera via Punta Callán pass. Finally there is the northern route via the Río Santa valley and the Canon del Pato, much

Cajamarca's cathedral dates from the seventeenth century.

of it unpaved. Total driving time from Huaraz to Trujillo is about 10 hours via either of these two alternate routes. There are daily buses from Lima, Trujillo, Chimbote, La Unión and Casma to Huaraz.

CAJAMARCA

As the major city of the Northern Andes, Cajamarca is an important transportation node and market town. The surrounding region with its fertile farmland is often called "Peru's Dairyland," and the gentle rolling hills are an open invitation to hiking and camping.

But the city is also celebrated for its history, albeit the notorious variety. In pre-Columbian times, Cajamarca was a powerful Inca outpost controlling trade routes in the north. In September of 1532, Inca ruler Atahualpa and his army were encamped near the hot springs at Los Baños del Inca when Francisco Pizarro arrived in the area with about 160 Spanish troops. Atahualpa provided for their accommodation in the city and arranged a rendezvous with Pizarro. But instead of a peaceful reception the Spaniards plotted an ambush. The Inca warriors with their hand axes and slingshot were overwhelmed by a much smaller force of Spanish cavalry and cannons. Atahualpa was easily captured and held for ransom. It took nearly a year for royal retainers to gather a royal ransom estimated at more than 6,000 kg (over 13,000 lb) of gold and 12,000 kg (over 26,000 lb) of silver. But Pizarro never kept his word: after receiving the loot he ordered Atahualpa's execution and marched on Cusco.

GENERAL INFORMATION

Cajamarca's **tourist office** is located inside the Complejo de Belén on Calle Belén. It is open weekdays from around 7:30 AM to around 5:30 PM, but usually closes an hour or two for lunch.

WHAT TO SEE AND DO

The town's **Plaza de Armas** is built on the site of the original courtyard where Pizarro captured the Inca leader Atahualpa in 1532. The central fountain was built in 1692 to

celebrate the arrival of Columbus in the Americas some 200 years earlier. Looming over the square are the seventeenth-century **cathedral** and the **Iglesia San Francisco**, which is supposed to house the bones of Atahualpa. In the attached convent is small but fascinating **Museo de Arte Religioso** (Museum of Religious Art) which is open Monday to Friday for a small entrance fee.

Cajamarca's most famous sight is **El Cuarto del Rescate** (Ransom Chamber), at Amalia Puga 722, the only Inca structure that wasn't destroyed by the Spanish. According to legend, Atahualpa promised to fill this room with gold in return for his freedom from Pizarro. However, historians are still not in agreement as to whether this was Atahualpa's actual ransom room or just his prison cell. Whichever, it's not a very impressive building. The chamber is closed Tuesday and there is an entrance fee.

The city's most impressive architectural statement is the seventeenth-century **Complejo de Belén**, a sprawling baroque compound that includes two hospitals, a fine little church, the **National Institute of Culture** and an ethnographic museum. Holding pride of place inside the men's hospital is a peaceful stone patio with fountains. The women's hospital, located across the road from the main complex, houses the **Museo de Etnografía** with its collection of regional ceramics and clothing, agricultural tools, and handicrafts. At the entrance to the museum, a stone carving depicts a woman with four breasts — a symbol of female fertility which dates back to ancient times. The museum is closed Tuesday and there is an entrance fee.

The thermal waters of **Baños del Inca** lie about five kilometers (three miles) outside of Cajamarca. Atahualpa was camped next to the springs when Pizarro arrived on his mission of conquest and total submission. Today there is a public pool and several private cubicles for relaxing in the hot water. Several hours walk up the Río Chanta from the baths is **Ventanillas de Otuzco**, a huge pre-Inca necropolis which comprise hundreds of niches where chieftains of the Cajamarca culture were buried.

Cerro Santa Apolonia, a grassy hill on the outskirts of Cajamarca, offers great views of the city and across the valley. On the back side of the hill is a path that leads to **Cumbe Mayo**, a well-preserved pre-Inca aqueduct and canal network which originally carried water from the eastern to western slopes of the Andes. Close by is a manmade cave which contains 3,000-year-old Chavín petroglyphs with feline images. It takes about three hours to reach Cumbe Mayo on foot.

WHERE TO STAY

Moderate

On the outskirts of town is a small resort called the **Hotel Laguna Seca** ((44) 823149 FAX (44) 823915 E-MAIL lag.seca@infotex .com.pe, Manco Capac 1098, situated next to the Baños del Inca hot springs. This four-star establishment features swimming pool, fitness center with sauna, air conditioning, cable television, and a restaurant. Some suites have their own thermal baths.

Inexpensive

Best of the budget abodes is the **Hotel Sierra Galana** ((44) 822470 FAX (44) 822472 E-MAIL sgalana@telematic.edu.pe, Jirón del Comercio 773, with its own restaurant and room service. Another choice is the **Hotel Continental** ((44) 822758 FAX (44) 823024, Avenida Amazonas 760. The rooms are clean and comfortable, but with a shopping mall underneath the place can get a bit noisy at times.

If antique charm is your top priority try the **Hotel Casa Blanca** ((44) 822141 FAX (44) 822013, Jirón Dos de Mayo 446 on the Plaza de Armas. The spacious rooms feature private bath and television. Also situated in an old colonial building is the **Hotel Cajamarca** ((44) 822532 FAX (44) 822813, Jirón Dos de Mayo 311, which offers comfortable rooms and a pretty good restaurant.

Hostal Peru ((44) 924030, Amalia Puga 605, is centrally located and relatively clean but quite basic. **Hotel Plaza** ((44) 922058, Amalia Puga 669, has lots of character but is a bit run down. You have a choice of rooms with private or shared bath.

WHERE TO EAT

Cajamarca doesn't get many foreign tourists, but those who come this way usually end up at **Restaurant Salas (** (44) 922876, Avenida Amalia Puga 637 on the Plaza de Armas. The menu includes a wide variety of Peruvian dishes at very reasonable prices. Similar food and ambience at the lively **Restaurant El Zarco (** (44) 923421, Jirón del Batan 170. For a change of pace you can try **Rocco's Pizza** at Calle Cruz de la Piedra 653.

HOW TO GET THERE

Cajamarca lies about five hours' drive due east of Pacasmayo on the Pan-American Highway. The route is paved and passes through a wide fertile valley with many small villages. There are frequent buses from both Trujillo and Chiclayo, as well as daily long-distance service from Lima. As an alternative, there are daily flights from both Lima as well as air service from Trujillo, Chachapoyas, and Chimbote several times a week. Cajamarca's airport is only three kilometers (just under two miles) outside town; buses run about every 20 minutes from the terminal to the city center.

TARAPOTO

Perched on the edge of the eastern Andean foothills, Tarapoto lies at 420 m (1,377 ft) above sea level and is the largest town in the department of San Martín. If you're coming overland rather than flying, this is the gateway to the northern Amazon. With its "high jungle" vegetation and frontier ambience, Tarapoto seems far removed from coastal Peru. Many of the local residents are Quechua-speaking Lamista Indians, descendants of the Chancas who fled to this region in the late fifteenth century. Most travelers pass right through Tarapoto on their way to somewhere else in northern Peru. But whitewater enthusiasts come here for a chance to battle the rapids of the Mayo and Huallaga rivers.

GENERAL INFORMATION

Your best bet for **tourist information** is probably the Ministry of Tourism on Avenida Palma (between Ursua and Levau), two blocks southeast of the central market. Otherwise ask at your hotel front desk or the adventure travel agencies around the Plaza de Armas.

WHAT TO SEE AND DO

While there isn't much to do in Tarapoto itself, there are some interesting excursions nearby. **Lamas**, an Indian village about 30 minutes away, is surrounded by pineapple plantations. The inhabitants are the descendants of the Chanca tribe that migrated here from the Central Andes in the fifteenth century to escape the brutal Inca conquest of their traditional homeland. There is an early morning market and a small museum.

Two whitewater rivers flank the town. The **Río Mayo** and **Río Huallaga** can be run in either kayaks or rafts, adventures that take you through jungle canyons where monkeys, toucans, and river otters make their home. The middle section of the Mayo is rated a breathtaking Class 4. July to September is the best time to explore the rivers. Bring fishing line and bait: typical Amazon fish species like piranha and arawana frequent both of these wild rivers.

Half-day, one-day, three-day, and five-day river trips are available from local outfitters. **Los Chancas Expeditions (** (94) 522616 FAX (94) 525279 E-MAIL amazon.raft@usa.net, Jirón Rioja 357, offers whitewater tours with English-speaking guides. Next to their office is a small arts and crafts store selling typical Andean weavings, pottery, and musical instruments.

There are also several jungle lakes in the vicinity of Tarapoto including **Laguna de Sauce** on the opposite side of the Río Huallaga, and **Laguna Venecia** with its nearby waterfalls.

WHERE TO STAY

Moderate

The best hotels are on the outskirts of town. **Hotel Río Shilcayo (** (94) 522225 Pasaje Las Flores 224, is situated two kilometers (just over a mile) from the city center. The relaxed atmosphere includes gardens and a swimming pool. One of the newer places is **Puerto Palmeras Resort (** (94) 523978 or (1) 2425550 (in Lima) FAX (1) 4449663 or (1) 2425552 (in Lima). Three kilometers (just under two miles) out of town on the road to Juanjuí, it offers comfortable, modern accommodation.

Inexpensive

Hostal Central ((94) 522234, Jirón San Martín, offers clean rooms with private baths, but its location next to a disco doesn't make for peaceful nights. Another cheap option is **Hostal Pasquelandia** ((94) 522290, on Avenida Pimental, which has rooms with and without private baths.

WHERE TO EAT

One of the best places in town for river shrimp (cooked half a dozen ways) is **El Camarón** on Jirón San Pablo de la Cruz. **Restaurant Real**, Jirón Moyobamba 331, offers up various Peruvian dishes as well as river shrimp prepared in various ways. Another good spot for local food is **Restaurant El Mesón** on the Plaza de Armas which serves a variety of reasonably priced dishes. The set lunch is especially good value.

HOW TO GET THERE

Tarapoto airport is one of the busiest in northern Andes with daily flights from Lima and several weekly services from Iquitos, Moyobamba, and Yurimaguas. There are no buses from the airport into town but plenty of taxis that will take you the short journey.

Tarapoto is also an important bus depot, with roads spreading west to Moyobamba, north to Yurimaguas and the Amazon Basin, and south to Juanjuí and Tingo María. The bus journey from Chiclayo to Tarapoto takes 20 to 22 hours; the service from Moyobamba to Tarapoto takes about five hours.

The Yanacocha gold mine in Cajamarca province.

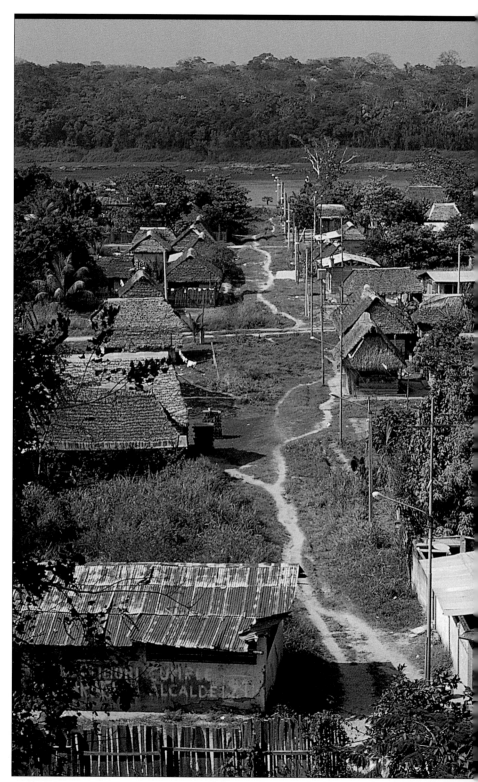

North and Central Amazon

THE AMAZON IS FAR MORE THAN JUST A RIVER, more than a tangle of tributaries and torpid brown streams. The Amazon is a mystery. Its origins are disputed endlessly; its resources raped since the eighteenth century. It's not a particularly pretty place except when a fat full moon bounces reflections in a black lagoon. Yet it always leaves me yearning for more.

All Amazon journeys involve countless encounters with vengeful spiders, no-see-ums, and ants. Endless hours drifting through rain and steam. Sweaty hikes along slippery trails, mud sucking at your feet. The best times are packed with memorable scenes. Flocks of scarlet and emerald macaws perched just out of reach. Sly, silent monkeys slithering through the rainforest canopy.

Sinister caimans sunning along murky streams. Despite the Amazon Basin's appeal to international oil, rubber, and lumber companies, it remains a wild and untamable place where travelers can still catch a sense of the river's mystique.

"The Amazon cannot be understood just as a river. It is a whole wilderness, a great integrated system of rivers and jungles, taking up about half of Brazil and parts of eight other South American countries," writes Joe Kane in *Running the Amazon*. "Defining the source of the Amazon is like unwinding a ball of string and trying to decide which of the tiny frayed threads at the core is, in fact, the end." Some believe the Amazon begins in the southern highlands of Peru at the Río Apurimac. Others say it starts in Ecuador.

In the north, travelers find easy access to primary forest, teeming lagoons, and wildlife along the rivers and tributaries flowing to Colombia and Brazil. Adventure tour operators have established reliable systems of river transportation and accommodations in this area. Iquitos is also the entry point for the remote Reserva Pacaya-Samiria, and is the largest river port in the country. Pucallpa, located in the middle of the Amazon basin near Brazil, is headquarters for the lumber, oil, and mining industries.

BACKGROUND

Spanish explorer Francisco de Orellana is credited with discovering the Amazon in 1542, opening the floodgates to a steady stream of explorers, industrialists, missionaries, and scientists searching to conquer or understand this primeval region. The indigenous Amazonian tribes scattered through the river basin had little interest in being conquered. They had survived and thrived in the jungle amid an abundance of food from the water and land, and had developed social structures and belief systems based on their existence with nature. Shamans, storytellers, traders, and hunters linked isolated communities together by transmitting information along their routes. Their Andean counterparts brought news from the highlands. But for the most part, the Amazonian tribes were autonomous, much like those in remote regions of Australia or Africa.

The Amazonian peoples did not take kindly to the Spanish incursion upon their territory, and the conquistadors faced a hostile, unnavigable terrain filled with danger. The promise of gold in the rivers kept explorers coming, however, and the tribes moved ever farther away from the most accessible settlements. Rubber became their downfall in the nineteenth century, when Europeans and North Americans developed a craving for the inventions based on a substance abundant in the Amazon Basin. Rubber barons descended upon the river's main settlements, enslaving the Amazonian peoples and decimating their population. The rubber tree became a valued property,

Either way, the mighty river which has given its name to a jungle basin stretching far beyond political boundaries begins with tiny rivulets and small streams throughout the Andes and flows through lowland jungles for nearly 6,400 km (4,000 miles) to the sea.

In Peru, the Amazon Basin is divided into several regions and encompasses nearly half of the country's land mass. Iquitos, a quirky river city serving the oil, lumber, and cocaine industries, is the gateway to the northern river basin. Puerto Maldonado, land of banana plantations, has the south's main airport and port. A chain of river-bound settlements and national reserves lie between the two, tempting adventurers with promises of wildlife sightings and encounters with Amazonian tribes.

Schoolchildren travel to class via shallow wooden boats in Belén.

and the jungle was destroyed in some areas as trees were tapped and logged. Huge vessels plied the deepest rivers, carrying slaves and masters to plantations and plunder to new cities. European-style mansions rose in Iquitos, where the barons thrived in a style nearly as cosmopolitan as that of Lima.

The rubber boom crashed in the early twentieth century when the international prospectors began plundering the jungles of Asia and Africa and scientists discovered synthetic recipes for rubber's elastic properties. But the Amazon would never return

to obscurity. Missionaries found it especially appealing; they began arriving in the sixteenth century and haven't stopped trying to convert the "savages" since. Multinational oil conglomerates have settled in for the long haul, claiming vast fields throughout the jungle for their pumps and rigs. The basin's rivers and plundered forests are perfect shelters for drug traffickers and revolutionaries.

The Amazon basin contains only six to ten percent of Peru's population. Census counters claim there are still 65 indigenous groups in the region, many of which have retained distinct dialects and customs. Amazon tours typically include a visit to an "indigenous" community, though the site is often constructed strictly for tourists. The Indians come from their homes across the river to demonstrate their cultural oddities then return to their normal lives, fishing the waters for an ever diminishing supply of food.

Peruvians are of mixed minds when it comes to the Amazon Basin; outside exploiters and preservationists complicate things.

As international agencies fight to protect the remaining jungle and rainforest, national economic interests become endangered. Mario Vargas Llosa, Peru's most famous novelist and politician, sums up the Amazon dilemma in his novel *The Storyteller*. The narrator is speaking with his friend Mascarita, who believes the Amazon and its peoples should be left in peace:

"Occasionally, to see how far his obsession might lead him, I would provoke him. What did he suggest, when all was said and done? That in order not to change the way of life and the beliefs of a handful of tribes still living, many of them, in the Stone Age, the rest of Peru abstain from developing the Amazon region? Should sixteen million Peruvians renounce the natural resources of three-quarters of their national territory so that seventy or eighty thousand Indians could quietly go on shooting at each other with bows and arrows, shrinking heads and worshiping boa constrictors? Should we forgo the agricultural, cattle-raising, and commercial potential of the region so that the world's ethnologists could enjoy studying at first-hand kinship ties, potlatches, the rites of puberty, marriage and death that these human oddities had been practicing, virtually unchanged, for hundreds of years?

"If the price to be paid for industrialization and development for sixteen million Peruvians meant that those few thousand naked Indians would have to cut their hair, wash off their tattoos, and become *mestizos* — or, to use the ethnologist's most despised word, become acculturated — well, there was no way round it."

IQUITOS

Steamy, languid and rather comical, Iquitos assails the senses upon impact. When I first visited on an August weekend in the dry season, there were few tourists on my plane from Lima. Most of the passengers were burly, sunburned men wearing boots, worn-down jeans, wide leather belts, and stretched-out T-shirts. Their conversations focused on "the field" and machinery; oil was their game. A few others bore briefcases and wore shades and button-down shirts, the classic uniform of drug agents and spies.

We were met by a motley jumble of pickup trucks, beat-up vans, and motorcycle taxis — vehicles somewhat akin to Bangkok's tuk-tuks, basically consisting of a motorcycle with a long wooden seat behind the driver and a basket on the back. I boarded a non-air-conditioned van with a group of oil workers bound for the town's best hotel. We rode for what seemed like an hour (more like 20 minutes) past a maze of paved and dirt streets, and entered the city amid a swarm of braking, honking motorcycles and trucks. My relief at finding a cool, quiet room beside a clean swimming pool was overwhelming.

But Iquitos won me over quickly, despite the uncomfortable introduction. Within days I settled upon my favorite riverfront restaurants and shaded parks, and was in nodding acquaintance with many of downtown's denizens. Though the city's population hovers around 400,000 residents, its center seems home to a few dozen regulars and travelers sharing beers and idle conversation. I could imagine the indigenous Yagua Indians operating in much the same manner, living in huts scattered about the region and visiting the riverfront to barter for necessities and visit with friends. Jesuit missionaries built a church in their midst in 1739 (the church is gone). The town itself was established in 1864 as Peru's primary river port, strategically located on the deep waters of the Amazon.

Iquitos thrived during the rubber boom in the late 1800s, and vestiges of its former more glorious state are evident in the ornate mansions near the riverfront. Though mostly rundown, these buildings with their elaborate walls of hand-painted tiles and wrought-iron balconies give witness to a more romantic era when great fortunes were made from the exploitation of the forests and the indigenous populace. Around 1900, Iquitos was home to an enclave of Europeans, where a few wealthy families paraded about in the latest fashions while enslaved Indians tapped rubber trees and watched their jungle communities disintegrate. The rubber barons departed in the 1920s, but the infrastructure of an important river port remained. Since

An 1873 engraving by Riou depicts life on the Amazon.

then, the region's fortunes and population have waxed and waned with the flow of oil, cocaine, and tourists exploring the rainforest.

Logging, hunting, and oil prospecting all threaten the fragile Amazonian environment around Iquitos. A few environmental organizations and individual entrepreneurs continue to create private reserves to protect the northern Amazon's forests and wildlife. The government has done a bit to help by creating the Pacaya-Samiria Reserve along the Río Marañón south of the city. Politics and nature have protected much of the north.

Iquitos sits on the border of a long-disputed, wild and undeveloped region of mountains and jungle claimed by both Peru and Ecuador. Skirmishes between the two countries' military forces have yet to resolve the border question; some negotiators hope the area will someday be an international nature reserve, much like the Parque de la Amistad shared by Costa Rica and Panama. For now, the areas northwest of Iquitos are lightly controlled by military personnel and ruled by drug lords, who find the region a safe haven for growing, cultivating, and marketing cocaine. Travelers are strongly advised to stay away from this area.

But there is still much to explore. The city is the customs and immigration station for travelers entering the country by river from Colombia and Brazil, and a prime shipping area for goods en route to the Atlantic. It's also the entry point for travelers wishing to explore this region of the Amazon, and there are a few excellent tour companies offering worthwhile experiences for adventuresome travelers.

GENERAL INFORMATION

The **Tourist Information Office** ((94) 235621 is located at Jirón Napo 176 across from the Plaza de Armas. It's open Monday to Saturday from 7 AM to 2:45 PM, and sometimes on Sundays. Maps and tour-company brochures are available here. The tour operators and travel agencies around town are also valuable sources of information.

The major festivals in Iquitos include the Iquitos Tourism Festival held around June 24, corresponding with the Festival of San Juan, patron saint of the department of Loreto

(of which Iquitos is the capital). Parades and fiestas mark the anniversary of the founding of Iquitos on January 5, and Carnaval is celebrated with fervor.

Iquitos has two seasons. The rainy season lasts from December through March, when the river rises as much as 12 m (40 ft). The dry season, from April through November, is cooler.

WHAT TO SEE AND DO

Iquitos is a confusing, sprawling town with few street signs or numbered buildings. As mentioned above, it has an overabundance of motorcycle taxis, with rides all over town costing less than US$1. The drivers are adept at finding the most obscure addresses. It's

far easier to board one of these transports than to try to walk to your destination (and far more comfortable in the jungle heat).

Most nonbusiness travelers spend less than a day in Iquitos, and stay overnight only to conform with their tour itineraries. But I find the city well worth exploring, and its relatively comfortable accommodations and varied restaurants provide much-needed comforts after lengthy stays in the jungle.

The **Plaza de Armas**, bounded by Jirón Napo and Avenidas Putumayo, Fitzcarrald and Raymondi, is the center of the city's limited social and cultural scene. Remodeled in 1998, the square plaza is fronted by the **Casa de Hierro** (Iron House), a fanciful structure created by the Eiffel company in 1898 and shipped to Peru by a wealthy rubber baron.

The building now houses a café, one of several facing the plaza.

One block east is the **malecón**, a riverfront walkway lined with restaurants, hotels, and private businesses. The sidewalk changes names when it intersects with Jirón Napo. The north side is called Malecón Maldonado, where the best cafés are located. The south side is called Malecón Tarapacá; it's a quieter section with a few hotels and an early nineteenth-century tiled mansion housing military offices. The malecón is *the* place to be in the evening, when children peddle miniature moto-taxis along the concrete sidewalks while grownups quaff chilled beers at outdoor cafés. Roving vendors display

Rivers are the main thoroughfares for villagers and produce in the Iquitos region.

beaded necklaces and blowguns for interested buyers. The women carrying swaths of cream-colored fabric woven with dark brown geometric designs are from the Shipibo tribe, one of the most intriguing groups in the Ecuadorian and Peruvian Amazon. Their textiles are all the rage among folkart collectors, and are used by fashion designers for pricey jackets and skirts sold in Lima's boutiques. Many of the vendors have been corralled into semipermanent stands on the streets intersecting with the malecón.

Taxi drivers, vendors, and shoeshine boys also congregate at the inner city **Plaza 28 de Julio** at Avenidas Grau and Caceres, less than a 10-minute walk northwest of the malecón. A few tourist hotels are located in this neighborhood; many of the buses for outlying areas depart from here as well. The small **Museo Municipal** on the third block of Jirón Távara at Avenida Fitzcarrald has exhibits about native culture and a musty collection of unfortunate animals from the region.

The main port for Iquitos used to be located at the malecón, but has been moved three kilometers (just under two miles) down river to the truly squalid **Puerto Masusa**. Travelers boarding cruise ships or freighters bound up or down river may be directed here by their guides; independent backpackers who chat up workers at the port may find a captain willing to take them on board for a lengthy, down-to-basics Amazon journey.

Puerto Belén, a small settlement with an outdoor riverfront market, is located three kilometers (just under two miles) south of downtown Iquitos. It was the setting for Herzog's classic Amazon film *Fitzcarraldo*, and still appears like a vision from the nineteenth century. Rattletrap wooden houses on stilts face the river, where residents from outlying areas arrive in dugout canoes to purchase vegetables, fruit, and meat. Belén is included on most city tours, and can seem a bit trite when viewed with a bunch of gringos. It's at its best in early morning and evening, when locals head back and forth to work or school via river transport.

Several areas make for good day-trips from town. **Quistococha**, 13.5 km (just over eight miles) south of Iquitos, sits at the edge of a lagoon surrounded by jungle that's particularly lush during rainy season. Attractions include the rather horrid Parque Zoológica de Quistococha, where a few pathetic creatures are kept in cruel conditions. Skip the zoo and take a hike on the **marked trails** into the jungle instead. Though you may not see any wildlife, at least you'll see the jungle in its semi-natural state. There are small bars and restaurants on the shores of the lagoon, where the water is supposedly safe for swimming (I wouldn't go near it without hepatitis inoculations).

The sandy beach at **Bellavista**, five kilometers (three miles) from Iquitos, is a popular swimming area crowded with locals on weekends. There are restaurants on the beach, and you can arrange a canoe trip to the juncture of the Nanay and Amazon rivers, with stops at villages along the way. The small towns of **Santa Clara** and **Santo Tomás** are known for their handicrafts. Many beaches have biting flies or mosquitoes. Be sure to bring repellent.

OPPOSITE TOP: Snake-oil potions from the Uña de Gato are used for nearly every ailment. BOTTOM: Motorcycle taxis clog narrow streets in Iquitos. ABOVE: Chicken restaurants abound, though travelers prefer sampling river fish.

WHERE TO STAY

The constant influx of business travelers for the oil fields and logging operations has created a demand for upscale hotels with direct-dial phones, satellite television, minibars, and other amenities. But even the most luxurious places are modest when compared with those in Lima, and the average hotel is a simple establishment. Most travelers spend only a night or two in Iquitos before and after jungle excursions, but it's best

243530 FAX 243532 E-MAIL riogrande@tvs.com.pe, overlooking the Plaza 28 de Julio at Jirón Próspero 644. The 49 rooms and suites are large and tastefully decorated and have air conditioning, mini bars and bathtubs (a rarity) along with showers. Facilities include a restaurant and bar; a swimming pool is in the planning stages.

Moderate

Facing the river, the **Real Hotel Iquitos** ((94)231011 FAX (94) 236222 at Malecón Tarapacá between Jirón Napo and Jirón

to book your room in advance as hotels fill up when large tour groups are in town.

Moderate/Expensive

By far the most lavish establishment in town, the **El Dorado** ((94) 237326 or (94) 221985 FAX (94) 232203 E-MAIL dorado@rail.org.pe, at Jirón Napo 362, has a delightful swimming pool and a very good restaurant. The rooms have air conditioning, small refrigerators, and satellite television. Scheduled to open in early 1999 is the Dorado's sister establishment, the **Plaza Hotel** ((94) 231405, on Jirón Napo across from the Plaza de Armas. The hotel is expected to be the best in town, with 60 rooms and a pool and restaurant. Also new on the scene is the **Río Grande Hotel** ((94)

Avenidas Putumayo has 73 air-conditioned rooms, a restaurant, and good views of the riverbed from some rooms. The swimming pool is a major plus at the **Victoria Regia** ((94)231983 FAX (94) 232499 at Jirón Ricardo Palma 252. The **Amazonas Hostal** ((94) 223574 FAX 242471, at Avenida Arica 108, is nicely located across from the Plaza de Armas. The 20 unremarkable rooms have air conditioning. The **Hostal Acosta** ((94) 235974, at Avenida Calvo de Araujo and Jirón Huallaga, has all the comforts except for a swimming pool.

Inexpensive

The **Hostal Safari** ((94) 233828 FAX (94) 234934, Jirón Napo 118, is my first choice in the budget range for its location right off the malecón and its friendly staff. **Hostal la Pacana** ((94) 231418 FAX (94) 232974, Jirón Pevas 133, is a favorite with the backpacker set. Hot water is rarely available, but the simple rooms are clean and the courtyard is a good spot to hook up with like-minded travelers.

WHERE TO EAT

Iquitos is no culinary paradise, but its restaurants do offer a sampling of regional and

international dishes. *Paiche*, said to be the world's largest freshwater fish, is a local specialty, as are fried green plantains, *tacacho* (fried bananas and pork rolled into balls), and palm-heart salads. All restaurants are casual, though the waiters have the same worried looks and harried attitude as those in the cities.

Moderate–Inexpensive

My first night in town I followed a blond woman to the malecón; when she stopped and abruptly asked why I was dogging her heels I said I figured she would know the restaurant I was looking for. She certainly did; she kept a beer mug in the freezer at **La Casa de Jaime** ((94) 236376 at Malecón

Maldonado 177. She was involved in monkey research deep in the jungle and looked forward to a meal at Jaime's like it was the finest bistro in her native Manhattan. We shared a dinner of fresh mozzarella, an excellent version of *sopa criolla* (a soup with chicken broth, noodles, cream, and spices) and fresh fish served *a la loretana*, the local style of presentation with white rice, fried plantains, and salad. Many claim Jaime's is the best restaurant in Iquitos; I tend to have at least one meal a day there. The salads are fresh and abundant, the meats tender and savory, and the clientele friendly. Jaime spends much of his time helping diners set up jungle trips. The book exchange in the interior dining room is an added blessing.

The most popular hangout in town is **Ari's Burger** ((94) 231470, Jirón Próspero 127 near Plaza de Armas. The place is packed at breakfast — try the *clasico* combo of eggs, potatoes, and toast, or the homemade yogurt — and draws crowds throughout the day and night with its 10 versions of hamburgers, individual pizzas and ice cream. The air-conditioned dining room at **Gran Maloca** ((94) 233126, Jirón Lores 170, is a pleasant

OPPOSITE: Rundown buildings in Iquitos show the effects of the damp river climate. ABOVE: Fried bananas serve as instant street snacks.

surprise with its pale pink walls, low lighting, fine paintings, and subdued ambience. Try the surprisingly tasty risotto with steak and mushrooms or the vegetarian lasagna.

The **Chifa Pekin**, at Jirón Avenidas Putumayo 901, is the best place for inexpensive Chinese food. **Café La Casa de Hierro (** (94) 221160, in the iron house at Jirón Próspero 190, has second-story tables overlooking the plaza and is a good place for coffee and ice cream. The breakfast buffet and other meals at the **El Dorado** (see WHERE TO STAY, page 242) are consistently good. **El Nuevo Mesón (** (94) 231197, Malecón Maldonado 153, has a truly amusing English-language menu offering "chicken bespattered with hearts of palm" (it's actually pretty good) and the delightful sounding "bleeding pitcher" (aka sangria).

HOW TO GET THERE

Most travelers arrive at the Aeropuerto Francisco Secada Vigneta from Lima; daily flights are available on AeroContinente. AeroPeru flies to Iquitos from Lima and Miami. There are no roads leading from the coast or mountains to Iquitos.

JUNGLE EXCURSIONS

Travelers who have put off planning their jungle expeditions can spend days visiting the plethora of tour operators around the plaza in Iquitos; in the long run, most offer the same transportation and jungle accommodations. There are options for every expectation. Diehard budget travelers can set

working in the region for over three decades, and is as involved in scientific research as he is in tourism. The heart of his operation is the ACEER (Amazon Center for Environmental Education and Research) Station, on a tributary of the Río Napo three hours northeast of Iquitos by boat. Near the ACEER laboratories is the **Explornapo Camp**, a remote river lodge with thatched cabins, kerosene lighting, and shower facilities. A two-hour walk through the jungle leads to **Explortambos**, a primitive camp with rustic open-air dwellings and beds covered by mosquito netting. Though these two options require an investment of time (the company suggests a minimum of four nights combining the camps and their more accessible lodges) they provide your best chances for wildlife viewing. The greatest attraction is a canopied walkway suspended up to 35 m (115 ft) above the jungle treetops. There are twelve platforms along the walkway where hikers can spend hours spotting monkeys and birds.

Closer to Iquitos is the **Explorama Lodge**, 80 km (50 miles) northeast of the city. The lodge, which has palm-thatched houses with private rooms and shared bathrooms and shower facilities, is located on the banks of the Río Yanamono in a 250,000-hectare (600,000-acre) reserve. It offers treks through primary forest and tours to indigenous communities in the area. The **Explorama Inn**, just 40 km (25 miles) from Iquitos has 26 comfortable bungalows with private bath, electric lights, and fans. Construction of 72 additional rooms at the inn is expected to occur soon, and there are plans for a more luxurious jungle resort with swimming pools and air conditioning. Explorama uses comfortable motorboats for transport to the camps; their guides are usually local people trained by ACEER scientists. Though the company's rates are higher than others in the area, travelers are sure to find comfortable lodgings, good food, efficient transport, and a wealth of educational opportunities.

Yacumama Lodge, contacted through Explorandes ((1) 4450532 FAX (1) 4454686 at

up their own trips by visiting with boat captains at Puerto Masusa. Many river boats have space for passengers, with options ranging from basic private cabins to floor space on the main deck. If you wish to travel this way be sure to bring drinking water, bug repellent, food, a rain poncho, and a hammock, and show up hours before the boat is scheduled to depart. Find a place to string up your hammock on the main deck away from the engines; you'll spend many long hours here.

More expensive and efficient options are available through **Explorama Tours** ((94) 252530 FAX (94) 252533 TOLL-FREE (800) 2236764 E-MAIL amazon@explorama.com WEB SITE www.explorama.com, on Avenida de la Marina. Owner Peter Jenson has been

Beaches line the Río Nanay, a watery roadway into the jungle.

San Fernando 320, Miraflores, Lima, was constructed in the late 1980s on the banks of the Río Yarapa about 145 km (90 miles) from Iquitos. Up to 30 guests can be accommodated in private cabins, shared dorms, and hammock huts (thatched shelters with plenty of hammock hooks), and travelers can use the lodge as their base camp for further explorations into the jungle. Yacumama has reliable boats for river transport and a yacht for longer trips; trails lead from the lodge into primary forest. Rates vary drastically depending on the accommodations and tours

up the Yarapa River from Iquitos. **Amazon River Dolphin Expeditions** ((94) 242596, at Jirón Pevas 116, Iquitos, or in the United States ((818) 572-0233 FAX (818) 572-9521, 3302 North Burton Avenue, Rosemead, California 91770, organize educational trips and prefer, but don't require, advance booking.

Independent travelers may want to specialize their trips by using local guides and agencies. Qualified, highly experienced guides can be hired through most agencies; ask around at Casa Jaime and Ari's Burger for recommendations. Reliable local agen-

you choose; it's hard to resist the overnight river cruise.

More economical are the trips offered by **Amazon River House** FAX (94) 231111, PO Box 181, Iquitos, about 60 km (37 miles) upstream from Iquitos. Travel agencies in Iquitos can arrange your stay. **Expediciones Jungle Amazonia** ((94) 236119 FAX (94) 231111, at Jirón Brasil 217, is run by the very competent Moises Torres Viena and his sons. Trips varying from several days to three weeks long can be arranged, with stops at jungle lodges and camps along the way.

If you don't mind sleeping on floor platforms, check out **Ecological Jungle Trips** ((94) 237154 FAX (94) 241198, at Jirón Soledad 1329. Their lodge is about 150 km (93 miles)

cies include **Carrusel Tours** (/FAX (94) 232173, which represents several lodges; and **Paucar Tours** ((94) 232648 FAX (94) 222177, Jirón Próspero 648, which does the booking for Zungarococha Lodge, 22 km (almost 14 miles) from Iquitos.

Several Amazon cruises begin in Iquitos. **Planet Expeditions** ((303) 449-3462 FAX (303) 449-3462 TOLL-FREE (800) 233-2433, 2945 Center Green Court, Suite H, Boulder, Colorado 80301, books the 100-passenger MS *Explorer* for eight-day cruises from Iquitos to Leticia, Colombia and back. The ship is geared toward adventure travelers and carries along plenty of rubber Zodiac crafts for side trips to oxbow lakes and shallow lagoons. Other international com-

panies offering high-end Amazon cruises are listed in TAKING A TOUR, page 56 in YOUR CHOICE. **Amazon Tours and Cruises** ((94) 231611 or (94) 233931 FAX (94) 231265, offers three-day boat trips from Iquitos to the border at Leticia, Colombia. Some passengers take the return voyage as well, turning it into a six-day cruise. Book in advance through the United States office ((305) 227-2266 TOLL-FREE (800) 423-2791 FAX (305) 227-1880, 8700 W. Flagler Street, Suite 190, Miami, Florida 33174. They also run **Tambo Yarapa Lodge** on the Río Yarapa 169 km (105 miles) from Iquitos. **Expreso Turistico Loreto** ((94) 238021, Jirón Loreto 171, has speedboats that connect Iquitos with the borders at Colombia and Brazil.

RESERVA PACAYA-SAMIRIA

The remote Pacaya-Samiria Reserve encompasses two million hectares (five million acres) of jungle, swamp and virgin forest southwest of Iquitos. The reserve is not easily accessed; it takes at least twelve hours to travel along the Ríos Huallaga and Marañón from Iquitos to Lagunas, the starting point for trips into the jungle. There are no facilities in the reserve, and explorers are required to register for permits through INRENA (Instituto Nacional de Recursos Naturales) at the Ministerio de Agricultura in Lima Ministry of Agriculture

OPPOSITE: Yagua indians preserve their traditions despite the rise of tourism along the rivers. ABOVE: Hot peppers thrive in the steamy climate of Pucallpa.

((1) 4323150 at Natalio Sanchez 220, Lima. You can also get information from the South American Explorer's Club (/FAX (1) 4250142 E-MAIL montague@amauta.rcp.net WEB SITE www.samexplo.org, Avenida Portugal 146, Lima. This area is a swamp land during rainy season (December to March) when rivers rise and the wildlife is more easily spotted.

PUCALLPA

The fast-growing town of Pucallpa, capital of the department of Marañón, now has a

population of 400,000 souls. You can guess the reason for this boom without much trouble: large deposits of petroleum and natural gas have been found in the area and are now being explored and exploited. Timber, paper, gold, and fishing are other important industries. Large ships navigate the Río Marañón between Pucallpa and Iquitos, 530 nautical miles (981 km or 609 miles) to the north. It is possible to take a cargo/passenger boat to Iquitos from Pucallpa, although as more cargo is shipped, space left over for tourists has become more scarce. There is little of interest for the tourist here; in fact, Pucallpa can be depressing for those who would prefer to see the rainforest staying in good health.

WHAT TO SEE AND DO

Laguna Yarinacocha, a large lake on the Río Ucayali nine kilometers (five and a half miles) north of Pucallpa, is a far more pleasant place than the city. The large lake and surrounding river tributaries are favored by the mythical pink river dolphins so beloved by Amazonian explorers. The main settlement on the lake is **Puerto Callao**, where there are a few small hostels, bars and boat captains willing to ferry sightseers around the area in their motorized canoes (called *peke-pekes*). Callao is home to the Moroti-Shobo Cooperative, an indigenous cooperative selling traditional wares. The Shipibo people who inhabit the area are very friendly and still practice some of their native crafts, most notably ceramics and textiles. There are several indigenous villages in the region (some researchers have counted at least 35 separate groups); explorers with time, patience, and a bit of cash can visit some of the villages and learn much about traditional Amazonian lifestyles. The **Chullachaqui Botanical Garden** is an hourlong boat trip from Puerto Callao and then another hour walk from the town of Nueva Luz de Fatima; entrance is free.

WHERE TO STAY AND EAT

There are quite a few hotels in Pucallpa and Callao; most of the nicer ones are found in the last few blocks of Jirón Tacna and Jirón Marañón near Parque San Martín in the city. It's much more pleasant, however, to stay at one of the lodges along the Yarinacocha lakeshore. **La Cabaña** ((64) 571120 is located across the lake from Callao; their office is in Pucallpa at Jirón 7 de Junio 1043.

HOW TO GET THERE

Pucallpa is connected to Lima and Cusco by air, and to Iquitos and other river towns by boat.

LEFT: An 1873 engraving depicts the simple dignity of the Marahua peoples. RIGHT: The Marahua people of Pucallpa create weaving and pottery in a distinct pattern coveted by collectors worldwide.

Southern Amazon

MACAWS, PARROTS, MONKEYS, AND JAGUARS find safe haven in Peru's southern Amazon Basin. The Madre de Dios department sprawls to the borders with Brazil and Bolivia, and is largely inaccessible except by boat. It is less developed (and less exploited) than the northern area. Federal and private reserves encompass oxbow lakes formed by U-shaped bends in the rivers, steep cliffs of salt-laden clay, and masses of undisturbed rainforest.

Parque Nacional Manú, located east of Cusco at the base of the Cordillera Vilcanota, is Peru's most famous Amazonia park, known for its abundance of tropical plants and birds. Puerto Maldonado on the Río Madre de Dios near Bolivia, is the department's largest city, with some 25,000 residents. Tambopata, near the city, is gradually being incorporated into a series of private and governmental reserves with relatively easy access to wilderness and civilized comforts.

MANÚ BIOSPHERE RESERVE

Birders, biologists and naturalists speak of Manú with utter reverence. UNESCO has declared it a World Heritage Site, a precious region vital to earth's survival. The park covers 2,233,700 hectares (roughly 7,000 sq miles) of high jungle and lowlands, and is home to at least 850 species of birds. Giant river otters, capybaras, peccaries, howler monkeys, and Andean bears called *ucuman* all thrive in their isolation.

Manú and the Río Madre de Dios (called Amaru Mayu or the Serpent River by its Amazonian residents) remained largely unexplored until 1946, when American adventurer Leonard Clark approached it in search of medicinal plants and gold deposits. In 1973, the Peruvian government hired British zoologist Ian Greenwood to search the country for a virgin, natural region worth preserving. Greenwood met up with Celestino Kalinowski, who had lived in the Andean jungle. Together, they determined that Manú warranted protection. Every wildlife and conservation organization one can imagine took interest in this valuable pocket of natural resources; Manú has since evolved from a simple national park to an internationally protected UNESCO-designated biosphere reserve.

Manú's highest point is **Shintuya**, a tiny settlement 4,100 m (12,500 ft) above sea level, about 30 hours by road east of Cusco. Though few travelers access the park from this direction, those who do encounter a region of incomparable beauty. It can easily take three days to travel from Cusco to Manú, depending on the condition of rough mountain roads. The road travels northeast from the city to the traditional Andean village of **Paucartambo**, where the annual Fiesta de la Virgen de Carmen attracts hundreds of visitors in mid-July.

The strip of broken asphalt climbs and twists ever higher to **Tres Cruces**, 162 km (100 miles) from Cusco. Overlooking the Amazon Basin from atop the Andes, the town is home to the Apa Kanahuey people, "Those

who are close to God" in Quechua. Tres Cruces sits above the clouds; its vistas are described as "awesome, breathtaking, spectacular," but words can't really capture the overwhelming sensations that come from watching the sun rise for three hours or more. May and June are the best months for the sun's show, a spectacle of rosy gray mist dissolving into shimmering treetops.

From here, the road crawls to Shintuya, where the park begins in misty cloud-forest and *puna*, Andean plateaus covered with gnarled and twisted trees. The highlands give way to massive groves of bamboo, which clatter and sing in the rain like a forest of wind chimes. Travelers en-route to the park's varied lodges board canoes by a small park office, where they must register before entering Manú. It can take a full day or two to reach a lodge from here; approaching the park in this manner is a time-consuming matter.

Most travelers arrive via plane, which allows them more time in the reserve rather than on rough roads. Boats are the only means of transportation allowed in Manú, and visitors quickly find they want more and more time to travel deep into the subtropical forest. The Río Madre de Dios and other smaller rivers trickle into swamps within Manú. In the rainy season from December to March the region is filled with rushing rivers; in the dry season (April to November) the rivers dissolve into vast floodplains.

Roads leading to oil wells slash through the jungle.

The Manú Biosphere Reserve consists of four separate entities. The National Park, which comprises over half the area, may be visited only by scientists with a purpose and a permit from Lima. Indigenous groups and ecotourism workers inhabit the Multiple-Use Zone, in which there are several lodges with tourist accommodations. The third zone is a reserve for indigenous people who still live according to their ancestral way of life. The fourth is designated for research and ecotourism; the only accommodations here are in the Manú Lodge, although tent

species of parrots and macaws; one can spot dozens on most mornings when the birds swarm to the clay hillside for their daily feeding.

A simple boat ride can result in amazing wildlife sightings. Capuchin monkeys, squirrel monkeys, black caiman, and otters all sun and feed at the river's edge. Trails into the jungle provide up-close views of liana vines creeping and braiding into each other up fig trees, along with rare wildflowers covered with butterflies, and troops of leaf-cutter ants headed to their nests.

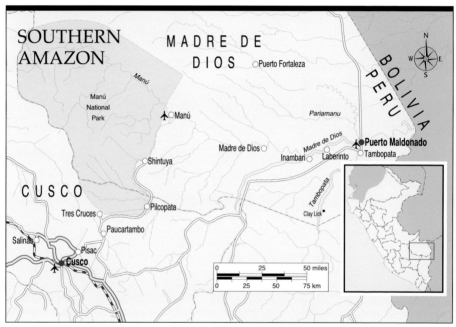

camps are available to those with permission.

Manú is a cult destination for nature lovers because of its diverse biospheres and rare birds, mammals, and plants. Researchers are constantly combing the shrubs, vines, and trees for medicinal plants; Amazonian shamans and healers have become invaluable to the international scientific community. **Birders** are in awe of the region and carry their life lists, identification books, and binoculars from cloud-forests to swamps. Everyone is enamored with the **Tambo Blanquillo** clay lick (or *collpa*), in the southern end of the park (there are smaller licks in the park as well). Blanquillo is famed for its abundant

ORGANIZED TOURS

Many of the tour operators offering Manú trips are based in Cusco, the traditional starting point for trips into the reserve. The most established companies are represented by international travel agencies, and you can easily set up your journey before leaving home. Manú doesn't come cheap; a typical tour with meals and accommodations costs US$1,200 for a four-day tour, and in addition you'll pay for air or road travel and for additional tours within the reserve. Advance reservations are strongly advised in the dry season, as all the lodges combined can only handle a few hundred people per day. Some lodges are closed during the rainy season, and the wild conditions of the terrain can throw schedules off even during times of peak tourism.

Eco-Tour Manú ((84) 252721 FAX (84) 234793 E-MAIL postmaster@mnt.com.pe, Avenida Pardo 1046, Cusco, is an organization of Manú operators committed to rainforest conservation. They can recommended members whose services best meet your interests and budget.

Manú Nature Tours ((84) 252721 FAX (84) 234793 E-MAIL postmaster@mnt.com.pe, Avenida Pardo 1046, Cusco, or in Lima (/FAX (1) 428990, Centro Plaza Conquistadores 396,

Expediciones Manú ((84) 226671 FAX (84) 236706, Avenida el Sol 582, Cusco, operates expeditions of four to nine days, at the inexpensive **Parrot Inn**, two hours down river from Boca Manú on the Madre de Dios river. The comfortable lodge is located right on a small oxbow lake outside the Manú Reserve's boundaries but within the private Reserva Blanquillo and is close to the Blanquillo macaw lick, one of the region's main attractions. Multiple species of macaws and parrots congregate at the lick each morning to eat the clay, which aids their digestion.

S-101, San Isidro, operates **Manú Lodge**, the only lodge in the Reserve Zone, slightly over six kilometers (four miles) by boat from Boca Manú. The company's owners are highly regarded for their work in organizing the lodge owners, training local guides, and providing a wealth of touring options, from professional birdwatching to river rafting. **Pantiacolla Tours** ((84) 238323 FAX (84) 233727, Calle Plateros 360, Cusco, offers eight- or nine-day jungle trips, either camping or staying at the inexpensive **Pantiacolla Lodge**, 30 minutes down-river from the end of the road at Shintuya in the Cultural Zone. Members of the South American Explorer's Club consistently rave about the couple who own Pantiacolla and their commitment to ecotourism.

HOW TO GET THERE

The only way tourists can get into Manú is with an organized tour headed to one of the lodges. You must make arrangements in advance either in Cusco or Lima (or before your trip). Most companies arrange charter flights from Cusco to Boca Manú, where the small airstrip is located. Those traveling overland from Cusco can board a public bus in the city — though the buses are usually just pickup trucks with wooden seats packed with passengers and supplies. The bus-trucks make stops in Paucartambo and Pilcopata, where you might want to

Boats clog the shores at busy river ports.

break up the grueling trip with a night in one of the two towns' small *hostals*. You can also reach Manú via boat from Puerto Maldonado, a ill-advised journey of three to five days.

PUERTO MALDONADO

There's not much reason to stay in Puerto Maldonado, capital of the largely undeveloped department of Madre de Dios. About 25,000 residents live around the town, which sits at the confluence of the Madre de Dios

There isn't much to do in this laid-back town; for most visitors it is just a stopover on the way to the jungle. There are some decent restaurants, however, specializing in fish. Socializing means strolling along the main street, Avenida León Velarde, sitting in the main square, the Plaza de Armas (which has a strange Asian-looking clock-tower at one end) or stopping in at one of the bars. The port itself is a rather bizarre spot, with a huge dirt parking lot and a lineup of shacks where water, snacks, and last-minute jungle supplies can be purchased. Today, this

and Tambopata rivers. Like Iquitos to the north, the city was created to serve the rubber industry of the early twentieth century; the barons did not settle in elegant mansions, however, and the city has little charm. Gold has always drawn prospectors to the rivers here, which rush down steep flows from the Andes. Oil has replaced rubber as the natural resource well worth tapping, but locals and foreign gold miners still pan for nuggets at lonely outposts. Because it is a center for gold mining and logging, the jungle surrounding the town has been stripped. The subtropical forest in the surrounding area around the Madre de Dios river, however, is still impressive and, in fact, more intact than the jungle around Iquitos.

port is a point of departure for trips to Bolivia and into the southern jungle, including Tambopata Reserves.

Puerto Maldonado is one of the few places in Peru where yellow-fever vaccine is sometimes required. There is a yellow fever vaccination checkpoint at Puerto Maldonado airport; proof of the vaccination wasn't required in late 1998. If they are checking and you don't have proof, you may be required to get the shot on the spot at an airport clinic.

WHERE TO STAY AND EAT

The peak tourism season occurs from June through October, but you can usually find a room in town any time. The hotels cater to business travelers and workers headed to the oil and lumber fields. The fanciest digs in town are at the **Hotel Don Carlos (** /FAX (84) 571323, Avenida León Velarde 1271, with 15 air-conditioned rooms and a good restaurant overlooking the Río Tambopata. **Cabaña-quinta (** (84) 571863 FAX (84) 571890 has no air conditioning, but does have a pleasant garden, friendly staff, and a restaurant.

HOW TO GET THERE

There is daily air service from and to Lima and Cusco on AeroContinente and AeroPeru. The arduous overland trip from Cusco to Puerto Maldonado via Mazuko involves some buses but mainly trucks, on a bad road for about 50 bone-jarring hours. Most of the road is unpaved; it is a definite miss in the rainy season. The scenery is predictably magnificent.

Most people prefer to arrange their jungle trips before leaving home or in Cusco to avoid delay or last-minute surprises.

TAMBOPATA

Puerto Maldonado is the entry point for the Tambopata region, where accessibility and an abundance of wildlife are attracting ever-increasing numbers of tourists and entrepreneurs. For me, Tambopata has the perfect combination of rustic novelties and natural challenges. Perhaps that's because I arrived with the winds from Patagonia called *freajas*. The first day I sweated and gasped from the heat, then watched a storm build in the jungle as winds lashed the trees and thunder rumbled from afar. The temperature dropped from 32°C (90°F) to 10°C (50°F). The next day I bundled up in a silk thermal shirt (don't leave home without one), two T-shirts, long pants, and a double layer of socks, and asked for two wool blankets for my open-air room. I refused to shower for nearly three days, and resorted to two-minute sponge baths. Yet I watched hundreds of macaws and parrots dine on salty clay every morning at dawn, and saw shy capybaras (like a prehistoric link between an anteater and a pig) sun themselves on riverbanks at the end of the storm.

Tambopata's lodges are all located within a few hours' boat ride from Puerto Maldo-

nado near a **clay lick** (called a *collpa*) that is said to be larger than any in Manú. Guests and guides ride small motorboats before dawn to various mud and pebble beaches facing the lick. Clouds of small gray and white swifts swoop over a stark, dark hillside and settle in the forest canopy above the river. Parrots and macaws soon follow, squawking and screeching in their approach. The din continues for several minutes, and then the birds descend in a ribbon of vibrant colors along the red-gray clay. Streams of macaws — scarlet, chestnut-headed, and blue-and-yellow birds some nearly two-foot tall — settle in the hill's cracks and fissures as swarms of green parrots flock from one favored spot to the next. The show can continue for an hour or more — I filled a 60-minute cassette tape with bird cries one morning and still missed the finale.

A surprising number of large mammals cavort about in Tambopata as well. On one hike I saw a large circle cleared in dense jungle — a tapir and jaguar had fought several rounds a week earlier. Parts of the tapir's bones lay about the gutted earth. Another morning I spotted dusty titi, tamarind, and squirrel monkeys during a three-hour hike. It took six hours by boat to reach my jungle camp, a research center deep in the jungle. But there are several lodges closer to Puerto Maldonado that offer similar experiences.

Tambopata is divided into several public and private reserves with changing boundaries and names. The **Tambopata Reserved Zone** was created in 1977; it comprises 5,500 hectares (13,500 acres) surrounding the Explorer's Inn Lodge. The area is known for its abundance of birds. In fact, this area has a high density of many species, from trees to butterflies to beetles, which is why it was designated a reserve. The **Tambopata-Candamo Reserved Zone** was created in 1990 after lobbying by British and United States conservation groups. It encompasses the entire Tambopata drainage basin, which includes cloud-forests and tropical savanna in addition to the subtropical forests of the lower Tambopata near Puerto Maldonado. Oxbow lakes and lagoons are sandwiched between the Madre de Dios, Tambopata and

Children parade down the streets in Puerto Maldonado, the largest town in the Southern Amazon.

Heath rivers, offering havens for giant river otters and caiman.

River travel in this area can be fascinating. It is not uncommon to see crocodiles and sideneck turtles along the river, or puma or capybara (or at least their tracks) in the mud at water's edge. When the water is low, vast deposits of volcanic rock are exposed as long beaches. River residents travel past tour boats in *peke-pekes*, the ubiquitous long canoe-like structure with something like a lawnmower motor dangling into the water at the back. Some lodges and boat captains at the port

wings. The baby birds use the claws to climb back to their roosts after falling into the river. Watson's bell birds bark their distinctive calls, hummingbirds flutter amid wild lilies. You can also spot kingfishers, herons, flamingos, tinamous, curacaos and the Pavonine quetzal — along with parrots and macaws. **Anglers** are drawn to the corvina, piranha and catfish in the rivers and lakes.

The Tambopata region is as endangered as every other part of the Amazonian basin. It is littered with petroleum reserves; reserves are edged by oil fields. Get there soon.

offer trips to **Lago Valencia**, about 60 km (37 miles) from Puerto Maldonado, near the Bolivian border. It takes two to four hours to get there (depending on the strength of the outboard motor), and twice as long to come back. Smaller lakes dot the jungle's interior; access depends on the water level.

The Río Tambopata is becoming popular with **river rafters** and has been featured in nature and travel television shows. The rivers are highest in April and May; lodges can assist with rafting trips, though you may need to bring your own gear.

Birders are particularly fond of this region, for good reason. Among the most fascinating creatures is the prehistoric-looking hoatzín, with small claws at the end of its

LODGES AND TOURS

The easiest way to visit Tambopata is to set up a tour and accommodations in advance through an international or Peruvian agency. **Rainforest Expeditions** ((01) 4218347 E-MAIL rforest@perunature.com WEB SITE www.perunature.com, Galeon 120, San Borja, Lima, arranges excellent trips to **Posada Amazonas** and the **Tambopata Research Center**. The Posada, two hours by boat from Puerto Maldonado, has 23 rooms in a series of wood structures set in the jungle. The uncovered windows offer limitless wildlife and star sightings; private bathrooms with fairly consistent hot water make this a more luxurious hostelry than most. Generous meals are served buffet style in the large dining room, where lectures on insects and birds are held most evenings.

The Posada is partially owned by the local Ese'eja Native Community. Indigenous guides lead hikers through the jungle, explaining traditional uses of plants. Giant river otters are sometimes spotted on excursions to Lago Tres Chimbadas; harpy eagle nests can sometimes be spotted from a 30-m (98-ft)-tall tower near the Posada. The Research Center, another five or six hours along the river, is blissfully secluded and comfortably

rustic. The rooms have open-air windows (changing clothes in those at the front of the lodge can be a challenge), comfy beds with mosquito nets, and hooks for hanging damp clothes. Shared baths have flush toilets and cold-water showers; meals are served in a central dining room presided over by a troop of semi-tame scarlet macaws called *los chicos*. The center is close to what may be the world's largest clay lick. Eagle-eyed hikers on the Ocelot Trail sometimes spot jaguar, puma, and ocelot tracks. Trips can be set up through Rainforest Expeditions (see above) or Wildland Adventures in the United States ((202) 365-0686 TOLL-FREE (800) 345-4453 FAX (206) 363-6615 WEB SITE www.wildland.com, 3516 NE 155th Street, Seattle, Washington 98155.

Tambopata Jungle Lodge ((84) 238911, Avenida Pardo 705 in Cusco, is located on the Río Tambopata just before it merges with the Río Malinowski. The bungalows have double and quad rooms with private baths. **Explorer's Inn**, ᶜ/o Peruvian Safaris ((1) 316330 or (1) 313047 FAX (1) 328866, Avenida Garcilaso de la Vega 1334, Lima; in Cusco ((84) 235342, Plateros 365, is found within the Tambopata Reserve, about three hours upriver from Puerto Maldonado. This lodge also serves as a research center and is set in one of the most beautiful remaining patches of rainforest anywhere on the earth. This lodge has around 30 km (nearly 19 miles) of trails in the surrounding jungle. About an hour by boat from Puerto Maldonado and another hour's hike through the jungle brings you to Lago Sandoval, site of the **Sandoval Lodge** booked through Turismo de los Angeles ((84) 571070, Jirón Puno 657 in Cusco.

Cusco Amazonica Lodge ((1) 462775 FAX (1) 455598, Andalucia 174, Miraflores, Lima; or in Cusco ((84) 232161 or (84) 223769, Procuradures 48, has been around since 1975 and is the most accessible lodge just 50 minutes from Puerto Maldonado. **Amazonia Lodge** (/FAX (84) 231370 in Cusco is on the Río Alto Madre de Dios, across the river from village of Atalaya. **Eco Amazonia Lodge** (/FAX (1) 462286, Pasaje Los Piños 114, Oficina 306 in Miraflores, Lima; or in Cusco ((84) 236159 at Plateros 351, is located about two hours down river from Puerto Maldonado. Oxbow lakes abound here.

Sachavachayoc Lodge ᶜ/o CEDCON office ((1) 4228800 or 4790540 FAX (1) 4790430 at Newton College, Lima, is a research center with a recently opened lodge about 60 km (37 miles) from Puerto Maldonado; there are two other "outposts" within the forest. Visits of two to eight days are structured around educational programs of interest to rainforest enthusiasts. One of the newest offerings, **Baguaja River Lodge** (/FAX (84) 228978 in Cusco, is located just 10 km (six miles) from Puerto Maldonado and has a few rooms in thatched huts.

OPPOSITE LEFT: Students from urban universities learn about semi-wild macaws in Tambopata. RIGHT: Trees tower above riverbanks, providing perches for monkeys and macaws. ABOVE: A Conibo Indian bearing the fruits of a river expedition is depicted in an engraving.

Travelers'
Tips

GETTING TO PERU

BY AIR

There are three international airports in Peru: Aeropuerto Internacional Jorge Chavez in Lima, Iquitos's Aeropuerto Internacional Francisco Secada Vigneta in the northeastern Amazon basin and Cusco's Aeropuerto Velasco Astete. Airlines with flights from the United States and Canada to Peru include AeroPeru, Aeroméxico, Avianca, Aerolineas Argentinas, American, Continental, Lan Chile, Lacsa, United, and Varig. Those flying from Europe include Air France, Alitalia, British Airways, Iberia, KLM, and Lufthansa. Service from other South American countries is available on Aerolineas Argentinas, AeroPeru, Ecuatoriana de Aviación, Lan Chile, Lineas Aéreas Parguayas, Lloyd Aereo Boliviano, and Varig. Air New Zealand and Qantas Airways provide flights from Australia and are generally routed through Los Angeles, with a connecting flight to Lima on Lan Chile.

Flights from the United States generally arrive in Peru by way of Miami or Houston. Travel time from New York is eight hours, five and a half hours from Miami, and eight and a half hours from Houston. Travelers from London can expect to be in the air for over 17 hours.

Travel agencies offering general and special interest tours of Peru are listed in TAKING A TOUR, page 56.

to Manaus, in the heart of the Brazilian Amazon. From there you'll probably switch boats for the trip to Benjamin Constante at the borders of Brazil, Colombia, and Peru. Travel time depends on currents and tides, but it's approximately two weeks. From here it's generally smaller boats to Ramón Castilla, Peru for a journey of two or three days to Iquitos. Ferry boats travel across Lake Titicaca from La Paz, Bolivia to Puno, Peru. Travel agencies offering boat tours are listed in TAKING A TOUR, page 56.

By Car

The *Panamericana* (Pan-American Highway) runs through Peru along the coast connecting Peru with Ecuador to the north and Chile to the south. The last Ecuadorian stop before entering Peru is Huaquillas, after which you'll cross the international bridge over the Río Zarumilla and enter Peru at the small town of Aguas Verdes, about two kilometers (just over a mile) from the border. The northernmost city before leaving Chile for Peru is Arica. From there you'll enter Tacna, which is about 42 km (26 miles) from the border.

ARRIVING AND LEAVING

The transportation system at Peru's airports can be dreadfully confusing. Typically, the most expensive taxis are located right outside baggage claim. Less expensive taxis park outside the airport parking lots; drivers solicit passengers at the airport exits. In some areas, minibuses called *colectivos* offer the least expensive transportation, but may stop at several hotels on the way to your destination.

Most international travelers do not need a visa to enter Peru. A valid passport is sufficient to receive a tourist card good for 90 days. The passport should be valid for six months beyond your intended stay. Immigration officials may also request proof that you have purchased a ticket to leave the country. Once your passport has been stamped, make a copy of your photo page, the immigration stamp, and your tourist card. Keep it with you at all times. A copy usually

By Bus

Bus service is available between Peru and its neighbors Ecuador, Brazil, and Bolivia, though travel times are extensive and services limited.

By Ship

It is possible to get from the mouth of the Amazon at Belém, Brazil all the way to Iquitos, Peru. This is budget, adventure travel for the most part, although tour companies offer more expensive and comfortable alternatives for some segments. Travelers should bring a hammock and sheet/bedding for sleeping, snacks, sunscreen, and shade hat. The first leg of the trip takes you from Belém

Wooden plows and sturdy cows are used to cultivate Andean farms.

suffices; if not, you can retrieve the original from your hotel safe. Visa extensions and other immigration problems are handled through the Dirección de Migración ((1) 330 4020, Avenida España 700 in Lima's Breña neighborhood, which is open Monday through Friday from 8 AM to noon.

Upon departing the country by air, there is an airport tax of US$25 payable in dollars or *soles*. Keep the cash stashed away with your ticket to avoid last-minute hassles, as some airports do not have money exchange offices and airlines will not accept traveler's checks

or credit cards. Always reconfirm your flight 48 hours in advance of your departure and check on the exact time of the flight. Schedules change with appalling frequency, and reservations can be canceled if you have not reconfirmed. Though it may be inconvenient, it's best to do so in person at the airline office. For international flights you must be at the airport at least two hours before your scheduled departure.

CONSULATES AND EMBASSIES

ABROAD

Peruvian embassies or consulates in other countries include:

Australia ((02) 9-262 6464 FAX (02) 9-290 2939, Level Three, 30 Clarence Street, New South Wales 2000, Australia.
Canada ((416) 963-9696 or (416) 963-5561 FAX (416) 963-9074, 10 Saint Mary Street, Suite 301, Toronto, Ontario M4Y 1P9.
England ((0171) 235-6867 FAX (0171) 823-2789, 52 Sloane Street, London SW1 95P.

France ((01) 42893013 FAX (01) 42895509 E-MAIL comperparis@i-t.fr, 102 avenue des Champs Élysées 75008 Paris.
Germany ((30) 2291455 or (30) 2291587 FAX (30) 2292857 E-MAIL conper.berlin@t-online.de, Schadowstrasse 6, 10117 Berlin.
Italy ((06) 8848230 FAX (06) 8848273 E-MAIL c.peru@flashnet.it, Via Degli Appennini, 746-Interno 2, 00198 Rome.
Japan ((03) 57934444 or (03) 57934445 FAX (03) 5793 4446, Gitana Fuji Building 1-13-12 Higashi Gotanda Shinagawa — KU Tokyo 141 0022.
Mexico ((5) 525 5618 or (5) 208 0606 FAX (525) 525 5618 E-MAIL comperu@data.mx, Sala Manca No. 34 Despacho 401, Colonia Roma, C.P. 06700, Mexico, D.F.
Netherlands ((20) 622 8580 FAX (20) 638 5639 E-MAIL postbus@conperamsterdam.demon .nl, Weteringschans 102, 1017 XS Amsterdam.
Spain ((01) 562 9022 or (01) 562 9012 FAX (01) 562 9111 E-MAIL 100627.2233@compuserve .com, C/o Maldonado No. 29, Bajos, 28006 Madrid.
Switzerland ((22) 7311912 or (22) 7311323 FAX (22) 7311347 E-MAIL consulate.peru @itu.ch, 50 Rue Rothschild, 1202 Geneva.
United States ((202) 462-1084 or (202) 462-1085 FAX (202) 462-1088 E-MAIL conwash@erols.com, 1625 Massachusetts Avenue NW, Sixth Floor, Washington, DC 20036.

IN PERU

Foreign embassies or consulates located within Peru, all in greater Lima, are:
Canada ((1) 4444015 or (1) 4443893 FAX (1) 2424050, Calle Libertad 130, Miraflores.
France ((1) 2217598, Arequipa 3415, San Isidro.
Germany ((1) 4224919, Arequipa 4210, Miraflores.
Great Britain ((1) 4334735 or (1) 4334839 FAX (1) 433 4735, Edificio El Pacifico Washington, 12th floor, Plaza Washington, Avenida Arequipa, Lima 100.
Italy ((1) 4632727 or (1) 4632728 or (1) 4632729 FAX (1) 463 5317, Avenida Gregorio Escobedo 298, Jesús María.
Japan ((1) 4639854 or (1) 4639144, San Felipe 356, Jesús María.
Mexico ((1) 2211173, Avenida Santa Cruz 330, San Isidro.

Netherlands ((1) 4761069 Principal 190, Fourth floor, Santa Catalina, La Victoria.
Portugal ((1) 4409905, Avenida Central 643, Fourth floor, San Isidro.
Spain ((1) 2217704 or (1) 2217207, Jorge Basadre 498, San Isidro.
Switzerland ((1) 2640305, Salaverry 3240, San Isidro.
United States ((1) 4343000 FAX (1) 4343037 Avenida La Encalada, block 17, Monterrico, Lima 33.

TOURIST INFORMATION

There are tourist information offices or booths at most major destinations, including Lima, Cusco, Puno, and Arequipa. City maps are typically poor in quality, and there are few printed brochures or tourist pamphlets. Information is less accessible in smaller towns. The addresses of local information offices are listed in the regional chapters.

One of the most valuable sources of overall information is the **South American Explorer's Club** (/FAX (1) 4250142 E-MAIL montague@amauta.rcp.net WEB SITE www .samexplo.org, Avenida Portugal 146, Lima, a nonprofit organization helping members share information about travel. They have many services, including equipment storage, book exchange, mail service and sale of books, maps, handicrafts and used equipment.

GETTING AROUND

By Air

Flying is the fastest way to travel within Peru. Several airlines offer domestic air travel with connections between Lima and other cities, including Arequipa, Cusco, Iquitos, Puerto Maldonado, and Trujillo. Some airlines offer passes, usually good for 30 days. The price of the pass depends on how many flights you book. Check with your travel agent. An airport tax of S/10 is charged for every domestic departure. Regional airlines traveling within Peru include **AeroPeru** ((1) 2411797 in Miraflores, Lima and **AeroContinente** ((1) 2424260 in Miraflores, Lima.

Always book your flight far in advance and claim your seat with a credit-card deposit.

Be sure to confirm and reconfirm your reservation, know which airport you're flying from, and arrive at least 90 minutes before the scheduled departure. Overbookings are common, and flight check-in typically involves waiting in several lines while one person checks your ticket, another screens your luggage, another checks your bags and so on.

By Train

Train travel within Peru was once a highlight of the journey. This is no longer true. The train

between Lima and Huancayo, the highest rail line in the world, ceased functioning in the early 1990s. Rumors of its imminent revival run rampant, but none have proven true thus far. The most popular train in the country runs between Cusco and Machu Picchu; the train passes through several small villages along rushing rivers beneath glacier-topped mountains. There are several classes of service; the most comfortable is the auto-vagon tourist train. The only other lines recommended for tourists run from Arequipa to Juliaca and Puno, and from Puno and Juliaca to Cusco. Inexpensive local trains stop

OPPOSITE: Cusco's airport is one of the busiest in the country. ABOVE: A Chancay mummy boasts a false head and traditional crown.

frequently and have little in the way of comfort or services. The *Trenes de Turistas*, are more comfortable (though far from luxurious), faster, and more expensive. Schedules change without warning, so make sure and check them the day before you wish to leave.

Some rules for train travel: Always carry drinking water, snacks, toilet paper, and a warm sweater or poncho; be acutely cautious with your possessions at all times (pickpockets and thieves abound); and expect significant delays. Arrive early for your train and try to snag a window seat (though the glass may be grimy). Expect considerable discomfort as the rail lines and coaches are poorly maintained.

By Bus

Bus travel is cheap, easy, and relatively comfortable in Peru. Buses are run by private companies, which often have separate terminals within a city. Always know which line you're looking for when asking directions to the *Terminal de Autobuses*. See the regional sections for information on local routes.

The condition of the buses ranges from comfortable to downright dangerous. **Cruz del Sur** and **Ormeño** are two of the larger companies, offering first-class buses with food services and video entertainment. Follow the suggestions for train travel to better your chances for a safe and comfortable trip. Expect delays, especially during inclement weather. While traveling at night is tempting, especially if you're trying to save money on hotel rooms, don't take the risk. More travelers die from road accidents than from all tropical diseases combined.

By Rental Car

Rental cars are expensive and can be hard to find during peak tourism periods. Four-wheel-drive vehicles are best for those headed to the hinterlands. Weekly rentals for a standard sedan start at US$350 plus insurance and taxes, though a car at that price is a real bargain. Most agencies quote rates in the US$500 per week range. Some rental agencies restrict the areas where you can take their cars. All require a credit card to be used as a guarantee.

International rental agencies with offices in Lima include: **Avis** ((1) 4341111 TOLL-FREE IN THE UNITED STATES (800) 831-2847 WEB SITE www.avis.com; **Hertz** ((1) 4424509 TOLL-FREE IN THE UNITED STATES (800) 654-3131 WEB SITE www.hertz.com; **Budget** ((1) 5751674 TOLL-FREE IN THE UNITED STATES (800) 472-3325; **Thrifty** ((1) 5751791 TOLL-FREE IN THE UNITED STATES (800) 367-2277 WEB SITE www.thrifty.com; **Alamo** ((1) 4447000 or (1) 4443934 TOLL-FREE IN THE UNITED STATES (800) 327-9633 WEB SITE www.goalamo.com; and **National** ((1) 5751111 TOLL-FREE IN THE UNITED STATES (800) 227-7368 WEB SITE www.nationalcar.com.

Local rental companies include **Fiesta Rent-a-Car** ((1) 2413058 and **Inka's Rent-a-Car** ((1) 5751390. Some agencies will arrange for you to hire a driver at about US$25 per day plus their food and accommodations.

It is also possible to hire a car and driver through tour companies. Prices are high, starting at about US$200 per day. For information see TAKING A TOUR, page 56.

The *Panamericana* (Pan-American Highway) runs north to south through the coast of Peru from Ecuador to Chile. The Carretera Central runs from Lima into the Andes. Few roads and highways are named or numbered. For information on specific road conditions, contact the **Asociación Automotriz del Peru** ((1) 4400495, Avenida Dos de Mayo 299, San Isidro, Lima. A foreign driving license is good for six months. If the vehicle is registered to someone other than the driver, he must carry a notarized letter of permission from the owner. Security checkpoints are common in outlying areas; always carry your passport, tourist card, and rental agreement.

Driving in Lima is a frightening experience and not for the faint of heart. The pace is swift and most traffic signs and lights are looked at merely as suggestions often to be ignored. When traveling by car in Peru, it is best to do so during daylight hours. Many roads are poorly marked and in need of repair. A good spare tire and a full tank of gas are priorities. In the more remote areas, road services are few and far between. Be aware of trucks and buses trying to pass you on narrow roads and major highways; let them by or risk your life. Gas is *extra* (84 octane) and *importada* (95 octane). A gas station is called *grifo*. The Instituto Geografico

Nacional ((1) 4759960 or (1) 4743030, Avenida Aramburu 1198, Surquillo district in Lima, has maps and aerial photographs as does Servicio Aerofotografico Nacional ((1) 4671341, Las Palmas Airforce Base, Surco.

HITCHHIKING

If you attempt to hitch a ride in Peru, it is unlikely that a passenger car will veer over to pick you up. Your only hope is a truck driver, and he will almost certainly except to be paid. Establish the price before the driver takes off.

tors or ramps and many have seemingly endless stairways. If you have difficulty walking, be sure to confirm a groundfloor room.

Advance reservations are strongly advised for times of peak tourism including the months of July and August and all religious holidays. The sole hotel beside the ruins at Machu Picchu books up a year in advance, and Cusco hotels book solid during the Inti Raymi festival in June. Ayacucho is particularly popular for Semana Santa (Easter week), and the Amazon region books

ACCOMMODATIONS

Parts of Peru are experiencing a hotel boom, and major hotel chains are investing heavily in Lima. First-class modern hotels with satellite television, restaurants, and pools are available in Lima, Iquitos, Puno, and Cusco. More moderate establishments are the norm, but the real pleasures are found in small inns all over the country. Some in the Andes are built beside mineral springs; others are housed in converted monasteries and convents. Budget hotels abound in small towns, where a double room with private bath can run as low as US$10 per night. Facilities for travelers with disabilities are limited. Few hotels outside the major cities have eleva-

up far in advance during peak birdwatching season in October. Make your reservations through the fax numbers in hotel listings; expect delays in getting a response, and be persistent. If your itinerary is tight, have a travel agent at home or in Peru pre-book all your rooms.

Room rates in Lima are extraordinarily high; prices drop the farther away you get from the main tourism areas. Lodges in nature reserves sometimes include meals in their rates; when it's your only option, you might as well pay the whole fee up front and not worry about each meal. Peru's hotel tax

Copper hulls provide strength for boats burdened with fresh-cut logs from the Iquitos jungle.

is a whopping 18%, which is often, but not always included in the room rate. Ask about the tax and any service charges (10% is often added to the tab) in advance. If booking ahead, make sure your voucher includes all charges that are covered. Many hotels include a complimentary breakfast buffet. Hotels in some areas drop their rates when tourism is low; don't accept the first price offered. On the other hand, when tourism is high you often get a better rate by booking in advance. Rates used in this book for a double room in high season are as follows:

Very Expensive	over US$150
Expensive	US$76 to US$150
Moderate	US$40 to US$75
Inexpensive	under $40

RESTAURANTS

Peruvian cuisine has experienced vast improvement over the past decade, and international dishes are available at most hotels and in restaurants in major cities. Regional dishes vary greatly throughout the country; see GALLOPING GOURMETS, page 50, for details. For information on the top restaurants in the country see LIVING IT UP, page 34.

Fish from the sea and mountain rivers factors heavily on most menus, as does chicken, which may well be the national dish. Beef is surprisingly inferior, considering the wide swaths of cattle ranges etched in the Andes. Most prime beef is destined for export, as is the best mountain coffee.

Lunch is the main meal of the day, usually served between 1 PM and 4 PM. Many restaurants serve a set lunch, called the *menú*, which includes soup, starter, the main course (the *segundo*), and dessert. There is often confusion over this meal, since those asking for the menu will be given a list of the set meals. If you wish to order à la carte, ask for *la carta*. Dinner is a lighter meal, saved for 8 PM or 9 PM. Snacks are ubiquitous, served with drinks and at street stands.

Our restaurant prices are based on the average cost of a three-course meal per person, not including drinks.

Very Expensive	more than US$50
Expensive	US$21 to US$50
Moderate	US$10 to US$20
Inexpensive	under US$10

TIPPING

Tips are generally not expected in the budget restaurants. A tip of 10% to 15% is expected in the more expensive restaurants unless a service charge has already been added to the bill. Taxi drivers do not need to be tipped. You should establish the price of the ride before you set out and then stick to your guns. Local guides and drivers should be tipped 10% of the cost of the tour for a day's outing.

BANKING

Banks are usually open weekdays from 9:30 AM to 4 PM. Banks, hotels and most shops readily accept United States dollars; travelers checks work best for other currencies. It can be difficult to change other Latin American currencies. If you're traveling to several countries, try to use up your money in each country and start afresh with travelers checks in the next. There are a few automatic teller machines in Lima. The quickest way to exchange money is at *casas de cambio*, which usually offer better rates than hotels. Some charge a commission. Avoid using the "street changers" if you're not familiar with the currency. You can get confused and cheated easily.

CURRENCY

The currency of Peru is the *nuevo sol*. There are 100 *centimos* in one nuevo sol. Bill notes are in denominations of 100, 50, 20, and 10 nuevo sols, with coins in 5, 2, 1, 0.55, 0.20, 0.10, and 0.05 sol denominations. The current exchange rate is S/3.1 to US$1.

BASICS

TIME

Peru time is five hours behind Greenwich mean time, and does not observe daylight savings.

ELECTRICITY

Peru operates on 220 volts AC (60-cycle) nationwide. Bring your own converter and adapter. Many of the outlets in Peru have two round prongs. Some fancier hotels have 110-volt outlets in the bathrooms for shavers only. Electricity blackouts are common; always carry a small flashlight.

WATER

Always drink bottled water, and be sure the seal on the bottle is secure. Hotels are often stingy with their supply of complementary bottled water, and charge exorbitant prices for additional bottles. Carry small bottles with you and stock up on gallon jugs for your room. Water shortages are common even in the major cities, and hot water is often a rare luxury. If hot showers are a must, stay in hotels that have their own water tanks.

WEIGHTS AND MEASURES

Peru uses the Metric System. Liquids are sold in liters, fruits and vegetables by the kilo.

Units of Distance
1 kilometer = 0.625 (⅝) mile
1 meter = 3.28 feet

Units of Weight
1 gram = 0.035 ounces
1 kilogram (kilo) = 2.2 pounds

Units of volume
1 liter = 2.1 US pints = 1.76 UK pints

CLIMATE

Peru's climate is as variable as its terrain, with hot, muggy jungles and snowcapped mountain peaks. There are two basic seasons — wet and dry. Summer lasts from December to April; winter from May through November. The coastal lands are arid except during the summer months, when it can be hot and sticky. January and February are usually the clearest months along the coast. A dense fog (called *garua*) settles over Lima and the sur-

rounding area from May through October. There is usually little rain throughout the year. The summer of 1997–1998 was a dramatic exception, however, when El Niño-driven rains wreaked havoc with much of South America's Pacific coast.

In the mountains, the temperature ranges from -7°C to 21°C (about 20°F to 70°F). Temperatures vary considerably with the altitude; from May through September temperatures in Cusco range from 0°C (32°F) to 22°C (71°F). The heaviest rains occur from October to April, and there is negligible rainfall the rest of the year. The jungle areas are usually hot and humid, except when cold winds from Patagonia (called *freajes*) occasionally sweep through the southern area. Jungle temperatures vary between 20°C (69°F) and 32°C (90°F). The heaviest rainfall occurs from January through April; touring outlying areas can be quite difficult at this time.

OPPOSITE: Colonial tiles back a modern ATM machine in Iquitos. ABOVE: Professional writers set up their machines at street stands to assist locals and tourists with correspondence.

COMMUNICATION AND MEDIA

TELEPHONES

The country code for Peru is 51, with different area codes for cities and towns, followed by a six or seven-digit telephone number. To dial long distance within Peru you must first dial a 0 before the two-digit area code. Dial 108 for an international operator. Most Peruvian towns have a Telefónica del Peru office, which is usually the best place to make both local and international calls. The connection is quick and the receptionist will tell you after you finish the call how much you owe. Street phones, called *kioskos telefónico* are operated by using coins or phone cards, sold in markets, pharmacies, and by street vendors in varying denominations. Hotels almost always tack on a surcharge for all calls.

EMERGENCY PHONE NUMBERS

Directory Assistance (103
Emergencies (105
Operator (100
International Operator (108
24-Hour Tourist Hot Line ((1) 2247888 or (1) 2248600

THE INTERNET

Public Internet offices are available all over the country, in places you would least expect them. Lima has several elaborate cybercafés; in smaller areas you may find a university office with one or two computers available for use by the hour.

MAIL

Postal facilities are adequate in Lima, limited elsewhere. First class airmail to Europe or the United States takes at least a week. The main post office in Lima is located near the Plaza de Armas and is open Monday through Saturday, 8 AM to 8 PM, and Sundays from 9 AM to 2 PM. If you wish to receive mail during your travels, have your letters addressed with your full name, in care of *poste restante*, to the main post office in the city you

are visiting. It is better to make hotel and tour reservations by phone or fax than to rely on the mail.

NEWSPAPERS AND MAGAZINES

Most newspapers are printed in Spanish; daily papers include *El Comercio, Ojo, Expreso, La República, El Mundo, El Peruano*, and *Sintesis*. The English-language *Lima Herald* is published weekly and is available from the larger hotels or bookstores. The *International Herald Tribune* is available at some news stands in Lima.

The English-language *Lima Times* magazine is published monthly. PromPerú, the government tourism authority, publishes a gorgeous monthly magazine called *El Dorado*, with articles in Spanish and English. Some book shops carry back issues. *Bien Venida*, another bilingual magazine, contains excellent articles on cultural themes. Tourist information publications include the *Peru Guide*, a small monthly magazine available in hotels and tourist information offices.

RADIO AND TELEVISION

The national broadcast media operate only in Spanish, and radio and television reception is shaky in all areas outside Lima. Satellite television service with movie and news channels in English is available in a few high-end hotels.

ETIQUETTE

Peru is a conservative, mainly Roman Catholic country where manners and dress are of considerable importance. The polite, soft-spoken approach always works better than a confrontational or demanding one. Begin and end all conversations with a few words in Spanish; *gracias* (thank you) goes a long way in making a good impression.

Peruvians dress conservatively, but casually, and expect the same from travelers. Shorts are frowned upon in the cities, and should not be worn in churches. Stay away from wearing camouflage-style clothing, which could arouse suspicions that you are affiliated with insurgents or the military.

HEALTH

Peru is rife with health risks and offers the unprepared traveler ample exposure to hepatitis, dengue fever, malaria, altitude sickness, cholera, rabies, and typhoid. The insects are enough to intimidate stalwart biologists, and bites, scrapes, bruises, and burns are all signs of the traveler who has been about the country a bit. Common concerns and precautions to take are found below.

Even a mild case can bring on all the symptoms Kane lists, along with a general lassitude that can severely hamper your ability to hike about Inca ruins and explore Andean cities.

Vendors hawking coca leaves greet bus travelers at nearly every mountainous city, offering bundles of the green leaves and a bit of charcoal. Chewing the leaves and charcoal together cuts many of the effects of *soroche*; it also gives one a green tongue and saliva and a slight buzz. *Mate de coca* (coca tea) is available in the lobbies of better hotels

ALTITUDE SICKNESS

Called *soroche* in Peru, altitude sickness is a very real problem for anyone traveling from coastal Lima to Cusco, Machu Picchu, Puno, and Lake Titicaca. One can easily experience dramatic shifts in altitude frequently when traveling about the country; those most affected by such changes should shape their itineraries accordingly.

"Altitude sickness is, in its own perverse way, wonderfully egalitarian," writes Joe Kane in *Running the Amazon*. "An old, fat, chainsmoking drunk is no more likely to suffer its headaches, vomiting, dehydration, confusion, diarrhea, nausea and shortterm memory loss than is a champion athlete."

and at most restaurants, and helps fight altitude symptoms. Prescription medications for altitude sickness are also available in the United States, Canada and Europe; purchase them before heading to South America and follow your doctor's instructions. You can usually cut back on any of these remedies after a few days of acclimation.

Drink plenty of water and little alcohol when in the mountains, where the altitude exacerbates the effects of liquor and the resultant hangovers. Take it slowly the first day or two and get plenty of rest. Try not to smoke. Hikers and climbers should pace themselves and ascend no more than 300 m (1,000 ft) per

Roads are few in the Ancash province and in most rural areas of Peru.

day when above 1,800 m (6,000 ft), and only 150 m (500 ft) per day when over 3,600 m (12,000 ft). If the symptoms are severe, get back to sea level and you should recover quickly.

IMMUNIZATIONS

All travelers to South America should be immunized for Hepatitis A and B; typhoid is also advised. A yellow fever vaccination may be required for travel in the eastern slopes of the Andes or the Amazon Basin. It is a good idea to carry a record of your immunizations along with your passport, and check with your public health service for recommended immunizations before traveling. In the United States, the Center for Disease Control and Prevention operates an international travelers' hotline at ((404) 332-4559 WEB SITE www.cdc.gov.

INSECTS

The truly paranoid should avoid reading *Tropical Nature, Life and Death in the Rainforests of Central and South America*, by Adrian Forsyth and Kenneth Miyata (see RECOMMENDED READING, page 281). The truly curious will love it, especially the chapter entitled "Jerry's Maggot." These two young Harvard-trained biologists spent years in the rainforests, watching beetles and botflies and chronicling their adventures in a most entertaining manner.

The authors inspire a caution which the uninitiated should emulate. Like most guides in the Amazon region, they wear long-sleeved shorts, long pants, socks, and shoes everywhere. Shorts and ingenuously designed sandals might seem sensible when you're browsing through catalogs at home, but they're utterly impractical in the river basin. One of the worst miseries known to river travelers is a chance encounter with a cloud of biting gnats or no-see-ums who appear utterly impervious to any form of repellent. Only long pants, socks, and long sleeves hold them at bay. Ample clothing also helps protect the skin from searing sunlight, and hats not only shade the face but also protect sweaty scalps from stings. Heavy hiking boots can be a drawback on muddy ground; lightweight sneakers fare better and collect less mud. Good traction is a must, as those who have slipped off rickety wooden planks above rivers can attest.

Your chances of being bitten by a snake or mammal are far less than those of enduring a mean, unpredictable sting. Forsyth and Miyata write reverently of the "Creeping Socialists," the ants that populate the rain-forest.

"One of the most painful nonlethal experiences a person can endure is the sting of the giant ant *paraponera clavata*," Miyata wrote. "These ants, with their glistening black bodies over an inch long, sport massive hypodermic syringes and large venom reservoirs. They call upon these weapons with wild abandon when provoked, and they are easily offended beasts. Unlike the stings of honeybees and polybiine wasps, the stings of *Paraponera* are not one-shot affairs."

Most insect stings are nonfatal, but they can cause considerable discomfort. The best protection other than clothing is insect repellent containing a high percentage of DEET. Repellents such as Permethrin can be sprayed on clothing and bedding and last through several washings. Mosquito nets and/or screens are imperative when sleeping in the jungle.

MALARIA, DENGUE FEVER, AND CHOLERA

Malaria is always a concern when you are traveling around water in third-world countries. The mosquitoes that carry the disease bite between dusk and dawn, and the disease may not become apparent until weeks after you've been bitten. Antimalarial medications do not ensure protection against malaria, but they do help and are worth taking in areas where the disease is found. These medications have some nasty side effects, from headaches to reported psychotic episodes, and must be taken for an extended period of time before and after your trip. Check with a specialist in travel medicine if you're concerned about side effects. Even with the drugs, you should take all the clothing and insect repellent precautions discussed above.

Dengue fever is a concern during rainy seasons and unusual weather patterns such as El Niño. The mosquitoes that carry the disease bite during the day and are more common in urban areas. There are no immunizations or prophylactic drugs for Dengue, which is rarely fatal except among the poor who do not receive adequate treatment. The symptoms include headache, fever, muscle pain, and chills and can make you feel miserable. Drink plenty of fluids and get medical care if the symptoms persist more than a couple of days.

Cholera outbreaks occur with disconcerting frequency, usually in times of heavy rains.

well stocked and staffed as the private ones. Many will not accept foreign health insurance coverage and will require a cash payment for services. You may want to purchase supplemental medical insurance with specific coverage for overseas care before you leave your country.

SECURITY

While the Peruvian government has been fairly successful in suppressing the two active terrorists groups in Peru, Sendero

Be particularly cautious with food and water at such times. If you have persistent diarrhea, get tested and treated for cholera.

SEXUAL DISEASES

Sexually transmitted diseases including AIDS (SIDA) are of utmost concern. Carry well-made condoms from home and use them religiously. Don't rely on local condoms; they can tear easily.

MEDICAL FACILITIES

There are good hospitals and clinics in Peru's major cities, but medical care is scarce in rural areas. Public and rural hospitals are not as

Luminoso (Shining Path) and MRTA (Túpac Amaru Revolutionary Movement), they are still considered dangerous and capable of terrorist actions. During 1996 and 1997, the MRTA held hostages at the Japanese Embassy residence in San Isidro, a suburb of Lima, for four months. The Sendero Luminoso bombed police installations in central Lima and Ate Vitarte, as well as a Shell Oil facility in San Borja. Visitors to Peru should be advised of the potential danger from these groups and are strongly advised to consult with their embassy for current security information. Certain areas are worse than others. Ayacucho, long the stronghold for revolutionary groups,

Televisions have arrived in Iquitos, where antennas sprout from humble huts.

has finally returned to peaceful state. Outlying areas around the city are less secure, however. Regions in the northern jungle are ruled by drug lords — stay away.

Peru is certainly not the safest country in the world — poverty and politics have always created conflict among the country's different racial, economic, and religious factions. Protests and uprisings occur far too frequently for comfort, though the country is calmer now than it was in the 1980s. Do not get involved in political protests and meetings, and try to keep your opinions to yourself.

Think of drugs in the same manner. Don't buy drugs, don't use them, don't talk about them. Dealers are delighted to use naive tourists as couriers — never accept an unopened package. Clean out your luggage before packing to go home and make sure everything in it belongs to you. It's a good idea to keep your luggage locked at all times, even in your hotel room. Antidrug agents are as prolific as dealers; if they target you as suspicious you can be followed on your travels — a disconcerting feeling.

Commonsense safety guidelines should be followed throughout the country. Grasp your purses, cameras and wallets tightly; don't flash money or wear gold jewelry; don't wander down deserted streets at night. Stow your passport, plane ticket and extra money in your hotel's safe, but carry a copy of your passport in a money belt. The police can ask you for identification at any time.

Rental cars are easy targets for thieves more interested in what's inside than the vehicle itself. Resist the temptation to leave your car, crammed with your belongings, by the side of the road while exploring. Drop off your gear at your hotel before parking in remote areas. Use guarded parking lots.

Robberies at airports and bus and train stations are common. In some cases, one crook distracts you while an accomplice steals your luggage. Smash and grab attacks on occupied cars are also common. In Cusco, "choke and rob" attacks are on the rise, particularly around the train station and the Plaza de Armas. These are also occurring in Arequipa, around Calle Jerusalén and near the main square, in particular. Traveling with a group will decrease your risk of attack.

If you are attacked or robbed, contact your embassy and the local police department.

WOMEN ALONE

The feminist movement in Peru is still relatively young and confined generally to the urban areas; the *machismo* attitude continues to be prevalent among the male population. Women traveling alone are more prone to annoying whistles, winks and slang comments than any real danger. Worse than the stares and hissing sounds are the occasional gropings in crowded situations, such as on a bus or in a busy market. Blonde and fair women are more often targeted than their darker counterparts. Your best bet is to just ignore these behaviors. If it is possible to travel with a friend, do so.

WHEN TO GO

Peru's varied terrain and climates make it difficult to reach all parts of the country during the best seasons. In general, tourism is highest throughout the country from June through August and during Christmas, Carnaval, and Easter. The mountain areas are most popular from June through September, when rain is scarce and hiking easiest. However, a dense fog blankets the coast during these months and Lima is quite dreary. Though dry season travel provides more comforts, it does have its drawbacks. The most popular attractions are overwhelmed by large tour groups; it's hard to soak in the spiritual essence of Machu Picchu or the wild beauty of the jungle when surrounded by chattering hordes. If you have sufficient time and flexibility, you may enjoy traveling toward the end of the rainy season from March through May. Though you may encounter travel delays and other hardships, you'll be rewarded with the sights of rushing rivers, miles of fields ready for harvest, vast patches of wildflowers, and velvet green mountains.

WHAT TO TAKE

Though travel gear, clothing and books are available in Peru, you're best off bringing what you'll need along with you. Prices for toiletries and all imported goods are quite high, and the quality is often lacking. Pack lightweight, comfortable long pants, shorts, skirts and shirts, and one warm jacket or sweater and thermal underwear for mountain climates. A waterproof, breathable poncho is essential most times of the year; rain and cloud-forests have no dry season. A lightweight umbrella comes in handy as well, and you'll need at least two pairs of sturdy walking shoes. Double the pairs of socks you think you'll need, and throw in one knee-high pair to wear under rubber

PHOTOGRAPHY

Bring more film than you think you could possibly need, along with extra batteries. There are good camera shops in most major cities, and it is possible to get most types of cameras repaired.

LANGUAGE BASICS

Peruvians are extraordinarily patient with travelers who mangle their language, and

boots. Camera buffs should bring all the film and batteries they'll need, since supplies are scarce and expensive. Disposable waterproof cameras come in handy for boat trips. You'll be sorry if you don't bring binoculars for wildlife sightings.

Bug bites, scratches and bruises are a part of any Peruvian adventure; your first-aid kit should include strong bug repellent (DEET), lotion for itches and stings, an antiseptic such as Bactine and gauze or bandages for covering wounds.

Foreign language books are expensive and though some hotels have book exchanges with selections in English, German, Italian, and French (depending on the recent clientele), the choice is often very limited.

appreciate all attempts regardless of the ridiculous content. Practice your Spanish everywhere, using basic phrases to show your respect for the country and the people. Educated Peruvians refer to their use of Spanish as *castellano*, and speak with very proper grammar and very little slang. Expressions you've learned in other Latin American countries such as Mexico may not be acceptable here.

About 50% of Peruvians consider Spanish to be their second language. In fact, indigenous people in remote areas speak no Spanish at all. Quechua was the lingua franca at the time of the conquest, and is still spoken

Peru's golden riches are displayed at the Brüning Museum in Lambayeque.

by native peoples today in varying dialects. In the Amazon basin, locals speak at least a dozen different dialects, though those who work in tourism usually have a good command of basic Spanish phrases. "Creole slang" is used in some areas, while in the northern Amazon Basin the vocabulary is influenced by Brazilian Portuguese.

Below are some common Peruvian words and phrases and general Spanish useful for travelers.

PERUVIAN SPANISH FOR TRAVELERS

Places and Things
airport *aeropuerto*
barren Andean region *paramo*
beach *playa*
bookshop *librería*
bribe *coima*
bridge *puente*
bus station / stop *estación/parada de autobus*
cathedral *catedral*
church *iglesia*
cigarette *cigarrillo*
cigar *puro*
city *ciudad*
complaint *queja*
harbor, port *puerto*
lane or alley *callejón*
market *mercado*
mountain *montaña*
mountain range *cordillera*
mountain dweller *serrano*
museum *museo*
nightclub *peña*
person of mixed indigenous and
    Spanish blood *criollo*
police station *delegación*
post office *oficina de correo*
river *río*
road *jirón*
street *calle*
tourist office *oficina de turismo*
travelers checks *cheques de viajeros*
train *tren*
viewpoint *mirador*
weekly market *feria*

Food and Restaurants
avocado *palta*
baked *al horno*
bakery, cake shop *panadería, pastelería*

barbecue *churrasco*
beans *frijoles*
beef *carne de res*
beefsteak *bistek, lomito*
beer *cerveza*
bill, check *cuenta*
blackberry *mora*
boiled *hervido*
bread *pan*
breakfast *desayuno*
brochette *anticucho*
butter *mantequilla*
cake *torta*
carbonated water *agua con gas*
charcoal grilled *a la parrilla*
cheese *queso*
chicken *pollo*
coffee with milk *café con leche*
corn *choclo*
crêpe *panqueque*
dessert *postre*
dinner *cena*
eggs *huevos*
fermented alcoholic drink *chicha*
fermented alcoholic drink made from
    purple corn *chicha morena*
fish *pescado*
fixed-price menu *menú del día*
fruit *fruta*
fruit juice *jugo de fruta*
garlic *ajo*
glass *vaso*
goat *cabra*
green salad *ensalada verde*
grilled *a la plancha*
ham *jamón*
hot sauce *aji*
ice *hielo*
ice cream *helado*
lobster *langosta*
lunch *almuerzo*
meat *carne*
medium *tres cuartos*
menu *menú*
milk *leche*
mineral water *agua mineral*
mushroom *champiñón/hongo*
octopus *pulpo*
olives *aceitunas*
onion *cebolla*
orange *naranja*
pineapple *piña*
pork *cancho*

potatoes *papas*
pepper *pimienta*
rare *poco hecho*
red wine *vino tinto*
restaurant *restaurante*
rice *arroz*
rosé wine *vino rosa*
salad *ensalada*
salt *sal*
sandwich *sandwich*
sea bass *corvina*
shrimp *camarones*
soup *chupe*
spicy, hot *picante*
squid *calamar*
stewed *estofado/a*
still water *agua natural*
strawberry *fresa*
sugar *azúcar*
supermarket *supermercado*
tavern *chicheria*
tea *té*
trout *trucha*
tuna *atún*
vegetables *verduras*
watermelon *sandía*
well done *bien cocido, entero*
white wine *vino blanco*
wine list *lista de vinos*

Arts and Crafts

bead *chaquira, cuenta*
bracelet *pulsera*
belt *chumpi*
ceramics *cerámica*
clay *barro*
cotton *algodón*
cowhide *cuero*
earring *arete*
folk art *arte popular*
gold *oro, dorado*
handicrafts *artesanías*
jewelry *joyas*
necklace *collar*
ring *anillo*
shawl *chaul*
shirt *camisa*
shoulder wrap *manta*
silver *plata*
sweater *suéter*
pottery *alfarería*
woodcarving *tallados de madera*
wool *lana*

On the Road

accident *accidente*
brakes *frenos*
bus *autobus*
diesel *diesel*
fill it up *lleno*
gas *gasolina*
lights *luces*
oil *aceite*
petrol station *grifo*
pothole *hueco*
road *jirón*
tire *llanta*
water *agua*

Road Signs

detour *desvio*
slow down *despacio*
stop *parada*

Key Words and Phrases

beautiful *bello(a), hermoso(a)*
big *grande*
can/may I…? *¿puedo…?*
cheap *barato(a)*
closed *cerrado(a)*
cold *frío(a)*
do you have…? *¿tiene….? ¿hay…?*
do you speak English? *¿Habla usted inglés?*
excuse me *con permiso, desculpe, perdon*
expensive *caro(a)*
far *lejos*
get in line *haga fila*
good afternoon *buenas tardes*
good morning *buenos días*
good evening/night *buenas noches*
goodbye *adios/chau*
he/she/it is/you are *está*
hello *alo, hola?*
here *aquí*
hot *caliente*
how? *¿cómo?*
how are you? *¿cómo está?*
how many? *¿cuánto(a)s?*
how much is it? *¿cuánto vale?/¿cuánto es?*
I don't know *no sé*
I don't speak Spanish *no hablo español*
I don't understand *no entiendo*
I understand *entiendo*
I would like *quisiera*
I'm sorry *desculpe, lo siento*
left *izquierda*
money *dinero*

much, very, a lot (of)   *mucho/a*
near   *cerca*
new   *nuevo(a)*
no   *no*
none   *ningun(o)*
OK/fine/I agree   *está bien*
old   *viejo(a)*
open   *abierto(a)*
please   *por favor*
right   *derecha*
right there   *allí*
see you later   *hasta luego*
see you soon   *hasta pronto*

small   *pequeño(a)/chico(a)*
straight on   *derecho*
thank you (very much)   *(muchas) gracias*
that   *ese(a)*
there   *allá*
there is/there are   *hay*
this/this one   *éste(a)*
welcome   *bienvendios*
well/good   *bien/bueno*
what?   *¿qué?/¿como?*
where is?   *¿dónde está?*
who?   *¿quién?*
why?   *¿por qué?*
yes   *sí*
you're welcome   *de nada*

In the Hotel
double room   *habitación doble*
room   *habitación, cuarto*
key   *llave*
laundry   *lavandería*
shower   *ducha*
single room   *habitación sencilla*
soap   *jabón*
toilet paper   *papel higénico*

towel   *toalla*
with a bathroom   *con baño*
with a double bed   *con cama matrimonial*
without a bathroom   *sin baño*

In the Post Office
air mail   *por avión*
general delivery   *poste restante*
letter   *carta*
parcel   *paquete*
postcard   *tarjeta postal*
stamp   *sello*

In Emergencies
altitude sickness   *soroche*
clinic   *clínica*
cough   *tos*
diarrhea   *diarrea*
doctor   *médico(a), doctor*
fever   *fiebre*
flu   *gripe*
head cold   *resfriado*
healer   *curandera/o*
help   *ayuda*
hospital   *hospital*
I am allergic to…   *tengo alergia a…*
I am diabetic   *soy diabética*
I have a toothache   *tengo dolor de muela,
   me duelen los dientes*
It hurts   *duele*
nurse   *enfermera*
pain, ache   *dolor*
pharmacy   *farmacia*
sick, ill   *enfermo(a)*
stomach ache   *dolor de estomago*
sunburn   *quemadura del sol*

Animals
bat   *murciélago*
bird   *ave, pájaro*
butterfly   *mariposa*
cougar, mountain lion   *puma, león*
crocodile   *cocodrilo*
deer   *venado*
frog   *rana*
howler monkey   *mono congo*
jaguar   *jaguar, tigre*
macaw   *lapa*
parrot   *loro*
river otter   *nutria*
sloth   *perezoso, perica*
snake   *culebra, serpiente*
spider monkey   *mono araña, mono colorado*

squirrel monkey   *mono ardilla, mono tití*
tapir   *danta*
turtle   *tortuga*

Numbers

1   *uno*
2   *dos*
3   *tres*
4   *cuatro*
5   *cinco*
6   *seis*
7   *siete*
8   *ocho*
9   *nueve*
10   *diez*
11   *once*
12   *doce*
13   *trece*
14   *catorce*
15   *quince*
16   *dieciséis*
17   *diecisiete*
18   *dieciocho*
19   *diecinueve*
20   *veinte*
21   *veintiuno*
30   *treinta*
40   *cuarenta*
50   *cincuenta*
60   *sesenta*
70   *setenta*
80   *ochenta*
90   *noventa*
100   *cien*
200   *doscientos*
500   *quinientos*
1,000   *mil*
2,000   *dos mil*
100,000   *cien mil*
1,000,000   *millón*
2,000,000   *dos millones*

Calendar

Sunday   *domingo*
Monday   *lunes*
Tuesday   *martes*
Wednesday   *miércoles*
Thursday   *jueves*
Friday   *viernes*
Saturday   *sábado*
January   *enero*
February   *febrero*
March   *marzo*

April   *abril*
May   *mayo*
June   *junio*
July   *julio*
August   *agosto*
September   *septiembre*
October   *octubre*
November   *noviembre*
December   *diciembre*
spring   *primavera*
summer   *verano*
autumn   *otoño*
winter   *invierno*

day   *día*
week   *semana*
month   *mes*
year   *año*

Time

morning   *mañana*
noon   *mediodía*
afternoon/evening   *tarde*
night   *noche*
today   *hoy*
yesterday   *ayer*
tomorrow   *mañana*

OPPOSITE: Fetching water is a daily task in many villages. ABOVE: Ice cream is a favorite treat for Quechua kids.

what time is it? *¿Qué hora es?* *¿Qué horas son?*
now *ahora, ahorita*
later *más tarde*

stone *rumi*
stone wall *pirca*
thank you *yusulpayki*
where is/are *Maípi*

QUECHUA

Many words and phrases from the Quechua language spoken by the Andean Indian groups have made their way into everyday lingo. Words for places, gods and goddesses, and household items are commonly used in Cusco and other mountain towns. If you travel off the beaten path you may find that few locals speak Spanish, and knowledge of critical phrases in Quechua is helpful.

In Quechua the plural of a noun is formed by adding the suffix *kuna*, or *cuna*. Thus, "baby" is *wawa*, "babies" is *wawakuna*.

Pre-conquest Inca ethics could be summed up with three short precepts: don't steal, don't lie, don't be lazy. Today these phrases are still used as a greeting: "*Ama sua, ama llullia, ama quella.*" The suitable reply is "*Qampas hinallataq*," which translates as, "The same to you."

A Few Words and Expressions

Andean folk song *huayna*
baby *wawa*
bridge *chaca*
creator god, white gentleman *viracocha*
earth (also clothing) *pacha* (mother earth *mama pacha*)
food *mikúna*
fortress *pucara*
fruit *ruru*
good morning *wenos idas*
good evening *wenas nuchis*
hawk *huaman*
hangover *chuchaqui*
hello *napaykullayki*
hotel, rest stop *tambo*
lake, ocean *cocha* (mother ocean *mama cocha*)
marketplace, courtyard, enclosed place *cancha*
moon *quilla* (moon goddess *mama quilla*)
mountain, hill *orgu (urco)*
navel *cuzco*
no *manan*
peak *piccu*
rest stop *tambo*
sacred place or object *huaca*

The main Internet information source in Peru is called **Red Cientifica Peruana** and can be accessed at **www.rcp.net.pe**. There are many good web sites to visit which can provide all sorts of information regarding Peru before you leave home. Other sites to visit are:

www.interknowledge.com/peru A good, general description of the country, its history, people and regions.

www.cdc.gov/travel/tropsam.htm This is a United States government site (Center for Disease Control) and provides information regarding current health concerns and necessary precautions in foreign countries.

www.lanic.utexas.edu/la/Peru This University of Texas web site is put together by the Institute of Latin American Studies. Some of the information is in Spanish, but there is plenty there to intrigue and inform the English-speaking student of Peru as well.

http://travel.state.gov/peru.html This is a United States State Department site and provides information regarding passport requirements, and health and travel warnings for Peru.

www.pbs.org/wgbh/nova/Peru The Nova Online series offers an unique view of the Ice Mummies of the Incas, found in the Peruvian Andes in 1996.

www.odci.gov/cia/publications/factbook/pe.html A government publication by the CIA, you will find every statistic you could ever possibly want to know about Peru here.

www.spectrav.com This site lists every conceivable tour and adventure journey option in Peru, with dozens of categories to choose from.

Recommended Reading

BINGHAM, HIRAM. *Lost City of the Incas: The Story of Machu Picchu and Its Builders.* Greenwood, 1981. The most readable of Bingham's books, focusing on his explorations at Machu Picchu.

COUSTEAU SOCIETY. *An Adventure in the Amazon*. New York: Simon & Schuster Books for Young Readers, 1992.

CUMES, CAROL and RÓMULO LIZÁRRAGA VALENCIA. Journey to Machu Picchu. St. Paul, MN: Llewellyn Publications, 1998. The authors delve into the spiritual aspects of the ties between the Andean people and nature. The previous edition of this book was published under the title *Panchamama's Children*.

FORSYTH, ADRIAN and KENNETH MIYATA. *Tropical Nature*. New York: Charles Scriber's Sons, 1984. A fascinating and highly readable account of scientific explorations in the jungle.

HEMMING, JOHN. *Machu Picchu*. New York: Newsweek Books, 1981.

HEMMING, JOHN. *The Conquest of the Incas*. New York: Harvest Books, 1970. This widely acclaimed history is considered to be the best account of the Inca lifestyle and their ultimate defeat.

HOLLIGANDE DIAZ-LIMACO, JANE. *In Focus: Peru*. New York: Interlink Books, 1998. A useful overview of the political, economic, and social issues facing the country.

KANE, JOE. *Running the Amazon*. New York: Alfred A. Knopf, 1989. This amusing, exciting and engrossing tale covers the author's expedition from the Peruvian Andes to the coast of Brazil.

KRAMER, PAUL and ROBERT MCNICOLL, *Latin American Panorama: Key Writings by the Major Social and Historical Interpreters of Latin American Culture*. New York: G.P. Putnam's Sons, 1968.

LAMB, F. BRUCE. *Wizard of the Upper Amazon*. California: North Atlantic Books, 1971. The story of a young rubber prospector named Manuel Córdova-Rios who was kidnapped by the Amahuaca people of the upper Amazon forest at the turn of the twentieth century.

MCINTYRE, LOREN. *The Incredible Incas and Their Timeless Land*. Washington, DC: The National Geographic Society, 1975.

MARTIN, LUIS. *The Kingdom of the Sun: A Short History of Peru*. New York: Scribner, 1974.

MATTHIESSEN, PETER. *At Play in the Fields of the Lord*. New York: Random House, 1965. This novel examines the life and tribulations of missionaries working in Amazon villages.

MAYORGA, CESAR A. GUARDIA. *Diccionario Kechwa-Castellano, Castellano-Kechwa* (quinta edicion). 1971; Lima, Peru: Editora Los Andes. One of the best dictionaries for those wishing to learn Quechua.

MEISCH, LYNNE. *A Traveler's Guide to El Dorado & the Inca Empire*. New York: Penguin Books, 1980. This well-written journal includes excellent descriptions of Peruvian folk arts, music, and other cultural tidbits.

MORRISON, TONY. *Pathways to the Gods*. New York: HarperRow, 1979.

PERKINS, JOHN. *The World As You Dream It*. Rochester, Vermont: Destiny Books, 1994. Perkins delves into the shamanistic teachings of Amazonian tribes.

POPESCU, PETRU. *Amazon Beaming*. New York: Viking Penguin, 1991.

REDFELD, JAMES. *The Celestine Prophecy*. New York: Warner Books, Inc., 1993.

SANDEMAN, CHRISTOPHER. *A Wanderer in Inca Land*. London, England: Phoenix House, 1948.

SASSER, ELIZABETH S. *Architecture of Ancient Peru*. Lubbock, Texas: The Texas Tech Press, 1969.

TOOR, FRANCES. *Three Worlds of Peru*. New York: Crown Publishers, 1949.

VON HAGEN, VICTOR W. *The Ancient Sun Kingdoms of the Americas*. Cleveland, Ohio: The World Publishing Company, 1961.

VON HAGEN, VICTOR W. *The Golden Man: The Quest for El Dorado*. London, England: Book Club Associates, 1974.

WERLICH, DAVID P. *Peru: A Short History*. Southern Illinois University Press, 1978.

WORCESTER, DONALD. *Makers of Latin America*. New York: E.P. Dutton & Co., Inc., 1966.

WRIGHT, RONALD. *Cut Stones and Crossroads*. New York: Viking, 1984

VARGAS LLOSA, MARIO. *The Storyteller*. New York: Farrar Straus Giroux, 1989. The conflict over the development of the Amazon region is sentimentally described in this fictionalized account of a city boy turned Amazonian storyteller.

VARGAS LLOSA, MARIO. *Conversation in the Cathedral*. New York: HarperRow, 1975.

VARGAS LLOSA, MARIO. *Captain Pantoja and the Special Service*. New York: HarperRow, 1978.

VARGAS LLOSA, MARIO. *Death in the Andes*. New York: Penguin, 1993. An excellent novel about the Sendero Luminoso era.

WILDER, THORNTON. *The Bridge of San Luis Rey*. New York: HarperRow, 1967.

Quick Reference A–Z Guide to Places and Topics of Interest with Listed Accommodation, Restaurants and Useful Telephone Numbers

Photography Credits

All of the photographs in this book were taken by Mireille Vautier, except those on pages 114 and 258 (left), which were taken by Maribeth Mellin.